A Bay of Destiny

This book is dedicated to Celia, my mother

Published by Bantry Design Studios (Publications) Ltd., New Street, Bantry, Co. Cork, Ireland
First published 1996
First issued as a Bantry Design Studios Publications paperback 1996

British Library Cataloguing in Publication Data
Michael John Carroll
A Bay of Destiny
Ireland. Local History. Irish History.

ISBN : 0-9519415-2-6

Acknowledgements

I wish to thank all those who assisted me in my research, compiling notes, typing and the preparations in getting this book to print.

Especially Piers Gardner of the Department of Transport and Energy, Dr. Ivor A. J. MacCarthy of the Department of Geology, UCC: the archivists of the following institutions, the Archives de France, Cedex, Paris; The Heraklion Museum, Crete: The Greek National Museum, Athens: The Prado Museum, Madrid: The Barbados Museum and Historical Society, the Jamaica Archives, Spanish Town, Jamaica: The British Maritime Museum.

To those who were kind enough to supply information on aspects of local history, including Tim Cadogan, County Library, Cork, Noel O'Mahony, County Library, Bantry, Paddy O'Leary, Ballydehob, Connie Murphy, Castletownbere, Ted O'Sullivan, Bere Island and Cork, Michael Donoghue, Bantry and Donal Fitzgerald, Bantry.

Special thanks to The National Gallery, Dublin, the *Cork Examiner* and the *Southern Star* for their kind permission to reproduce photogrpahs and old reports.

Finally, to Brendan and Gloria of Red Barn Publishing, for editing and typesetting the contents to Roland and his staff at Anro Graphics for the preparation of photographs and illustrations: to Ian Vickery for some of his old photographs, and to all who had an input into this book, a special thanks.

Cover illustration:
The Battle of Bantry Bay 1 May 1689 by Willem Van Diest,
reproduced by courtesy of the National Maritime Museum, Greenwich.

Drawings and photographs courtesy of Caroline Daunt, Jack Roberts, Ian Vickery and the author.

Printed in Ireland by Colour Books Ltd., Dublin

A Bay of Destiny

A HISTORY OF BANTRY BAY AND BANTRY

MICHAEL J. CARROLL

This book is dedicated to Celia, my mother

Published by the author in April 1996

Acknowledgements

I wish to thank all those who assisted me in my research, compiling notes, typing and the preparations in getting this book to print.

Especially Piers Gardner of the Department of Transport and Energy; Dr. Ivor A. J. MacCarthy of the Department of Geology, UCC; the archivists of the following institutions: the Archives de France, Cedex, Paris; The Heraklion Museum, Crete; The Greek National Museum, Athens; The Prado Museum, Madrid; The Barbados Museum and Historical Society; the Jamaica Archives, Spanish Town, Jamaica; The British Maritime Museum.

To those who were king enough to supply information on aspects of local history, including Tim Cadogan, County Library, Cork; Noel O'Mahony, County Library, Bantry; Paddy O'Leary, Ballydehob; Connie Murphy, Castletownbere; Ted O'Sullivan, Bere Island and Cork; Michael Donoghue, Bantry and Donal Fitzgerald, Bantry.

Special thanks to The National Gallery, Dublin, the *Cork Examiner* and the *Southern Star* for their kind permission to reproduce photographs and old reports.

Finally, to Brendan and Gloria at Red Barn Publishing for editing and typesetting the contents; to Roland and his staff at Anro Graphics for the preparation of photographs and illustrations; to Ian Vickery for some of his old photographs, and to all who had an input into this book, a special thanks.

Cover illustration: *The Battle of Bantry Bay 1 May 1689* by Willem Van Diest, reproduced by courtesy of the National Maritime Museum, Greenwich.

Drawings and photographs courtesy of Caroline Daunt, Jack Roberts, Ian Vickery and the author.

Printed in Ireland by ColourBooks, Dublin

Part One

Part Two

Part Three

Part Four

Part Five

Introduction

During the early 1980s I became interested in local history and spent most of my spare time visiting all the known historical sites in the Bantry Bay region. In the course of time I collected a substantial amount of information, especially on the megalithic monuments of the area. This has been recorded in the *Guide to the Antiquities of the Bantry Region*.

Trekking over the mountainsides and glens, I found many sites which were not recorded, and I heard many tales of a vast number of others which had vanished off the face of the earth while successive governments did nothing to protect this ancient heritage of ours here in West Cork. Even the few monuments under the protection of the Board of Works receive very little attention over the years and are left to be vandalised at will. The Kilnaruane Stone is the best example of the government's complete lack of care for our ancient monuments.

Having concentrated on the fieldwork of researching the historical sites, I spent the next few years trying to piece together the prehistory of this region. Consulting the ancient Irish literature, as well as that of western Europe and the Mediterranean countries, I was able to put together a historical picture of the main events which influenced our local history up to the time of St. Patrick. In fact, the first part of this book in itself would constitute a substantial volume in its own right if all the accumulated information was used.

During the period from the fifth century to the twelfth, the history of this part of West Cork, due to its isolated situation, has been very poorly documented. In fact, the events in Bantry Bay were better known in France and Spain than in Cork, Dublin or London, because of our sea commerce with these countries.

Even the importance of the Bardic School of the O'Dalaig near Kilcrohane was better known on the Continent than in the rest of Ireland.

Not until after the migration southwards of the O'Mahonys, O'Sullivans, O'Donovans, and their followers do we get any reasonable documented history of local events. In the following centuries all our records are mostly those which were accumulated by the Normans/English who were inclined to record in writing everything important that happened.

Even after the battle of Kinsale, until the end of the nineteenth century, most of the recording of history was done by the ruling class (the English) and it was not until about the turn of the twentieth century that Irish historians began their work in earnest.

With only the sources of the religious writers and the plainly biased interpretation of historical fact by the English historians to work on, our historians faced an uphill task.

One of the greatest Arab writers of the fourteenth century, Ibn Khaldun, writing on the criticism of traditional history said:

> Since it is of the nature of tradition to incorporate false statements, we must examine the causes which produce them:
>
> 1 The attachment to certain opinions and schools of thought. Now if a man's mind is impartial in receiving tradition he examines it with all due care so that he can distinguish between the true and the false: but if he is pervaded by attachment to any particular opinion or sect he immediately accepts any tradition which supports it; and this tendency to attachment clouds the judgement so that he is unable to criticise and scrutinise what he hears, and straightaway accepts what is false and hands it on to others:
>
> a Over-confidence in the probity of those who hand on the tradition;

b Ignorance of the real significance of events; for many traditionalists, now know the significance of what they saw and heard, record events together with their own interpretation or conjectures and so give false information;

c Belief that one has the truth. This is widespread and comes generally from over-confidence in narrators of the past;

d Ignorance of the circumstances surrounding an event induced by ambiguity or embellishment. The narrator hands on the story as he understands it with these misleading and false elements.

With these tenets, or should I say guidelines, in mind how are we therefore to interpret our historical sources? The answer is not easily forthcoming, especially regarding a history of Ireland which has never escaped some influence or other in its numerous narratives.

The 'earliest' recorded history of the country contained in the annals is biased and imbued with a primitive Christian doctrine. These were written by the religious for the religious and not for 'human consumption'. The tales and events that they relate are sometimes taken out of the context of tradition and lose their true interpretation amidst the dogmas and accepted beliefs of the religious scribes. Anything that was contrary to the Christian thinking of the time was omitted and only those passages which could be accepted, or changed to suit Christian teaching, was included.

We may ask ourselves what were the main sources of history that the monks used? Many centuries had passed since the demise of the Druid Schools of Learning and the famous bardic tradition. Even though St. Patrick is reported to have 'burnt over 1,500 pagan books' on the Hill of Tara, some parchments or records must have survived throughout the early centuries of Christianity.

Bearing the above in mind, you, the reader, will find in the following pages a somewhat new interpretation of history which I hope is closer to fact than presented heretofore. Some people will find the contents controversial and not compatible with the accepted 'norms' of documenting history. I have not complied with the 'standard' interpretation of historical facts as laid out by many important and eminent historians of the past, but rather attempted to throw a new light on the subject matter.

I have used references sparingly and only in those instances where it might prove useful for future study by those interested in a particular episode of local history. However, the bibliography is substantial, and, if all the references were used, the content of this book would be changed completely into a serious and academic tome.

I have omitted various aspects of local history such as social development, rural history, education and the influence of the Catholic Church, as these have been well documented in other recent publications.

Finally, it must be pointed out that this is not a comprehensive chronicle of the region but rather an account of the major events, both local and otherwise, which have influenced local tradition, customs and the history of the region.

I do hope that in reading the following pages you will find many items of interest which will broaden your understanding of our past.

Michael Carroll

Preface

Situated on the south-west coast of Ireland on the outskirts of Europe, Bantry Bay has often been referred to as a 'Bay of Destiny'.

The events which have occurred here, from prehistoric times to almost the present day, have changed or influenced the history of Ireland, Europe and, to a lesser extent, the world.

Firstly, there are the accounts in the ancient Irish annals placing the first people to visit our shores as having arrived in Bantry Bay—namely, Cessair and her followers, who disembarked at the well-known location called 'Dun-na-mBarc', which is about a mile on the northern side out of Bantry town. This event, even though previously considered as a mere legend or myth, is now judged to contain a certain amount of fact, as it had been transcribed by Christian monks despite being a complete contradiction of the Old Testament account of the deluge.

Sometime during the period 6500 BC to 2500 BC came the megalithic builders, who, by erecting various types of stone edifices, converted the bleak and wild countryside into the greatest concentration of prehistoric monuments to be found in western Europe.

Then, as related in the *Leabhair Gabhala* (Book of Invasions), the Tuatha de Danaan landed here, to be followed by the Milesians (*c.*1700–1400 BC) whose ancestors were to rule and dominate the country, as well as the seas around the British Isles, for almost two millennia.

The Norsemen came and made one of their important bases on Dursey Island, from where they plundered and ruled the waves of the south-west coast for a century, before suffering their first defeat by a force made up of the local tribes.

At the end of the twelfth century, the Normans came and built their castles and tried to dominate the land, while the local tribes fought amongst themselves over territorial expansion and inter-tribal rivalry. However, realising that the Norman was the common enemy, they joined forces and entrapped the enemy at the battle of Callan in 1261, thus inflicting on the Normans their first defeat on Irish soil and also bringing into existence a type of warfare which later became known as guerrilla warfare.

The English settlers came and exploited the natural resources, including the fisheries, woods, forests, and the native population. The exported fish fed nations both on this side of the Atlantic and in the newly discovered colonies of the West Indies and the Americas. The timber from the despoliated woodland built the great warships of the English navy which was to dominate the oceans for centuries, and built the mansions and houses of that country, while the native Irish were treated no better than black slaves.

The remnants of the Spanish Armada passed our shores before their perilous journey home across the wide expanse of the Bay of Biscay. Even though no documented evidence of ships foundering in Bantry Bay is recorded, traditional eye-witness reports of ships disappearing off the Bay may lead to the conclusion that there are in actual fact some wrecks of the Armada in the vicinity.

The French invasion fleet came in 1689 and, beside landing a substantial force, inflicted on the English navy its first humiliating defeat in what was called the 'Battle of Bantry Bay'. Over a century later, in 1796, came Wolfe Tone and another French invasion force, which, due to severe weather conditions, failed to land a force of over 20,000 soldiers to liberate Ireland. If the invasion had been a success, Ireland would have been liberated, English defeated both on land and sea, and most of western Europe would have become a collection of socialist republics.

From the town, villages and hinterland emerged a group of dedicated men who infiltrated the British House of Commons by becoming MPs, where they used their influence to change the British attitude towards Ireland and who, by their efforts, became known as the 'Bantry Band'. The following is a traditional poem celebrating these men.

The Bantry Band

The 'Bantry Band', the 'Bantry Band',
Who blushes for the 'Bantry Band'?
Are truer men in all the land
Revilers than the 'Bantry Band'?

Not theirs in these or darker days
To tune their harps to tyrants' praise
Not theirs to gather venal bays
Where Honour warps and Truth decays.

Not theirs the part of sneering slave,
When good men leagued the land to save;
But theirs the grit that foiled the knave,
And theirs the cry that cheered the brave!

Though cradled not in halls built high
With rackrent wrung from misery—
Mere Irish just as you and I—
We cheer them yet with fearless cry.

For love of Erin fires their hearts,
And spite of foes and traitor arts,
Fell Faction reels beneath their darts,
And still the whipped oppressor smarts.

Could every town in Ireland show
Such Spartan bands to face the foe,
Not long we'd wait his overthrow
Not long we'd wail our country's woe!

Then, blessings on you, 'Bantry Band',
Speed on, speed on, brave 'Bantry Band',
'Til Freedom crowns your native land,
And ends your labours, 'Bantry Band'.

John MacCarthy

While England anxiously awaited news of the battle of Trafalgar in 1805, Bantry had already learned of the victory and Nelson's death, as the picket boat bearing the message to Plymouth had passed the news by signals to one of the watch towers at the end of the Bay.

The English built their sea fortifications making Bantry Bay one of their major naval ports from the 1800s, culminating in Berehaven harbour becoming their dominant position to control the sea lanes of the Western Approaches during the First World War, preserving England and her allies from naval defeat. The Prince of Wales and the German Kaiser partied, drank and finally shook hands on the local pier (at Bantry) before war was declared between their two nations.

From Bantry Bay (Berehaven) sailed the British fleet, under the command of Jellicoe, to the inconclusive battle of Jutland.

To Bantry Bay came English and European royalty, as well as famous writers, poets and personages of note, to spend their vacations cruising around the Bay in the idyllic surroundings of a semi-tropical climate. Meanwhile, the local Irish were marching on the hidden country roads, learning to drill and bear arms for the eventual struggle which would liberate the country from English rule. The achievements of these local Volunteers are well noted in history as having a direct bearing on the final outcome.

Towards the end of the Second World War, when the British presence was no longer visible, the arrival of the Spanish fishing fleet heralded a slight recovery for local trade and commerce. The adoption of Bantry as the second home port for the Spanish and French fleets brought back the importance of Bantry as a port and renewed its ties with Continental Europe.

The building of a crude oil terminal and the age of the supertanker created a drastic change in the transportation of oil from the Middle East to Europe, which in a way changed the economic growth of western Europe. However, the chance diversion of the tanker *Betelgeuse* from Portugal to Bantry Bay and the subsequent on-board explosion ended Bantry's boom era.

In the short period of time that has elapsed since that night of disaster, Bantry has once again dragged itself out of oblivion to become one of the major shellfish farming sites of western Europe, as well as a mecca for tourism.

And, now again, as the oil terminal on Whiddy Island is being brought back into operation, we shall experience a revitalisation of port activity with tanker traffic, as in the 1970s.

In the following pages the reader will discover events and facts which have only been partially recorded to date, or not at all. With the absence of written historic documentation, the writer has interpreted the various oral traditions so as to give as accurate an account as possible.

Also, it is not my intention to cast aspersions on any belief—local or otherwise—to change recorded facts, or to blame any person or groups for any past event.

Part One

From the Last Glaciation to *c.* 1500 BC

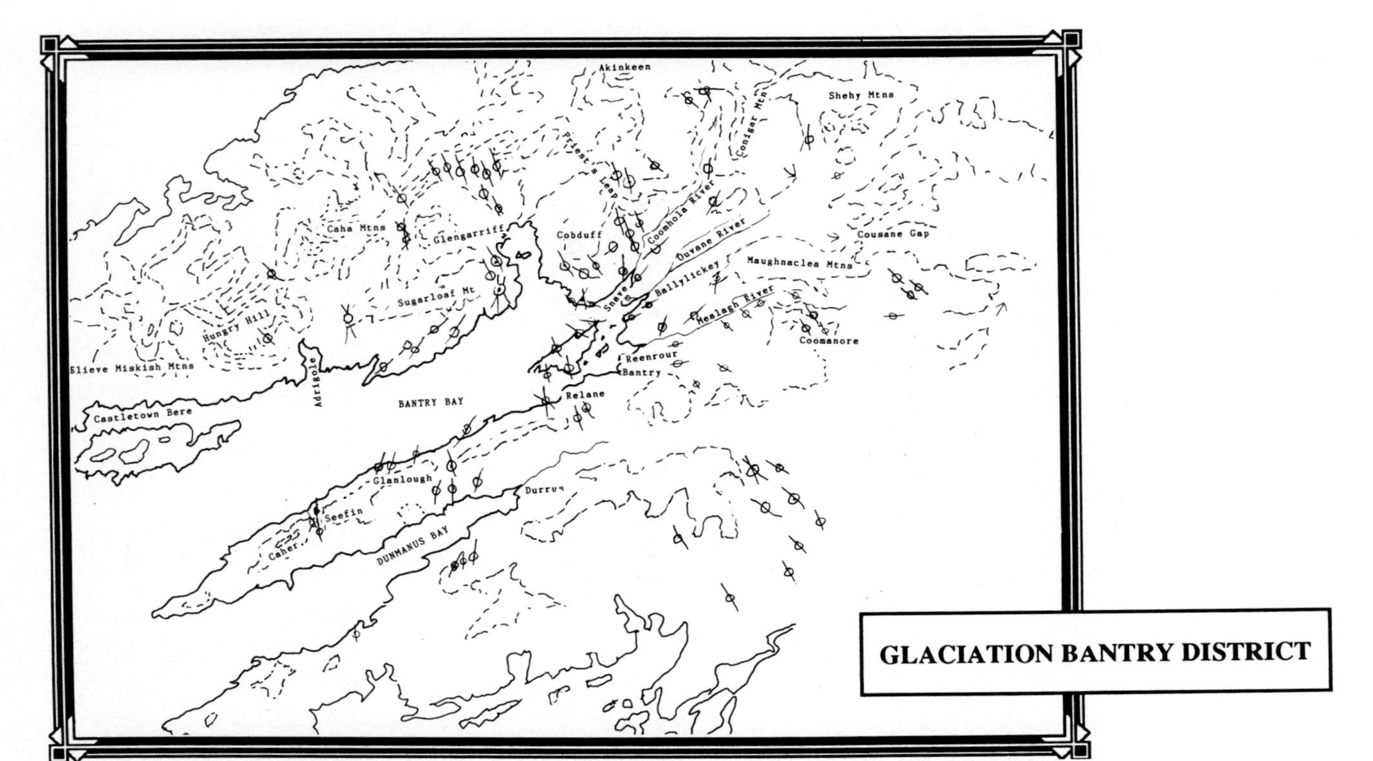

GLACIATION BANTRY DISTRICT

— I —

An Introduction to Ancient Ireland

If all the references to ancient Ireland are examined, it will be found that there are numerous names given to this country by the ancient historians and writers of pre-Christian times. Each of these names was based on the individual's interpretation of ancient history.

When we look closely at the ancient annals of Irish history, we must bear in mind that they were rewritten and framed by Christian bards and scribes. The products of these endeavours are confusing, owing to the revisions and alterations made as concessions to the vanity of their illustrious patrons—the Chieftains or Lord Abbots.

A good example of this practice is clearly demonstrated in the description and content of the *Book of Invasions* (*An Leabhair Gabhala*), where all events, people and dates were changed to suit Christian dogma at the time of writing. It is also evident that the transcribers were attempting to follow the early French custom of trying to prove a direct lineage back to Noah for their benefactors.

In this context, one could not omit mentioning the instance of the 'poor monk' who rewrote the *Tale of Cessair*—the history of the first inhabitant of Ireland. He placed her landing as before the deluge, the account of which survived afterwards, which is in complete contradiction of Biblical teaching. It can be asked, how was this event handed down by tradition if everyone perished in the deluge except those who were on Noah's Ark?

In light of the above, it is an extemely difficult task to extricate any facts from our ancient manuscripts. However, with the assistance of the early Hebrew, Egyptian, Minoan, Greek, and Roman historians, some parts of our early history can be clarified. However, in the light of modern-day research, some of the conclusions reached by our early historians—such as Keating and O'Flaherty—are found to be debatable. These eminent historians were over-reliant on existing Irish sources and did not, for one reason or another, consult the many 'foreign' records.

When the references to ancient Ireland, its inhabitants and Bantry Bay made by O'Flaherty and others are examined, it will be found that the name *Iernus* (Ireland) is used, and the inhabitants are called *Ierni* or *Classa Eibheir*.

Danva / "Refer to chapter 6, Early Myths & Legends"

Unlike O'Flaherty and Keating, who refer to Kenmare Bay as *Inmbear Sceine*, Ptolemy, the Greek historian, equates *Inmbear Sceine* with Bantry Bay. (*Sceine* or *Sceana* is sometimes interpreted as Danua, leader of the *Tuatha de Danaan.*) Yet, in another historical context both O'Flaherty and Keating equate *Inmbear Sceine* with *Ceann Mhara* which is in fact one of the old names for Bantry Bay.

Ptolemy, in his first map of Ireland, refers to the island of Ireland as 'Ivernia' and to the inhabitants of Bantry Bay as the 'Vodil' or 'Uodii'. The name 'Vodii' was placed over Whiddy Island on the map, while the inhabitants or Septs of the neighbouring coastline were referred to as the *Coriondii* (*Corunnaigh*) and the *Velaborii* (*Veliberi*). These tribes will be mentioned in a later chapter dealing with *Corca Laidhe*.

It has been suggested that Ptolemy's knowledge of the coastline of Western Europe and the British Isles was limited to what he had learnt from sea traders prior to committing himself to map making, and was therefore only secondhand and could not be considered reliable. In making this type of judgement, the critics have completely overlooked the fact that the Eastern Mediterranean seafarers, whoever they may have been, had a detailed knowledge of our coastline and especially of this area, even though they may have handed on some incorrect names.

The main sources of early Roman references to Ireland are Caesar's Commentaries (*De Bello Gallico*), Tacitus (*Vita Agriculae*), Dionysius Periegesis, Pomponius Mela, Juvenal, and Orosius. In these, Ireland is variously referred to as *Hibernia* (*Ibh-eir-in*), *I-er-ne*, *Juverna*, *Ivernia*, (*Iv-er-ni-a*) and *Iariin* (*Iar-i-in*). All of these mean the 'Western Isle' or 'Territory of the Western Isle'.

The term Gael, or Land of the Gael, has many connotations. The earliest reference to the *Gooidhil* (*Gael, Gaoidhealg, Gaodhal*) is found in ancient Hebrew as *Gadol*, according to Hector Boetius, the early historian. In this context, the name refers to the 'followers of *Gaodhal*' in Egypt at the time of Moses, later found in Crete and then in Scythia. Where this Hebrew tribe went from there is open to conjecture. In a chapter dealing with the Milesians, this matter will be expanded further. It is also interesting to note that Caesar and other Roman historians referred to the first settlers in Ireland as *Gaill* or *Godill*, which means herdsmen or hunters, not to be confused with the Goths, who are reputed to have fled to Ireland after being defeated by Vespasian *c.* AD 68.

If we examine the ancient Irish language, we discover that it contained sixteen letters, as in early Greek, and had the same basic structure. Taken as a whole, it was made up of forty per cent early Greek, thirty per cent early Etruscan (Latin), ten per cent Hebrew and ten per cent Berber dialect (North African). Taking these facts into consideration, it is strange to find that past historians disregarded the contact between the Eastern Mediterranean countries and the South of Ireland in their conclusions on the origins of the various prehistoric 'invaders'. In fact, they arrived at the erroneous conclusion that there was no similarity between Old Irish and the Scythian, Coptic, and early Cantabric letters and language. If a closer look is taken at early Irish, it is found that the numerals are Arabic: alphabetic numerals are early Roman (borrowed from Greek); Irish names of 1 to 100 are Latin; names of trees, etc., are early Cycladic Greek (from Phoenician).

In this context, it is of relevance to note the comments of three early historians. Tacitus, the Roman historian, wrote that 'the harbours of Ireland were better known to the seafarers of the Mediterranean than those of Britain'. Avenius, also Roman, wrote that 'the Carthagenians traded with Ireland which they called Oestrumnides' and Dionysius Periegesis of the third century AD wrote that 'the early Greeks knew it [Ireland] well'.

It is indeed surprising that most of those who wrote about the ancient history of Ireland were unwilling to accept that the early inhabitants of this country could have come from outside the boundaries of Western Europe. In fact, they often seem to have had a limited, or 'tunnel', vision as to the origins of the early inhabitants. If they had only studied the rites of the ancient Irish Druids, they could not but recognise their close resemblance to the rites and worship of the Sumerians (Persians). In the context of our own stone circles and places of ancient worship, we find that the Persians had no temples, as such, but altars on the high hills and dominant positions of the countryside where sacred fires were lit during the rites and ceremonies to the moon, sun and earth.

If we look at Greek references to Ireland, we find that the following historians—Heroditus, Hecataeus, Aristotle, Hellanicus and Ephories—mention that the 'land of the Gooidhil' lies beyond the 'Pillars of Hercules' (the entrance to the Mediterranean). It is very doubtful that the Greeks were referring to the Celts in Catalonia (Spain) or in Northern Gall (France) at that time, but is more likely that they were referring to a different race of people inhabiting Ireland.

Taken in this context, what follows is a singular viewpoint of the ancient history of Ireland.

— 2 —

The Geological Evolution of Bantry Bay

Bantry Bay is unique in its formation. We have only to look at an ordnance survey map of the area, or to ascend one of the many vantage points around the Bay, to recognise this fact. The first impression is of an almost rectangular stretch of water, bordered on the north and south by ridges of high mountains, with the eastern end occupied by the low-lying Whiddy Island and moderate river valleys, while the Bay itself opens—in the south-west—to the Atlantic Ocean.

In geological terms, Bantry Bay has been described as a 'sunken valley', and to explain this fact further we shall have to briefly go back in time to trace the reasons for the changes in the earth's crust in this general region. In the Jurassic Period (±150 million years ago), a shallow sea was formed which covered an area now consisting of the British Isles and the adjoining waters. This lasted only a short period of time, leaving little, if any, deposits. However, during the Mesozoic and subsequent Cainozoic Eras, this country seems to have risen and then submerged again, before finally re-emerging to resemble roughly what we see today.

The mountain folds had a slight covering of chalk rock, but with constant erosion and weathering it soon disappeared. This was also due to the slight tilt to the south which introduced our mostly south flowing rivers, which were the initial drainage system in the southern part of the country. These main rivers, such as the Bandon and the Lee, had offshoots—with their origins in the same mountain ridges—which became our south-westerly fast-flowing rivers and streams, such as the West Cork and Kerry rivers which emptied into the 'sunken valleys' of Bantry, Kenmare and Tralee Bays.

Then came the major Ice Age, with its dramatic results. It is important at this point to note that the ice cap that covered the south-western corner of Ireland, extending from Kerry to the east Cork coast, was distinct from the ice sheet which had covered Ireland at an earlier time in history.

There is only evidence of two Ice Ages in Ireland, while the rest of Europe suffered at least four. Prior to the advance of the first, the country was subject to intense weathering by frost in Arctic-like conditions. We find that scree deposits of giant angular rock fragments, caused by the freeze–thaw process, were precipitated in the boulder clay of West Cork at the end of the glacial period, before the temperature had risen, resulting in peat and other deposits being found in the different stratas of boulder clay. During the Ice Age, a great ice cap covered the Cork and Kerry region on at least one occasion. Ice sheets advanced south-eastwards over the Caha and Slieve Miskish mountains and over the numerous passes. These Cork–Kerry mountains acted as a great centre of accumulation, from which the south-western ice sheets grew.

Even the mountains were covered by this ice sheet, to a height of about 2,000 feet. The whole area was invaded by this advance, and Bantry Bay filled with ice which moved south-west towards the mouth of the Bay, north-eastwards up into the mountain valleys and south-eastwards towards Skibbereen and across Muintir mBaire.

The ice coming down the various valleys to the north (i.e. Healy Pass, Glengarriff, Coomhola and the Borlin Valley) was congested in the lower regions of the Bay and there were many different movements within the ice mass itself, as it sought passage in various directions. This led to various ice masses converging, in their quest for space to expand. The general direction of the striae (parallel scratches or grooves made by ice on rock) is north-west and south-east. The ice mass in the Bay sought other ways of escape, and, having reached the highest passes of the Muintir mBaire range, began to move southwards into Dunmanus Bay.

The direction of the striae along the south side of the Bay was clearly dictated by the topography as the ice moved south-westerwards and along the top of the ridges. The opposite happened in the lower Coomhola area around Snave, as the ice moved north-easterly, pushing into the mountain valleys to merge with the glaciers which had already occupied these valleys from the north. The power of this mass eventually changed the direction of the ice movement to right-angle across the main movement. The striae indicate that the ice mass diverged at Whiddy Island. As the Bay continued to fill with ice, the local topography dominated the normal movement, which moulded the drift to drumlin form at the maximum point of the ice sheet at the head of the Bay. The orientation of the drumlins along the southern shores (from Scart West to Gearhies) agrees with the normal uninterrupted flow of the base ice sheet, while the upper ice seems to have been moving south-east.

The numerous erratics (misplaced rocks on open spaces) around the Bay give us some idea of the power of the ice movement. This effect is particularly noticeable on the north side of the Bay between Glengarriff and Adrigole, where large ice-borne blocks of rock dot the bare landscape. This area has often been referred to as 'the playground of the gods' in local mythology, i.e. where the gods played by throwing boulders as if they were playing ball. These erratics are all derived from the grits, coarse sandstone and sandy shale which form the ridge of the Caha mountains, while a few other examples of carboniferous slate and purple grit are found at the eastern end of the Bay.

As the temperature slowly rose, the tops of the mountains appeared, and gradually the ridges became visible. The ice began to melt, commencing at the passes, and eventually the valleys were vacated. However, the lower reaches were still blocked by the ice sheet covering the Bay, and this caused the creation of 'water ponds' in many of the valleys, i.e. Owengar, Borlin and the Mealagh. Also, deposits of gravel and drumlins were made as the hidden streams and rivers coursed to the south-west, as dictated by the topography of the area.

The ice sheet over the Bay gradually melted while the rivers flowed beneath towards the south-west. The courses these ice-fed rivers took probably resemble what we can see today, as far as their estuaries went. However, where they went beneath the ever-decreasing ice mass occupying the lower end of the Bay is open to question. If we consult the old sea charts, the ordnance survey maps and take account of the geological features, we might find the solution.

It is evident that Whiddy Island was joined to the mainland at Beach, and that, earlier, only a small opening disgorged the waters from the harbour between Whiddy Point East and Eagle Point, where they joined the outflowing Coomhola river. Within the harbour itself, a strange natural phenomenon exists in the vicinity of Horse Island. To the west of the small island there exists a ridge of boulder stones running east–west for a distance of about 100 metres, and known locally as the western Horse Island 'bar'. Even though it consists of almost round boulder stones, the northern and southern sides of this ridge are almost perpendicular, from sea-bed to top—a height of some 50 feet. As to the course taken by the rivers and waters then existing in the harbour area when the beaches were breached, it is a matter of conjecture, but the deep gorge which exists south of Lousy Island and the deep channel running south-west off of the south shore from Gearhies to Horse Point can only fan the imagination.

On the northern peninsula of the Bay—Beara—there are many geological remains of the Ice Age. Some of the best national examples of hanging valleys, U-valleys, glacial valleys, cirques and aretes are to be found from Dursey Sound to Ceim an Fhia. The best examples of U-shaped valleys are on the Kenmare side of Beara, at Inchiquinn Lough, Glenmore and the Drumbeg river, whilst on the south side of Beara there is the Adrigole river, Commerkane and the Coomhola river. Barley, Commerkane and Coomadovallig Lakes are good examples of the form of high mountain lake known as cirques, and it is also worth mentioning the waterfall out of Coomadovallig which is over 500 feet high and in full spate after heavy rain.

After the final withdrawal of the ice from Ireland (c. 10500–9500 BC), the country was connected to Britain and mainland Europe for some time. Plant and animal life was able to migrate from the east and south. Trees and vegetation began to grow again. It is worth mentioning here that at some previous period in history, giant trees grew well out into the present Atlantic, especially on the vast area west of Galway known as the Porcupine Bank. Even today, fishermen refer to the area as the Wood or Forest, because of the giant stalks and roots which entangle their trawls and sometimes come to the surface. Ireland was now entering a Forest Period, as the climate became warm and damp. Shallow lakes covered the lowlands, as pine, oak and yew trees began to grow on the flat lands and up the mountain slopes.

With the retreat of the ice, the giant Irish deer and other animals invaded the tundra-like conditions of the countryside. The deer's sojourn was but brief, as it died without apparent reason.

The climate became increasingly more mild, and man made his appearance in Ireland *c.* 7500–6900 BC. Some historians record an earlier entry, but, as far as the evidence from those human remains that have been found to date goes, the above dates are as accurate as can be verified. Some experts say that man came across the landbridge that joined Northern Ireland to Scotland, while others say that he made his way in primitive crafts across from Wales. All that really matters is that the first primitive man had arrived.

— 3 —

Ireland's Early Inhabitants

It is not known for certain when Ireland was first inhabited. However, it is generally accepted by historians that there was a native aboriginal race on the island *c.* 8500 BC, referred to as 'native Neolithic Man', or the 'Beaker People'. The Neolithic Period extended from *c.*8500 BC to the Early Bronze Age, around 3000 BC.

However, it is also evident that primitive man existed in Europe during the Paleolithic Age (Old Stone Age, *c.* 100,000 BC). Even in 35,000 BC, it is estimated that some 20,0000 primitive people lived in southern England. As Ireland and Britain were part of the European continent during that time, and as similar animal bones have been found here, it is reasonable to suppose that a primitive caveman lived in this western section of the continent. However, with the ever-changing climate, from hot and tropical to Ice Age, primitive man had to be constantly on the move.

When he did finally arrive, whether by means of the land connection to the north, or by primitive boat along the east coast, he encountered a deeply forested and wooded region, with misty bogs, newly formed lakes, raging rivers and high mountains. The newly found country was inhabited by wild animals such as elk, wolves, deer, wild boar, foxes and bears, whilst the rivers and lakes abounded in fish.

The land was not very hospitable, and it was downright dangerous to advance inland. He would have moved slowly along the shoreline, either by boat or on foot. Living mostly near river mouths, he built a basic shelter with wicker, timber and mud. He surrounded this hut with a circle of fencing made out of thorn bushes and spikes, in order to protect himself, his family, domesticated animals and fowl from the attacks of wild animals such as packs of wolves.

It is interesting to note that, according to most historical sources, the Irish elk still existed on the arrival of man in Ireland. But the animal most feared was the wolf, which roamed Ireland in great numbers and attacked in packs. All early fortifications were built to guard against wolf attacks, rather than human foe. As a point of interest, the location where the last wolf in the country died, in 1827, was north of Kilgarvan. The wild boar, which can be a very dangerous animal, was plentiful in those early times and remained so, right down to the seventeenth century, in the wilds of Cork and Kerry. From the recent discovery of boar tusks, it is estimated that these early wild boar were larger than the common pig seen nowadays.

From the coastline and river estuaries, aboriginal man slowly explored the interior, following the rivers and streams. In the beginning, his journeys inland were taken with great trepidation. It is unlikely that he stayed away from his small fortified enclosure overnight, unless he had located a defensible cave. His major aim was to make safe shelters which could be visited in daylight hours as a kind of outpost.

When an ideal new location for his home was found, he immediately fortified it, and later on transferred his family and kin, at least until the day he found an even better site. Sometimes, caves were used as a transition home, as they could easily be defended from prowling wild animals.

In the Bantry region, suitable caves were scarce, due to the type of rock and glaciation. Yet, on the northern Caha ridge there are a number of habitable caves in such places as Borlin, Coomhola, Glengarriff and north-east of Adrigole. Some of these have yet to be examined by the archaeologists, and contain neolithic drawings and scribing. Some examples of this rock scribing are reproduced overleaf.

The question of when primitive man arrived in the Bantry region is difficult to answer. If we are to accept that the 'shell-midden' site at Ballyferriter, County Kerry, dates from *c.* 4300 BC, and that the two similar middens in Donemark and Glengarriff date from roughly the same period, then we are left with a serious question—why did it take primitive man almost 3,500 years to explore southwards from his 'accepted' arrival point on the north-east coast, in what is now County Down. Much of the early system of dating for prehistory was based on carbon dating alone. This system has recently been found to be defective when used on its own, and serious mistakes have been discovered. For example, Newgrange has been corrected by 800 years, to *c.* 3400 BC, placing its construction prior to that of Stonehenge and the Pyramids of Egypt. This new date for Newgrange, and the possibility that other important archaeological sites of that period have been incorrectly dated, points to a major historical problem, namely that this early primitive civilisation in Ireland possessed the knowledge of building these large stone monuments before the early European and Middle Eastern civilisations. This question of the accepted diffusion of civilisation will be explained in the following chapter. Meanwhile, the question remains: where did primitive man come from, and why did he choose this island? Was it from necessity, or was it the need to explore? The accepted explanation is that he was pushed westwards by the influx of nomadic tribes from Eastern Europe, and sought safety.

Maybe there is another answer to this question: that primitive man sought refuge here, not due to the fact that he was forced out of Europe, but because some natural disaster where he previously existed forced him to move on. From what is known about this early period of history, there were only two major events which occurred—and these can be accepted either as fact or myth.

The first is the account of the deluge, or flood, which has been recorded by most of the early Middle Eastern civilisations. However, most recent research has found that the deluge, as such, only affected that particular part of the world, and it was unlikely that the early Mediterranean people would have ventured out into the Atlantic.

The second possible answer lies to the west. Recently, it has been discovered that a meteorite hit the area around the Yucatan peninsula *c.* 9500–12000 BC. This discovery now supports the idea of the

A Standing Stone at Scart, Bantry

destruction of the legendary continent of Atlantis (as described by the Greek, Plato), which was situated in the North Atlantic between Europe and North America. Briefly, it was described as the most advanced culture of that time, with pyramids, buildings, and palaces which were the forerunners of those that appeared much later in the Middle East and Mexico. Its system of government was based on a monarchy of nepotism, with a powerful priestly class who practised monotheism to the sun-god. Up to the present time, there are approximately forty-eight books written on the subject of Atlantis, which, it is beleived, was destroyed by earthquake, fire and tidal wave, then sank to the bottom of the ocean.

The Vikings land at Gearhies / "Refer to chapter 17, The Vikings in Bantry Bay"

Returning to Plato, he states that the earliest inhabitants of the Nile Delta, before the emergence of the kingdom of Egypt, related that 'a great seafaring nation came out of the West and settled amongst us'. Who were these people? According to history they did not exist, as the known world was flat and ended in the Western Mediterranean. Were these early people in fact fugitives from the legendary kingdom of Atlantis and were they the same early inhabitants of this country?

If one wishes to study this matter more closely, one of the best references is *Lost Atlantis* by James Bramwell.

There are many conflicting ideas as to the type of ship or sea-going craft that was used by early aboriginal man. It has been almost unanimously agreed by Irish historians that the hide-skin curraghs were the main type of sea transport used here up to the arrival of the Vikings in about AD 840. This conclusion is based on the premise that only those types of boats are depicted in early documents, and no evidence has been produced of any other type of boat being used.

To say the least, the historians were rather insular in their beliefs, as modern-day research and discoveries have proved. For example, the recent 'findings' of dug-out canoes in the Midland bogs have been dated to *c.* 500 BC. There is also evidence of Mediterranean shipping to the south-west for minerals *c.* 1700 BC, and the ancient records of the Romans Tacitus and Caesar describe the sea-going vessels of the 'Western Galls' as being 'beyond imagination' in their size and construction—in other words, they were bigger and better than the Roman warships of the day.

However, the question remains as to how this early art of building large timber ships cound have disappeared. The answer is simple, as we know all too well today: when the craftsman dies, so too does his art.

Yet, the aboriginal man developed in other directions, and was noted for his ability in the shaping and making of primitive tools and weapons. After a period of time, certain individuals improved their flintstones and spearheads, made flint flakes, borers, scrapers, saws, arrowheads, javelins and axe-heads. With this advance in the rudiments of early production, the population along the seashore and river estuaries began to increase, and what followed was a gradual movement inland, as primitive man was no longer fearful of the threat of wild animals. And so a new age dawned—the Megalithic Age—for primitive man, also known as the Stone Builders.

The Stone Builders

If we agree that the greater Bantry region encompasses Beara peninsula and Muintir mBaire, we find that this area contains the greatest concentration of megalithic monuments in Western Europe, if not in the world. In light of this, it is difficult to accept that the engineering and astrological knowledge of those primitive builders had gradually infiltrated from the adjoining island. In this regard, I clash with the views and findings of the majority of historians, especially those of the latter part of the last century and the beginning of this.

From a detailed study and site investigation of early civilisation in the Middle East, the Mediterranean countries, Spain, Portugal, Brittany and the south coast of England, it is more than obvious that, early on, a westwards migration of a semi-civilised people occurred. What do we have to support this argument? We do not have parchment, or early papyri sketching out epochs of early history like the Egyptians, Sumerians, Minoans or Greeks. Nor do we have hieroglyphics or wall murals, like early Egypt or Crete.

What we do have are the best examples of early places of worship, burial grounds, dolmens and standing stones, the majority of them being in alignment with the sun, moon, stars and other natural phenomena such as tides and equinoxes (the commencement and ending of the seasons).

Unfortunately, our local monuments, which number about 200, are not as well preserved as Newgrange, Knowth, and Dowth. In a sense, they have been forgotten, and suffered the ravages of time, abuse and decay. We are surrounded by one of the greatest tourist attractions in the country, and few people realise it. I suppose it is one of the best kept secrets of our time, and the foundation of our proud heritage.

It is difficult to believe that, as the majority of historians suggest, primitive man in Ireland advanced by 'leaps and bounds' during the period 4500–1500 BC. We are led to believe that Ireland was extremely isolated, and visited only by those who dwelled in the neighbouring island. How primitive man could have advanced so much in knowledge of the sciences, religion, and basic culture without the influence of 'foreign' cultures defies logical thinking.

The supposition that sea-going vessels capable of making a long journey (say from Spain) did not exist during this period ruled out the possibility of early sea-going people visiting our shores. However, the fact that there are no artefacts or remains of large ships does not justify the conclusion that they did not visit. The Phoenicians, those early voyagers and explorers from the Eastern Mediterranean, were already circumnavigating the continent of Africa in *c.* 600 BC in sea-going vessels. There is no reason to doubt that they could also have voyaged northwards to Ireland. As a matter of fact, everything about megalithic man here points to this fact, regardless of what other historians believe.

The Phoenicians were extremely secretive about their sea-faring journeys and the lands they had found. Having explored the Mediterranean, around 3500 BC, they established a city, called Tartassos, at the mouth of the Gualdalquiver (south of modern-day Cadiz), and from this base they began to explore the lands to the north and south which bordered on the Atlantic. In contrast to the Egyptians, their vessels were built of cedar wood against bound rushes, and were held together by timber dowels. Prior to the introduction of the sea-going vessels of the Phoenicians, the Sumerians seem to have been the first to utilise river and sea transport *c.* 5500 BC.

If, for a moment, we examine the Uruk civilisation during the Ubaid Period of 6500–3500 BC, we find that they were already navigating the Tigris and Euphrates rivers by boat, and had already made use of the sail. These reed vessels are depicted on clay tablets found in the ruins of Nippur. In addition, they also had constructed large barges on which they transported cargoes of hewn stone of 1,000 tons down-river, where they constructed their cities of Ur, Kish and Erech. A point worth noting here is that the first known record of Noah and the flood was found on a broken clay tablet in the ruins of the city-state of Nippur, and it was some 500 years later that the Hebrews wrote their particular version, which had widely exaggerated the original account. Finally, these Uruk people were the first to introduce copper tools, they invented the wheel, wrote records on clay tablets with pictograph signs (hieroglyphics), and, most important of all, they had devised a system of navigation by using a metal lode which was pointed to the magnetic north.

Returning to the Phoenicians, we find that they had passed Agadir, and were already at the Cape by *c.* 600 BC. As they progressed southwards and established various outposts along the way, other vessels followed with families, animals, goods, etc., to establish a settlement. And as they moved northwards along the coast of Spain and Portugal, with vessels propelled by both oar and sail, the same system of early colonisation was followed.

We doubt whether they encountered much difficulty in crossing the Bay of Biscay, by use of the trade winds and their primitive compass. Early references show that they were already trading with the 'peoples of the Northern Isles' for precious metals well before 3500 BC, and no doubt they had set up their own trading outpost along our southern coastline.

In those early days of trading and bartering, many items of Middle Eastern culture found their way into usage here. Communication was probably by sign language at first, until certain important words came into usage. After a time, the interpreters would have come into play and there was a spreading of knowledge. No doubt, when winter and gales came early, these eastern traders were obliged to sojourn here for the winter months and intermarriage and relationships commenced. At this point in local history, our ancient heritage was born.

Our knowledge of prehistory only began in the 1870s and, therefore, we must realise, as many historians and archaeologists have pointed out that we are only dealing with 'the tip of the iceberg'. No statement is more true as far as this part of the country is concerned. With the absence of artefacts such as implements, utensils, cooking objects, urns, weapons, hieroglyphics, rock paintings, etc., such as are found in southern countries, we would expect to be totally in the dark as regards this most ancient civilisation and its culture. Fortunately, this is not the case, as we are able to trace the existence of these people by a variety of means:

1. religion and religious rites
2. their system of burial
3. their knowledge of astronomy
4. their gods
5. the survival of ancient placenames

Religion and Religious Rites

In order to consider the earliest of religious beliefs and practices here in southern Ireland, we must first briefly examine the religions of the ancient Sumerians (Iraq), Assyrians, Phoenicians and Carthaginians.

One of the most important tenets of the earliest Sumerian religion was dualism: the belief in the existence of two original uncreated principles—good and evil—which were two mighty beings in continuous conflict. One was the creator of life, earth, the heavens and all things spiritual, while the other was the creator of all that was evil. Both of these gods had a number of inferior spirits, and principal among them was the good spirit and leader of the angelic host, Serosh, on whom the Archangel Michael was fashioned. With the offering of sacrifices and the burning of the 'sacred fire', these were the origins of the priestly sect from which came our ancient druids. Later, this religion corrupted into the practice of worshipping the four elements of fire, air, earth and water, under the direction of a powerful priest-caste. The fire-altar on the mountain tops became the centrepiece of their religion, where the high-priest reigned as the chief mediator between the gods and the people. It was not unusual for a woman to be a high-priest (see Shubad's Tomb, discovered by Whooley).

The Assyrians

As far as the Assyrian religion is concerned, there are a few points worth noting. They believed in a supreme god—Ra—and under him there existed a triad of minor gods: Anu (chaos), Bel (creative spirit) and Hoa (animate matter), or, in other words, the gods of water, heaven and earth. Of these, Bel is the most important to us as he represents the maker of heaven, earth and the minor sun-god Shaman, who is represented as the 'lord of the fire' and 'the light of the gods'. The seventh month, Tisri, was dedicated to him, and he had nine festivals. In the ancient Sumerian 'deluge' tablets, it was he who caused the 'flood'.

The Phoenicians and Carthaginians

Within the limited polytheism of the Phoenicians we find a number of gods which bear a certain similarity to our own ancient gods: El, Baal, Moloch and Shamas. Of these, El had the personality of a supreme or most high god, Baal is the 'lord' or 'master', while Moloch is the 'king'. Baaltis was the feminine form of Baal, and so we find that the Phoenicians also worshipped goddesses, such as Baaltis (Baalti, Belthis, Belthes) and Ashtoreth. Baal was really the supreme god or eternal king to whom nearly all Phoenicians were dedicated or consecrated after birth. Another god worthy of note here is Dagon, whose worship spread throughout the Mediterranean and further. He is represented as the 'fish-god', deriving from dag, meaning fish. Shamas, or Shemesh, 'the sun', was worshipped separately from Baal, and this practice was accompanied by the use of 'sun-images'. The Phoenicians followed the custom of offering human sacrifices to placate the gods in time of great pestilence or calamity. They, however, were not idolators as such, but worshipped the 'ever-burning fire' to Baal. Instead of building temples and the like, they dedicated conical or large upright stones to the various deities, and these 'baetyli' (standing stones) were believed to possess certain mystical powers. Also, large wooden uprights, or 'asherahs' were used, and these, together with the stone monuments, were worshipped by sung praises, prayer and sacrifice. The 'asherahs' became sacred trees and from this came the worship of certain types of trees in later religious ceremonies. Their festivals were held mainly at the equinoxes, especially at the vernal, when everybody gathered for the festivals.

Ancient Burial Rites

In order to consider the profusion of megalithic monuments—stone circles, dolmens, standing stones, cromleich, etc.—in the area, we must trace back to the commencement of these burial practices in prehistory. Skirting along the western seaboard of the European continent, as far as southern Spain, we find almost identical monuments and practices—along the south coast of England, across into Brittany, in north-western Spain, Portugal and the south of Spain. From there, we can trace the same practices to Malta, Libya, Northern Africa, Crete, Lebanon, Syria, Iran, Hindustan and the Upper Nile. It appears that there was a general migration of early civilisation westwards. Some historians are of the opinion that this diffusion of early civilisation took place as far back as 8500 BC.

Taking but a few examples of this aspect of history, we have only to look at the similar customs of Catal Huytik (*c.* 6500 BC) in Anatolia (Eastern Turkey), Knossos (Crete), Nea Nikomedeia (Pella, Macedonia), Dhimini (Greece), Pylos and the Cycladic Islands to find evidence of this system of burial, such as tumulos, cist graves, tholii (burial mounds or cairns), stone circles, shaft graves and standing stones. If, in this context, we consider Newgrange, we find many identical examples in the eastern Mediterranean—for example, on the Mesara Plain, where the tholii were built entirely above ground, at Platanos in Crete, and Khiroktia in Cyprus, all of which have been carbon dated to *c.* 5800 BC. The early circular tombs were communal, for families or clans over numerous generations. Where this system of collective burial came from is open to question, but it seems to have originated in Anatolia (northern Turkey), and to have been introduced to the eastern Mediterranean by a nomadic race, whose custom was to live in round huts surrounded by either timber fencing or clay walls for protection. Artefacts prove that important families had the protection of two mounds, or walls, sometimes with a type of dyke between them. It is no wonder, therefore, that the burial places took on the shape of their existing living quarters as the abode of the dead in the after-life.

Primitive Astrology

To describe the unbelievable grasp, held by early civilisation, of the movements of the sun, moon and stars as 'primitive' would seem to me to be a great misnomer. When we consider astrology, we have to bear in mind its relationship with mathematics, geometry and the calendar.

Having discussed the systems of burial above, and compared them with what we find in Ireland, it is important to mention one major difference, and that is that most of our ancient burial places are surrounded by stone circles. This introduces another dimension, as their alignment coincides with the apparent movements of the sun, moon and stars. Newgrange, for example, is surrounded by a circle of some 35 to 36 stones.

Amongst the best examples of the ancient knowledge of astrology is the Solar Calendar of Heliopolos in the Upper Nile, while at Carnac in Brittany (named after Karnac on the Upper Nile) there is a wonderful example of the alignment of 'menhirs' (standing stones). Our own stone circles and standing stone alignments have a direct reference to the movement of the sun, moon and stars, including the equinoxes, solstices, tides and an overall grid system within the area.

At this point it is most important to clarify the question of standing stone circles. These are not druid circles of early Celtic times, but are of an age which predates the so-called Celtic invasion by thousands of years. The ancient circles of standing stones consisted of a ring of pillar stones (of any height) which were set on end and enclosed a circular patch of ground. In addition, there was a solitary stone outside the circle, whilst both within, and part of, the circle were the portal stones and a recumbent stone. By the use of these, the different times of the year could be ascertained. Some historians, including R. A. S. Macalister, were of the opinion that the various stones of a stone circle represented different deities.

Standing Stones at Scart, Bantry

Ancient Religious Symbols

It is in this context that we see the influence of the different religious beliefs of various civilisations of the Middle East. Before commenting on them in detail, we must first look at those elements of belief which were common to most, if not all, early religions, which have been depicted on our ancient stone monuments.

Spirals

This symbol is predominant in all burial rituals and sites. It represents the worship of the 'Earth Mother' or goddess of life and fertility and the return of the body of the deceased to the care of the Earth Mother. It also represents the cycle of life here on earth.

Sun Symbol

There are many variations and examples of this particular symbol, but the basic theme is that of a circle, or solar disc, with interior geometric patterns, or a surround of rays emitting from the centre. This symbol also denoted the place of burial of a ruler or leader, who was blessed by the sun-god through his priests, and marked his grave or territory.

Boat of the Sun-God

It is generally accepted that all our dolmens were originally covered by mud, earth and stones, to form a mound. Only the basic structure of the dolmen still exists, which comprises of three upright stones supporting a reclining top stone. I agree with some archaeologists and historians who state that this structure represents a ship with its high prow, supported by the three pillars (triad of the gods), which transported the spirits of the dead to the Other World.

The most common symbol of the above is that of a boat with some figures on board—the dead—being transported to the Other World by the sun-god on his nightly journeys. There is a clear indication here that there was a widespread belief in the transmigration of the spirits in most early civilisations, including Ireland.

— 4 —
The Legend of Cessair

There are many versions in the old manuscripts of the arrival on our shores of the first human being—in the person of Cessair. We must not forget that the early scribes who recorded these events, as well as other myths and legends, were imbued with the dominant tenets of early Christianity. They were translating the Irish language as well as writing down the spoken word of the bards, who recorded past history in verse. As the early Irish language did not conform to the grammatical structures of Latin, we must assume that most of the original stories would have lost something in translation. Therefore, their interpretation of these stories would have been coloured by their own beliefs, and the written records, such as early manuscripts, contain only what was acceptable to the church authorities.

The exact context of the Cessair legend will never be known. However, if we examine closely the various interpretations, we will be able to separate the pagan and Christian elements of the story. At the time of translating the old stories of the various 'invasions' (*An Leabhair Gabhala*), the notion and practice of filling in the genealogies of all famous people and events from the time of Noah was uppermost in the early Church's mind, so as to give a sense of identity and meaning to all that was written. Accordingly, the story of Cessair has been written in a semi-religious context, with an attempt to discard any pagan symbolism in the process. As the monk scribes were dealing with a very important event, namely the flood, they had to be extremely careful not to contradict the 'Word of God', as written in the Bible. As things turned out, they failed miserably in their attempts, as by mentioning the story at all they implied that there was another ark besides that of Noah. The story, as related by the early scribes, is briefly as follows:

Having been warned by Noah that a 'great flood' was imminent, Cessair, daughter of Bith, son of Noah, gathered her followers and constructed three 'arks'. When the vessels were ready they sailed out of Meroe, upon the Nile, for the open sea. During their voyage, which lasted for seven years and three months, two of the vessels were lost in a storm. Finally, some forty days before the deluge commenced, Cessair and her crew landed at Dun-na-mBarc, near Bantry.

Cessair arrives by longboat at Donemark

On the vessel with Cessair were three men—Bith, Ladra and Fintan—and fifty women. (No details were given as to the numbers on the vessels that were lost, except that they each also had fifty women aboard, but, since we are dealing with a repeated combinations of numbers here, we may assume that there were also three men on board each vessel lost.) There is no mention as to how long they remained at Dun-na-mBarc before setting off again for 'the meeting of the three rivers' (Suir, Nore and Barrow). Here the men divided the women amongst them—Fintan took Cessair and seventeen women, Bith took seventeen women, and Ladra, who only had sixteen, was very unhappy with the division. Fintan, Cessair and the seventeen women went north. In time, word reached Fintan and Bith that Ladra had died of an 'excess of women', so they came together again and divided Ladra's sixteen women equally between them. It is recorded that they all died some years later as a result of pestilence.

This is the first recorded 'incursion' to our shores, but when we examine it more closely we must ask the question, 'If nobody but Noah and his ark survived the flood, how was this tale of Cessair passed down?' The early writers explained this by asserting that Fintan, having been drowned in the flood, afterwards rose from the dead and passed his story on for posterity. So, according to our early Christian monks and scribes, Fintan was the first Lazarus.

However, it is assumed that the story of Cessair was originally placed after the flood, like all similar tales in the legends of other civilisations. In actual fact, the first written account of the deluge was found on a broken clay tablet in the ruins of Nippur (modern Iraq):

> For seven days and seven nights...the flood had swept over the land. And the huge boat had been tossed about by the wind storms of the great waters. Zuisundra opened a window on the huge boat and...'

Zuisundra was the favourite king of the city state of Sumer, and, like Noah, he was chosen to ride out the mighty deluge by the gods. Some four centuries later, the Hebrews wrote their version, replacing Zuisundra with Noah, and adding his family to the story.

It is interesting to note that Sir Bernard Wholley, the archaeologist, on his excavations of the cities of Ur and nearby Al-Ubaid, had to dig through eleven feet of mud deposits before he found traces of the famous cities of the Sumerians. These deposits of mud have been dated to between 12000 and 9500 BC which, according to recent studies, coincides with a meteorite hitting the earth off Yucatan,

Mexico, and the destruction of 'the lost continent of Atlantis', and give an approximate date of the 'great flood'.

Cessair disembarks at Donemark

The Greeks also adopted the tale of the great flood in their mythology of the gods. When the god Zeus decided to annihilate the human race by burying it beneath the waves of a deluge, Prometheus warned his son Deucalion and his wife Pyrrha to build an ark. For nine days and nine nights they rode the waves, and on the tenth day they both disembarked on Mount Parnassus, which was the only place still above the sea. When they prayed to Zeus to save the human race, they were spared and the seas subsided.

Whatever we may say about the other flood stories, the ancient Irish version, before it was tampered with by the scribes, must have been dated after the deluge, as Cessair means 'life to the world' and Fintan means 'the deathless son of Bochna' (or, 'the eternal son of the ocean'). They had set out on the ark, before the flood, on a holy day called 'Lam Di' (Day of Llama), so that they would have the blessings of the gods. We encounter the mystical number three: in their setting out seven years and three months before the flood; three men; and their second destination, 'the meeting of the three rivers'. As for the number of women being put at fifty, there is no explanation except to populate each and every area of Ireland at that time. We must also note that Fintan was portrayed as a good man, while Ladra was the opposite, being prone to excesses. Thus, together they represent good and evil. Finally, in some of the versions handed down to us, Dun-na-mBarc is placed off the coast of Kerry, and in some around Wexford, but the generally accepted location is Donemark, near Bantry.

— 5 —
Ancient Civilisations

As far as ancient Irish civilisation is concerned, we must examine what these early inhabitants left behind as proof of their existence, and what similarities there were with other early civilisations.

The evidence for early Irish culture consists of megalithic monuments, tumuli, passage graves, stone circles, hieroglyphics such as spirals, and other stone patterns or designs. In order to find a solution as to how these graves and monuments happened to be built in Ireland, we must first look at the approximate dates of the prehistoric 'invaders'.

It is fairly certain at this stage that Ireland was inhabited towards the end of the Neolithic era, *c.* 6500 BC, and that the builders of the megalithic monuments arrived either around this time or towards the beginning of the Bronze Age, *c.* 3500 BC.

These early people cremated their dead and buried them in 'boulder burials' and were small in stature (see R.A.S. Macalister, *Ireland in Prehistoric Times*). During the early Middle Bronze Age (2000–1600 BC), another race of tall people arrived, who buried their dead without cremation. Later, at the end of the Bronze Age (1600–1000 BC), yet another race arrived, who again cremated their dead before burying them with urns and implements. Finally, at the beginning of the Iron Age (1000–500 BC), small numbers of another war-like race arrived, who overran the country and dominated the previous inhabitants.

If we identify the above with those mentioned in the early Irish manuscripts as 'invasion' forces, we come up with the possibility that the first mentioned were the Fir Bolg, the tall people were the fair-haired Tuatha de Danaan, and the Iron Age invaders were the Milesians.

The question of where these various peoples came from has been a subject much debated by historians over the past one hundred and fifty years. Firstly, many question the authenticity of these ancient accounts, believing them to be pure fiction. Others believe that there is a degree of factual content in the tales, while a few are of the opinion that there is a substantial amount of fact shrouded amongst the legends.

If we are to assume that the various invasions mentioned came from Britain, as the nearest island, why has it been stated that the culture in Ireland was about eight hundred years more advanced than in Britain during the early prehistoric period. Newgrange, for instance, has recently been verified as dating from within about eighty-two years of 3880 BC, which places it earlier than Stonehenge, and even the Pyramids Egypt. As to the accepted theory of the diffusion of civilisation spreading from east to west, there are many unanswered questions, such as those regarding the incursions of the 'Sea People' into the Mediterranean, as related in Egyptian and Phoenician myths and legends, and the arrival of Kukulkan—otherwise known as Cuchulainn—at Yucatan in Mexico, as related in Mayan legends.

Examination of the burial places, rites, customs and hieroglyphics of the countries bordering on the Mediterranean, reveal a striking similarity with those found in Ireland. If we look at Newgrange, we find that this particular type of sepulchral burial is associated with a primitive race which inhabited the Upper Nile, Anatolia in Turkey, Greece, Crete, Cyprus, Libya, Malta and Iberia in Spain in early history. These tombs, or tumuli, were communal to families or clans over generations and are dated as Neolithic (8500–6500 BC).

One of the best examples of similarity with Newgrange is found at Platonos, on the Mesara Plain of southern Crete. It was constructed entirely above ground, with its floor sunk by about a metre. No roof remains, but certain evidence shows that it was domed and built in a corbelled, or bee-hived, pattern like the Tholos tombs. This particular type of burial was widespread throughout the area now known as Greece and the Islands. The thick passage walls lean inwards in an 'A' shape, supporting domes built from stone-bonded clay. The tomb at Platonos and another similar one at Khiroktia in Cyprus are carbon dated to prior to 5800 BC. This system of burial is reputed to have been brought by the Aryan people from the east, who themselves lived in a round type of hut. These Tholos style tombs are also found at Les Millares, Almeria, in Spain.

Returning to Newgrange, we find the influence of an earlier culture, that of the builders of the stone circles, as Newgrange mound was surrounded by about thirty-six standing stones. The alignment of the Newgrange passage and the stones gave an accurate table of the apparent and actual movements of the sun, moon and stars, and as such was a type of calendar, in common with most of the stone circles found in the Bantry region. The Palace of Knossos, in Crete, was built on top of a Neolithic mound like Newgrange, and has been dated to *c.* 6341 BC.

Standing stones are not unique to Ireland. If we examine closely the archaeological maps of Western Europe and the Mediterranean, we can see how the line of standing stones, also known as menhirs or baetyli, stretches from the east to these islands. It appears that they had different purposes, such as marking the grave of someone important, a division of land, a stellar or lunar alignment, or maybe directions to a particular site. There are many fine examples in the Bantry locality, especially at Ahil Mór, Kielnascarta and Millbeg.

As for the stone circles, they come in many different numbers of upright stones, varying from five to thirteen. They represent both a druidic temple and also calendar clocks, which were calculated to the accuracy of 365.242 days in the year, as compared to our modern calendar of 365.2422 days. As the druid astrologers did not foresee the slowing of the earth on its axes, their alignments with the sun, moon and stars are now slightly erroneous.

Stone Circles

There are quite a number of stone circles in West Cork and in the Bantry region, but very few of them now stand intact. The best examples are to be found at Kealkil (five stones), Breeny Mór (unknown), Cullamane (five stones), Baurgorm (five stones) and Millbeg (five stones). There are a number of other sites where exact numbers of stones cannot be proven.

A study of this particular type of megalithic monument is a lifetime occupation for some enthusiasts, and the various theories and findings as to their exact role in early civilisation would fill volumes. Therefore, we shall only have a brief look at their importance and past usage.

Firstly, when we speak of stone circles, we automatically conclude that they are all perfect, or near perfect, circles. This, in fact, is not true. Some are indeed perfect circles but others are well constructed ellipses and are deliberately constructed as modified circles—some with flattened arcs or others pulled out like an egg shape—to conform to their primary use as astronomical clocks, a means by which to tell the seasons, and then as a solar calendar and a means of foretelling both solar and lunar eclipses.

It must have taken a considerable time for Neolithic man to select a site which corresponded with known landmarks to give the position on the horizon of the sunrise and sunset at different times of the year. Taking the North Polar Star and the top of a well-known mountain peak as static points, they were able to chart out the sun's movements through the seasons using the knowledge they had of right angled triangles.

In addition, with this basic knowledge of geometry, they were able to correlate groups of stone circles with standing stones and foretell the lunar eclipses. In a word, in the form of standing stones, they have left their five-thousand-year-old computer, and their observational accuracy was not equalled until the Renaissance.

In establishing a lunar calendar by the study of the phases of the moon, they had approached the early Hebrew calendar, which is still based on the lunar month and alternate months of twenty-nine and thirty days. This calendar revolves around a period of nineteen years, twelve years having twelve months and seven years having thirteen months, making a total of two hundred and thirty-five months. It is brought back into line with the solar year by the use of the Metonic Cycle.

On the other hand, the Muslim calendar is purely lunar, making a complete revolution every thirty-three of our years, and the beginning of the year rotates around the seasons. It is much more likely that the early lunar calendar used here was similar to the Hebrew one.

If we are to examine the locations of both the stone circles and the standing stones in the Bantry Bay region, in order to try and correlate their positions with either the sun or the moon, we immediately run into difficulties, mainly due to the absence of stones in vital locations that would assist us in chacking alignments. However, by trial and error many possibilities of alignments do appear. Unfortunately, I have neither the time nor sufficient knowledge of physics and mathematics to carry out a detailed study, but, in the illustration I have marked out those alignments which seem important, and hope that this will be of some assistance to those who have an interest in this particular subject.

If we are to consider the stone circles as astronomical clocks, we should not use the word 'primitive' when we take into consideration the unbelievable grasp that early civilisation had of the movements of the heavenly bodies. Also, we must point out that they are not 'Celtic druid circles', as they predate any so called Celtic influence by thousands of years. (Some historians, including Macalister, were of the opinion that the various stones of a stone circle each represented one of the lesser deities of the ancient religion.)

Our boulder burials, or cromlechs, are believed to be the oldest type of ritual burials, and they are mostly found in the south-west of Ireland. It is argued that they were originally covered in mud and stone in a type of mound, not unlike Newgrange, but have been subjected to the elements and the influence of man over the milleniums, leaving them in their present state. The structure itself consists of a large tilted stone supported by two or, more usually, three vertical uprights at either side. Some authorities state that the inclination of the covering slab represents a ship with a high prow and that the three pillar stones represent the ancient triad of the gods (Father, Son and Mother Earth)—thus the spirits of the dead were carried in the

'Board of the Sun' to the Other World under the protection of the Trinity.

Some of the best examples are found at Colomane, Breeny Mór and Millbeg. As for cairns or rock mounds on top of hills or in high places, it used to be generally accepted that these were nothing more than piles of stones marking out territory. Now, however, after excavations, it appears that these were in fact burial mounds, with a number having underground passages to the burial chamber at the centre of the interior.

Unfortunately, some of the best examples in the region have been ravaged for building stones over the centuries, such as Curran, Maughanaclea and Colomane.

Rock art in general has been viewed rather sceptically by both archaeologists and historians, who believed them to be nothing more than the doodling of some farmer or herdsman. Now, however, attitudes have changed, following serious examination of various sites in south Kerry. The latest conclusion is that they possibly date from the Middle Bronze Age (2000–1600 BC). Rock art is peculiar to south Kerry and the Bantry region, and there are many fine examples, in particular those at Kealanine, Crooha West and Massmount (Adrigole) and Coom.

If we are to look at West Cork in general, we find that there are some 3,662 identified sites at the present time. In addition, there are about two hundred more sites to be examined and classified. It is estimated that the above number is approximately one third of what originally existed prior to the eighteenth century.

A breakdown of those early sites would be roughly as follows:

Period	*Number of sites*
Medieval	306 sites
Early Christian	1,893 sites
Celtic Iron Age	64 sites
Bronze Age	989 sites
Mezzolithic	4 sites
Neolithic	3 sites

(The sites which cannot be dated are included in the Bronze Age category.)

The ring forts which, even nowadays, are a common sight on elevated ground or on top of hillocks were built during the period 800 BC to AD 500, either as dwelling places for tribes or, to a lesser degree, as a type of fortified farmstead.

Scribed rock markings at Coom

— 6 —

Early Myths and Legends

Amongst the local myths and legends there are a few interesting tales which are worth noting here—the legend of Cessair and her followers, as well as the arrival of other people (incursions), like the Tuatha de Danaan and the Milesians. All of these are discussed in separate chapters, because of their overall importance.

These people brought with them their own myths and legends—in the form of pantheons of the gods, customs and beliefs—which have influenced the lives of people since their arrival. Those who were amongst the first to arrive in this country brought with them the Aryan customs and traditions of the Far East. This is exemplified by their use of tumuli in their burial ceremonies and the use of earth, fire and water as important elements of their religion.

It is believed that Eastern mysticism was at the root of the spiritual life of the early Irish inhabitants.

In examining the early invaders of this country, it should be noted that one of the first mentioned is Parthalon and his followers, who are reputed to have come from the West and not the East. It is one of the first, if not the first, reference in early literature to people arriving in Europe from the Atlantic—counter to the accepted belief that the diffusion of civilisation came westward from the East—and opens up a multitude of questions which cannot be discussed here.

Next to arrive were the Formorians, who were described as a cruel and uncouth people who practised the power of 'evil and darkness', living in the land of ice and gloom. Their god was called Balor (of the evil eye) and was represented as a giant, whose death 'by a stone in the eye' is almost a direct reference to the story of David and Goliath in the Bible.

Nothing much can be said about the Nemedians and the Fir Bolg, except that they were inferior and servile races.

The arrival of the Tuatha de Danaan—their pantheons of the gods, burial customs, ceremonial rites and the dominant priestly caste—introduced a completely new culture and attitude to life. The influence of their science and poetry permeated everyday life. They had four sacred objects in their mythology: the Stone of Destiny; the Invincible Sword; the Magic Spear and the Cauldron of Dagda.

These all have Greek mythological connotations. Even the name Danae has Greek connections, being the daughter of Acrisius who was to bear a son by Zeus called Perseus who journeyed to the western extremities of the earth. The story of Danae giving birth to a son through the intervention of the supreme god Zeus is another example of the 'virgin birth', which was a dominant factor in eastern mythology before the time of Christ. The last account of Danae in Greek mythology is of being in the city of Argos in a western land.

It was the Tuatha de Danaan who introduced the influence of music into early Irish society—as well as musical instruments—and also the influence of the seasons. Music was supposed to induce sleep and it also invoked various moods, whether of happiness or sadness. Ireland became known as the land of the harp. Even Hecataeus the Greek historian observed that 'the inhabitants were almost exclusively harpers and that Apollo must have an influence in this matter'. The harp was described as Orphean, an evident derivation from Orpheus, god of music, who is said to have held back the rivers in their course, made the woods listen and moved stones. The early Irish referred to the harp as 'Clearest' and 'Cruet'—the former identified the musical board and the latter the strings.

It is said that the harp was introduced to the Middle East by Indian priests, the followers of Buddha, who had been forced to flee their country by rival sects of Brahma. How it arrived in Ireland is debatable, but it dates from the time the Tuatha de Danaan were supposed to have arrived here. Through the millenniums, the music has not much changed and has mostly retained its original character, as mentioned in the Book of Genesis, Chapter Four—'and Jubal was the father of all such as handle the harp and organ'.

In early times, Ireland had native animals such as the elk, deer and wolf, etc. These had been left behind when the landbridge between Ireland and Scotland disappeared. Contrary to legend, Ireland did not have snakes and, when reference is made to St. Patrick banishing the snake from Ireland, it is not the cold-blooded reptile that is being alluded to but the snake god Dagda of the old pagan religion.

One interesting animal which deserves attention here is the humble donkey. This animal is not native to these isles or to northern Europe, but to the Middle East and Africa. How it arrived in Ireland before making an appearance in England is a question in need of further study.

The ancient names of some local important sites or physical structures might cast some light on these questions.

For instance, the Bull, the Cow and the Calf rocks, off Dursey Island, were known by these names only from *c.* AD 1500 and derive from folklore concerning the Cailleach Beara and her two sisters. However, according to earlier references to the south-west of Ireland, the names of these three rocks were completely different. The Bull Rock was known as *Mosdah* (Big Sea), *Mikologh* (Great Beyond) or *Teach Don* (meaning the house of Dagda, the supreme god). The Calf Rock was known as *Crelagh* (Ashes), referring to the cremated dead, while the Cow Rock was called *An Torann* or *Tonnai*, denoting a rough and stormy sea.

On the north side of the Bull Rock was a large cave, before the action of the sea tunnelled right through it. This cave, or aperture, was referred to as the Entrance to the Other World—a direct reference to the entrance to Hades, as related in Greek mythology, where Aeneas is helped by Sybil to cross the black river Cocytus when she offers a golden branch to the old ferryman, Charon, whose first refusal was because he only ferried those who had received proper burial rites.

It is interesting to note that Sybil, in Greek mythology, is said to have possessed prophetical powers and the power of magic. Maybe there is a link here between Sybil and Sceine (An Cailleach Beara). As for the local equivalent of Charon the ferryman, the only reference is to Manannan, who manned the ferryboat which departed from the location known as Coite (near the base of the cablecar hut).

Situated to the east of Bantry town is the mountain known as Mullaghmesha. This mountain, in ancient folklore, was regarded as a sacred place. The name lends itself to a variety of interpretations—(1) the high round summit, or (2) the altar to the god Molloch (Phoenician Melek or high god). Whether the top of the mountain was a ceremonial site in ancient times is open to debate and requires further site investigation. The tradition that a type of passage grave was to be found on the northern side of the mountain, as well as an extremely large cave which could hold a few thousand people on the south side, might lead to the conclusion that the mountain was indeed held sacred in ancient times.

As for the Mill Beg site, which has been mentioned elsewhere, there is a tradition that this apparently insignificant location was the burial ground of kings. Who these kings were, or what period of time is in question, nobody knows. Examination of the site itself has revealed very little, due to its almost complete destruction over the centuries.

There is no tradition of an ancient battle being fought in the vicinity, so it must have been a place of ceremonial ritual and burial. Maybe the sacrificial stone gives us a clue as to the exact type of sacred ritual.

As related elsewhere, the custom of building Christian settlements on old pagan sites was most common in this area—Colomane, Kilmacomoge and Kilcaskan (Adrigole). This latter site is most intriguing, as it contains a bullaun-type hollow on a large stone from where a snake-like concentration of boulders winds its way down to the nearby river.

This site, as well as others situated under the southern side of Hungry Hill, which were converted to Christian usage, must have had some influence in ancient times in the naming of Hungry Hill as Cnoc Da Dia (The Hill of Two Gods). Was it the conflict between the ancient pagan religion and the new Christian dogma of the Trinity?

One of the most important myths of the region is that of the Cailleach Beara. The word *cailleach* itself means priestess, witch or someone who has magic powers of some good but mainly evil. She has been referred to as *An Sceine*, *Boi* and *Bui*—in this context as *Inbhear Sceine*, *Cuan Bui* and *Cnoc Bui* (Knockboy mountain). There appears to be a direct reference here to An Cailleach.

She was the goddess of the harvest and wife of Lugh, the sun-god, who gave his name to Lughnasa which was the ancient harvest festival which fell on the last Sunday of July. An Cailleach was always associated with two other Cailleach—one of Dingle and the other of Bolus Head.

She is known also as the wife of Manannan, the god of the sea, who has been mentioned above as the Bull Rock ferryman to the Underworld. If Manannan is compared to the Greek god of the sea, Poseidon, we find that the scope of Manannan's power and identity is much greater and much older in history. Besides being the god of the sea, he was also the god of water, the god of the river and streams, as well as the snake god. However, Cailleach does not bear any resemblance to Amphitrite, the wife of Poseidon.

As to the connection of An Cailleach with the stone overlooking Ballycrovan Harbour, which bears the same name, the myth has to be further explored. When St. Catherine fell asleep outside her monastery at Coulagh, the Cailleach snatched her prayer book and ran away and ended up at Gortgarriff, where St. Catherine caught up with her. As a punishment for stealing the prayer book, St. Catherine turned the Cailleach into stone. This, of course, compares to the Greek myth of Medusa.

Another local legend is the tale of one of the exploits of Fionn MacCubhal at Inchinagaum, Coomhola, where he fought with the carrion of death. (This story is related in full in *Where the Deer Ran Wild*, by the author.)

One of the most popular myths in the area is that of the Priest's Leap, which deserves some clarification. The most common story relating to this is the account of a priest being pursued on horseback by English soldiers. Coming up the north side of the mountain with the pursuing detachment of horsemen closing, and having arrived at the summit of the pass, his further escape was doomed because of the terrain. With a price of £5 on his head, he had no option but to urge his horse to jump off the steep cliff face. However, instead of falling to their death, the horse and rider took off and flew through the air and finally came to earth leaving hoofprints on the rock at Newtown, just outside of Bantry. A commemorative plaque marks the spot.

Princess Beara

As far as can be ascertained, the story or tale seems to have originated *c.* 1603, after the fall of Denbigh Castle, and refers to an exploit of Fr. Archer, a Jesuit who was in the Beara locality at that time. This particular priest was not known for his pious behaviour, but rather for his other exploits, especially as far as the fair sex was concerned. The old traditions of the area around Curran and Coomhola state that, if Fr. Archer was the priest in question, it was not by the power of the God above, but of the 'man below' that the horse took off.

One of the interesting tales to emerge during my research was that there was a strong tradition of the existence of a leprechaun who often appeared at the top of the pass. This, combined with the free flow of poteen on the mountain, puts a different slant on the story! Emerging from this combination, there were many tales of men returning from the Kerry side who, resting after the climb, encountered the leprechaun, whose gift was to transport anyone who fell into a trance to wherever they wished to be. As a result, many a story exists of men finding themselves sitting by their own hearth, or in bed, or else in the outside stable when they woke up. The reader can draw his/her own conclusion.

Before completing this chapter, it might be worth mentioning some of the local, and more recent, myths or tales of the town. The first one to come to mind is that of the 'headless coachman and coach' which rushed through Blackrock Road at midnight on every 21 December. This was based on the hold-up at Colomane, where the assistant coachman was killed and the driver had his head sliced off with a scythe before the horses took flight. The horses, knowing the route, came through the old access road to Bantry House through Blackrock Road, with the headless driver still in his seat.

Old fishermen used to relate another tale, of how they used to see a black beast coming out from under the gateway of the old deal-yard when they were going fishing on a dark winter's morning. The dog never crossed the road but kept pace, snarling, with whoever was walking on the footpath, and then vanished as soon as they reached the old Bantry House wall.

Another, similar, tale existed about the strange wailing which used to be heard on passing the Abbey cemetery at night when the farmers were returning home. Their horses used to get so agitated that they reared up and refused to go any further until daybreak.

Finally, there was the spectre of an old woman which used to appear at the old Black Bridge, beyond the quarry fields. Various tales are told of how, when she touched anybody—usually on the shoulder—the imprint of her bony hand scorched the clothes of the victim to the skin.

The Priest's Leap

The priest is out upon the hill before the dawn of day;
Through shadows deep, o'er rugged ground he treads his painful way.
A peasants homely garb he wears, that none but friendly eyes,
May know who dares to walk abroad beneath that rough disguise.
Inside his coat and near his heart lies what he treasures most,
For there a tiny, silver case enshrines the Sacred Host.
Adoring as he goes, he seeks a cabin low and rude
To nourish there a fainting soul with God's appointed food.

For so it is within the land whose brave and faithful race,
In other days made all the isle a bright and holy place.
Its temples are in ruins now, its altars overthrown.
Its hermits' cells in cliff and cave are tenantless and lone.
The ancient race is broken down, their power is passed away,
Poor helots, plundered and despised, they read the soil today.
But yet, though fallen their fortunes be, through want and woe and ill,
Close hid and fondly loved, they keep their priests among them still,
Their faithful priests, who tho' by law condemned, denounced & banned
Will not forsake their suffering flocks or quit the stricken land.

The morning brightness as he goes, the little hut is near,
When runs a peasant to his side and speaks into his ear.
"Fly. Father, fly, the spies are out, they've watched you on your way,
They've brought the soldiers on your track to seize you or to slay.
Quick, Father dear, here stands my horse, no whip or spur he'll need,
Mount you at once upon his back, and put him to his speed,
And then what course you'd better take 'tis God alone that knows,
Before you spreads a stormy sea; behind you come your foes.
But mount at once and dash away; take chance for field or flood,
And God may raise His hand today to foil those men of blood".

Up sprang the priest, away he rode, but ere a mile was run,
Right in his path he saw the flash of bayonets in the sun.
He turned his horse's head, and sped along the way he came,
But, Oh! there too his hunters were fast closing on their game.
Straight forward then he faced his steed and urged him with his hand,
To where the cliff stood high and sheer above the sea-beat strand.
Then from the soldiers and the spies arose a joyful cheer,
Their toilsome chase was well-nigh o'er, the wished for end was near.
They stretched their eager hands to pluck the rider from his seat,
A few more lusty strides and they might swing him to their feet.

For now betwixt him and the verge are scarce ten feet of ground.
But, stay! Good God, out o'er the cliff the horse is seen to bound
The soldiers hasten to the spot, they gaze around, below,
No splash disturbs the waves that keep their smooth and even flow.
From their green depths, nor form of man or horse is seen to rise,
Far down upon the stony strand no mangled body lies.
"Look up! look up!" a soldier shouts, "Oh! what a sight is there,
Behold, the priest, on horseback still, is speeding through the air".
They looked, and lo, the words were true and trembling with affright,
They saw the vision pierce the blue and vanish from their sight.

Three miles away, across the bay, a group with wondering eyes,
Saw some strange speck come rushing fast towards them from the skies.
A bird, they deemed it first to be; they watched its course, and soon,
They thought it some black, burning mass flung from the sun or moon.
It neared the earth, their hearts beat fast, they held their breath with awe,
As clear and clearer still—the horse and then—the man—they saw.
They shut their eyes they stopped their ears to spare their hearts the shock
As steed and rider both came down and struck the solid rock.

Ay, on the solid rock they struck, but never made a sound.
No horrid mass of flesh and blood was scattered all around.
For when the horse fell on his knees, and when the priest was thrown.
A little forward, and his hands came down upon the stone,
That instant, by God's potent will, the flinty rock became,
Like moistened clay or wax that yields before a glowing flame.
Unhurt, unharmed the priest arose, and with a joyful start,
He pressed his hand upon his breast; the Host was near his heart.

Long years have passed away since then, in sun and wind and rain,
But still of that terrific leap the wonderous marks remain.
On the high cliff from which he sprang, now deemed a sacred place,
The prints left by the horse's hooves are plain for all to trace.
And still the stone where he alit whoever likes may view,
And see the signs and tokens there that prove the story true.
May feel and count each notch and line, may measure if he please,
The dint made by the horse's head, the grooves sunk by his knees.
And place his fingers in the holes for they are there to-day,
Made by the fingers of the priest who leaped across the bay.

— 7 —
Places of Historical Interest

It would be extremely difficult to give a detailed account of all the historical monuments in the Bantry region, which number in excess of six hundred sites. Most of these monuments have been noted and marked on the Ordnance Survey maps by the relevant authorities—the Board of Works, the Archaeology Department of University College Cork, and others. Full details can be found in the Archaeological Survey of West Cork. Therefore, this chapter will deal with the history, location and use of a limited number of these monuments and sites.

Generally speaking, the public have been brainwashed with the notion that all our prehistory dates from the so-called 'Celtic age'. As for the 'Celtic Invasion' of Ireland, many are now of the opinion that the idea itself is but a myth. It can be accepted that different groups of Celtic colonists did reach the shores of Ireland and integrated with the existing society, becoming part of that framework. These were not great inventors, as history suggests, but rather they improved or made better anything they considered worthwhile.

Much has been written about the Celtic druids and their influence in ancient Ireland, especially in the context of their ceremonial rites in and around the megalithic monuments, such as stone circles. This is presented as if the Celtic druids themselves were the instigators of the construction and usage of these monuments. Nothing could be further from the truth, and this idea should be obliterated from Irish history. In fact, some authors, when dealing with this particular subject, cannot escape from their own limited vision as to the exact origins of the megalithic monuments found in this country, and fail to realise that the so-called Celts did not come on the scene in Western Europe until *c.* 400 BC. They ignore the trail of similar and almost identical monuments extending from the Far East, through the Middle East, the Mediterranean, Portugal, Spain, western France, southwest England to Ireland. This trail automatically suggests the migration of certain races along its path; whether from east to west or west to east is another matter.

When the ancient myths and legends of Ireland are considered, there is a certain amount of fact and fiction intermingled in the various tales. It is extremely difficult to separate fact from fiction but, in the light of present-day scholarship, a certain amount of serious study is being undertaken.

Forgetting about the exact names given to the various waves of incursion into this country in prehistoric times, it is worth noting that they all seem to have come from the south and by the sea. The question of the existence of suitable boats for long sea journeys at that time has been discussed.

Some historians say that the Tuatha de Danaan were Minoans fleeing Crete at the time of the early Greek conquests, but palaeontologists have refuted this argument by showing that the Minoans were of small stature, with black hair and dark eyes. Also, there is no evidence (to date) in Ireland of exotic murals, for which the Minoans were renowned. Yet, evidence of bull-worship, the same pattern designs, and identical burials are to be found here.

A much more plausible explanation would be that the Tuatha de Danaan were Dorians who had overrun the Eastern Mediterranean *c.*2000 BC. Having been defeated by the Egyptians under Rameses II, the Dorians scattered all over the Mediterranean, even as far as southern Spain. They were noted for their fair hair and blue eyes, which was more akin to Nordic features than those found in the Near East.

During their short occupation of Crete, they had adopted some of the Minoan religious ceremonies and customs, such as reverence for the bull and the use of the double-headed bronze axe. No doubt, during their occupation of Crete, they had intermarried with the Minoans and adopted their way of life to a degree, including their burial rites.

After their decimation by the Egyptian forces, the defeated race fled in sea-going vessels. They were tall, fair haired, blue eyed, of an advanced culture with a pantheon of gods, who buried their dead in dolmens, tumuli and passage graves, they had emblems of a double-headed axe and a bull's head, and, more important still, their language had its roots in early Greek, Latin and Hebrew. Before leaving the eastern Mediterranean, it is worth noting that one of the most important natural disasters occurred in 1626 BC. This was the eruption and almost complete disappearance of the island of Santorini, which is north of Crete. The resulting clouding over of the atmosphere for thousands of miles caused consternation in the lands of Crete, Egypt and Palestine, when days were turned into night. This event even finds mention in the Bible—'when darkness fell over the lands of Egypt for three days' (Exodus).

The Dorians seem to have vanished off the face of the then civilised world of the eastern Mediterranean.

Monuments

The exact dating of the earliest monuments in Ireland and elsewhere is very difficult, as it mostly depends on two factors—the presence of wood (charcoal) and implements (ware, weapons, or bones). The dating processes for these are dendrochronology and carbon dating (carbon 14). If either of these two dating processes cannot be accomplished, then the approximate date of similar monuments elsewhere is taken into account.

Here in the Bantry region there are many ancient sites and monuments which for some reason or another cannot be accurately dated. The most important, and probably the oldest, of these are:

1. The stone circle, cromlech alignment, standing stone alignment and sacrificial stone at Mill Beg, Coomhola
2. The Kealkil ritual complex, which consists of a stone alignment, a five-stone circle and a radial stone cairn

3 The stone circle and cromlechs of the Breeny Mór site
4 The stone circle, quartz cromlech and cairn of Colomane.

Alignment, circle and radial cairn complex at Kealkil

Pilgrim's cromlech and cairn, Colomane

These four sites are believed to be amongst the oldest in Ireland and, as they were used, possibly over millenniums, as places of worship and ceremony, the exact time of their construction and their original meaning have now been lost, due to wanton desecration of the sites over the past four centuries.

Attempts were made from 1963, to try to date the Kealkil stone circle but, due to the lack of suitable material on the site, no date could be ascertained. Whether any attempt will be made to date the other sites remains to be seen. However, it is possible that these sites were in use *c*.4500 BC.

The next oldest type of megalithic monument which is considered important is the 'boulder burial', which consists of large boulders resting on smaller stones and is nearly always found adjacent to a stone circle or else in groups by themselves. They probably date from the Early Bronze Age, *c*.3500 BC. In addition to the 'cromlechs' (boulder burial), there are a number of other examples to be found at Dereenogreena, Ballycomane, Cappanaboul, and Maughanaclea.

Cappanaboul stone circle and cromlech

Alignment at Ahil Beg

There are many examples of standing stones in the region, too numerous to mention. They can be found in rows, in pairs or just singular. They usually stand on a NE–SW axis. Those in alignment are graded in height—with the tallest at the SW extremity. It is generally accepted that these also date from the Early Bronze Age and were either used to tell the change of seasons, or marked a grave, a battle site, or a boundary. In the countries bordering on the Mediterranean and the Near East, they are referred to as menhirs and baetyli.

Mill Little megalithic ritual complex

The next most important types of ancient heritage in the area are the various sites where rock art and rock scribing can be found. These consist of various motifs hacked out of rock, and are mostly based on circles with interior designs. Some, however, are of unique designs and appear to replicate constellations of the night sky. Most of these rock scribings and rock art are found in Kealanine, Coomhola and near the Mass Rock at Adrigole. Some years ago, the author took a sample of rock scribing found in the Coom of Coomhola which appeared to be a type of writing. Having being studied by the British Museum, Yale and Harvard, it was discovered to be early Cycladic script—a type of early Greek writing! How this writing found its way from the Aegean Sea to Bantry Bay is another question. It might be the key to the early prehistoric invaders as detailed in our ancient manuscripts (also dated from the Bronze Age).

The only other interesting sites or monuments dating from around the same period are the *Fulachta Fiadh*—sunken rectangular pits which were lined with wooden planks, filled with heated water and used for cooking. They are usually found near a source of water and in the vicinity of other megalithic monuments. Most of the examples in this region are to be found in the Coomhola, Borlin and Kealkil areas.

Some of the oldest monuments in Ireland are the cairns and tumuli, which are mounds of stones or mounds of earth. They date from the Neolithic Age, *c.*9500 BC–6500 BC, and were erected over burial places or tombs. Sometimes, however, they were erected to signify some event, or as a memorial. There are quite a number of these in the Bantry region, including Curran, Illane, Maughanaclea and Maulinward and Currane. Some of these have been found to contain burial urns, while others have a souterrain.

In the general archaeology field, it is worth noting the importance of 'shell middens'. These are mounds of discarded sea shells, encountered along or near the seashore. Here, in the Bantry region, two have been found—at Glengarriff and at Donemark. The Glengarriff midden has been dated to around the end of the Bronze Age. The recently discovered midden at Ferriter's Cove, near Dingle, has been dated to the Mesolithic/Neolithic period, *c.*12500 BC–10000 BC, proving that the south-west was inhabited in those early times.

The megalithic stone monuments mentioned above are of various types, as outlined. The cromlechs derive their name from Crom, meaning god (to adore), and leach, meaning stone. The worship of particular stones was widespread during prehistoric times and was practised by early western European civilisation. The custom seems to have originated in the Far East, where the early inhabitants of the upper plains of the Indus river in India adored stones and called them *Lithoi*. This religious practice came westwards, through the Middle East, the Mediterranean, North Africa, and Spain, where the stones were referred to as baetyli and were of Canaanite or Phoenician origin (see Appollonius, the Roman historian).

The practice was so prevalent in western Europe up to the Middle Ages that the Council of Latern, in 1672, prohibited it. Later, the

Council of Paris decided that all such stones connected with the ancient religious superstitions should be destroyed. Here in Ireland these stones were usually situated on high ground or in a prominent position overlooking the adjoining countryside. As most of the main pagan ritual sites had earlier been converted to Christian usage in Ireland by the building of Christian settlement and places of worship most of the stones escaped destruction.

Forts, ring forts, etc.

Generally speaking, most of the forts that existed in the countryside were built between 800 BC and AD 500. Some were built even later and were occupied up to the sixteenth century. Before describing the different types of forts, it would be useful to look at the society of the people who dwelt in Ireland.

The most important unit in land ownership was the *tuath*, which was an area of approximately six hundred square miles, and there were about eighty tuatha in Ireland. The size of the tuath varied according to the success or failure of its ruler or *Righ*. Usually, those who inhabited a tuath were of the same family and name, and the head of the family was chosen by members of the tuath. In practice, it was generally one particular family and its descendants who were most likely to rule. A number of families of the same name (descendants of the same ancestor) were called a *sept*. While a *clan* was a number of septs from the same common ancestor. Finally, a *tribe* was made up of several clans, where all the families were related to one another.

The forts, whether as abodes of families, clan leaders or tribal leaders, were of different types. First there was the ordinary small fort with the ring built of earth or mud, which was usually the abode of a single family unit. Then there was the double circular fort, which was where the head of the family, or sept, resided, and then the double walled fort with a dyke, which was usually occupied by the clan leader, and, finally, there was the three rings fort (with or without dyke), where the tribal chief dwelt.

Besides the above, there were also promontory forts which were built on headlands or on high ground overlooking the coastline. These were used to keep watch on the activities of boats, in case of attack from the sea. In addition, there were stone-built forts, which were built on main access routes to particular territories as a focal point of defence.

Generally speaking, the ring forts (*rath* or *lios*) were enclosed farmsteads with interior dwellings and stables built of timber posts. They were built with walls of wattle and mud, and thatched roofs, and families, or groups of families, occupied them. They were not very defensive, but were adequate as protection against predators such as wolves, and as a deterrent against cattle raids which were prevalent during that period.

Most of the ring forts had souterrains, which usually consisted of a number of chambers or cells linked together by small narrow passages which opened into the interior of the main dwelling. Opinions differ as to their exact usage—either as a place of refuge at time of attack, or else as a place of storage. In fact, there are two distinct types of souterrains—those that are interconnected within the fort complex and those that have an exit either near the boundaries of the outer ring or further away. These latter, which are to be found in the important forts, were used as means of escape at times of attack. Some of these were even cut through rock, as excavations have shown.

The forts in the Bantry region are too numerous to mention here, although one of the best examples is Ardrah (Ard Rath), which originally had three rings and a moat (dyke) and a souterrain running west.

Castles and Fortified Houses

Remains of castles and fortified houses are scarce in the region, mainly because the Normans did not get a foothold in the countryside. Moving from the extreme west, there was Dunboy Castle, Puxley's Mansion (part of which was fortified), Castletown Castle, Glengarriff Castle, Reendisert Fortified House, Carriganass Castle, Donemark Castle, Scart Castle, Castledonovan, Baurgorm Castle and Reenavanig Castle on Whiddy Island. Most, if not all, of these are discussed in other chapters dealing with the history of their particular locations.

There are many other important historical sites in the region which have yet to be examined and defined, such as *crannógs*, early caves, early mines, medieval settlements, possible beehive settlements and other sites. Only with the assistance of aerial photography and excavations can the true value of these be verified.

Before leaving this section, it is worth noting that there were a number of large residences in the area which were mainly built by the English settlers. These include, besides Bantry House and those mentioned above: Bantry Lodge at Glengarriff (White); Inchiclough (White); Balliliskey (Hutchinson); Gurteenroe (Lawlor); Dromore (White); Newtown (Murphy); Ardnagashel (Hutchins); and Beach House.

Castledonovan

Bantry Abbey

As the Abbey was totally demolished over the centuries, little or nothing remains today except for some stones—sculptured or plain—which now make up a type of altar on the grounds of the present graveyard. The exact location, however, is known. It occupied the ground to the north of the stone steps ascending at the top centre.

During the course of the years, the local monument and grave diggers have encountered sections of the cobbled floor area. As there are no plans in existence, it is difficult to know what was the exact shape or form of the monastery. One thing we do know is that there was a large bell tower at the north-west corner, where the choir was probably located. The records of the Franciscans in Ireland do not give any details, except for a brief paragraph. There is an ancient map of Bantry Bay, *c.* AD 1598, which gives some idea of what the Abbey looked like. This is outlined in one of the illustrated sketches, just to give a general impression.

There is controversy regarding the exact date of its foundation—whether in 1340 or 1460. It did not figure in local or Irish history until it was mentioned in military circles in the 1850s. Yet, during the preceding period, it had become well known in maritime affairs on the Continent as an *entrepot* or centre of wine and spirits smuggling from France and Spain. In fact, it had the reputation of being the centre of the smuggling trade on the south-west coast of Ireland. Whether the monks themselves were involved in this lucrative trade is open to conjecture.

The monastery was built by the O'Sullivan clan, as it was a growing custom amongst the various clan chieftains and leaders to patronise a monastery on their own particular territory. And, in time, many of the O'Sullivans, O'Mahonys, and other high-ranking clan members were buried there.

With the suppression of the monasteries and churches around 1542, the Abbey monastery seemed to have escaped due to its isolated location. However, *c.* 1580 the English army came and, having ousted the friars, occupied the building for a short period of time. They were put to flight by Donal Cam O'Sullivan, who partially demolished the Abbey so that it could not be used as a base by the British. Shortly afterwards, the Earl of Thomond sent a number of regiments to the area, one of which reoccupied the ruined monastery while the others attempted to march to Dunboy Castle.

The garrison remained in occupation for about a year until the Abbey was attacked again and all the English garrison were put to the sword. The Abbey suffered much further damage during the last assault, but some section must have been habitable as the Earl of Thomond, during his march on Dunboy with Carew, sojourned there while his army bivouacked across the harbour at Donemark fields and Whiddy Island (see Fall of Dunboy).

Following the 'scorch earth policy' of Carew after the fall of Dunboy Castle in 1602, little is recorded concerning the fate of the ruined Abbey except the removal of stone, first by Revd. Davys, local rector, to build a 'fish palace' in Bantry, then by Lord Bantry for the construction of the 'stables' and other buildings at Bantry House. It is not known what happened to the Abbey bell, but there is a tradition that it was dropped into the harbour off the Abbey Point *c.* 1582.

Within the walled enclosure there were walks, pathways and vegetable gardens. Outside, there were a number of houses (*bothans*) situated between the Clamp entrance roadway and the monastery itself. The old entrance road can still be seen running from J. J. Crowley's gate parallel to the main road, although it is now covered in bushes and difficult to distinguish.

Below the monastery, by the seashore, were at least two bothans which were later (in the 1800s) occupied by a John O'Sullivan and the Downey family. Below the monastery to the west, at the corner of the Black Strand, were a number of fishermen's huts, while at the end of Beach Road a coastguard station was built. Only some of the interior walls of this are now visible.

The Franciscans did not, however, leave Bantry after the destruction of the monastery. It is recorded that two friars remained in the area for some time afterwards. Over a hundred years later, two friars were captured by the English in 1667 and there were still reports of other friars in the area in 1703 and later. Whether they remained longer is debatable, as there is a reference to 'Friar's Walk' adjacent to the first convent in Bantry at Reenrour. (For further details on the monastery, see *Bantry Journal* No 1.)

Franciscan Abbey at Bantry

— 8 —
The Ancient Festivals

When we look at the concentration of megalithic monuments, including stone circles and other places of worship, in the Bantry region, it is interesting to try to imagine the activities of those early inhabitants during the sacred festivals of the year: the first of February, the first of May, Midsummer, and the first of November. Of these, the most important was the first of May, which was called *Lá Baal-Tinne* (*Bealthaine* in modern Irish). At this time fires were lit to Baal, the sun-god of these early people. It is more than a coincidence that the Phoenicians and the earlier Sumerians of modern-day Iraq worshipped the sun-god, Bel or Baal, on the same day, with almost the same ceremonies.

All domestic fires were put out on the eve of *Lá Baal-Tinne*, and, when the head priest had lit the sacred fire within the stone circle, burning embers were carried to the nearest hearths, and from these to others, until all the home fires were relit. Sometimes two fires were lit at the circle, through which a bull and cattle were driven in order to be 'marked by the fire'. This practice is something like the custom of the early Minoans of Crete, who worshipped the bull.

It has been said that the Baal fires were used for human sacrifice in those early times, but there is only one possible reference to this practice, which concerns a tribal ceremony in the midlands. It is more likely that the sacrifices offered were animals. However, people had to pass through the flames to be purified from evil spirits, and water that had been boiled over the fires was sprinkled on the recipients by the high priest as a sign of cleansing. It is worth mentioning that the fires were started by rubbing together two pieces of ash timber, which was considered sacred. As with the Sumerians and the Phoenicians, the early Irish religion had Baal as the Supreme Being and worshipped him by fire, trees and water. Fire was the most important aspect of the ancient religion as it protected people from the evil spirits.

As the dawn of Lá Baal-Tinne approached, with the fires burning high, the festivities commenced with the people dancing around a large may bush, decorated with multi-coloured garlands of cloth, which had been placed on a large mound of earth close to the circle. The girls wore ribbons in their hair while the men carried a branch of green leaves in their hand. Then, holding hands, they danced around in two circles to the sound of music and drums, which began in a steady rhythm and then built up to a pulsating and hypnotic beat, which put the dancers into a state of trance. This type of dance was, according to some sources, known as the *baila*, the dance of Baal.

The sacred fire of Baal was a source of revenue to the druids, who demanded some payment of food or goods in return for receiving the burning embers to light their own fires.

Every three years, the sacred fire of Tara (Tamhair-na-Righ) was ceremoniously lit, and from this all the sacred fires in Ireland were kindled at the feast of Baal. The fire was started with a primitive type of lens, which diverted the sun's rays onto dry straw, by the friction of rubbing two pieces of wood together or by the striking together of stones.

As the first of May was the beginning of the Old Calendar Year for the early Irish, there were many rituals to be performed. Amongst these was the gathering of herbs for curing diseases during the following year. These were usually collected on May Eve and, once blessed by the high priest, were distributed amongst those chosen ones who practised the 'curings' on the local population.

This was also a time of prophecy. The high priest, or members of the priestly caste, gave their predictions for the coming year by the 'signs' of nature visible on that morning, such as the direction of the wind, the fall of the ashes or the sighting or sound of a particular bird.

Chapter 8

Midsummer—the Festival of the Baal Fires and Dances

As the sun's rays disappeared behind the north-western hills, the people began to gather firewood and make preparation for the great festival, at the various sacred sites in the locality. These sites were usually the stone circles, which were built on high ground. There was a site held more sacred than any other for this particular celebration, and this was situated to the east of the region on a high vantage location within sight of the other sacred locations. We are not certain of the exact siting of this important circle, but it seems to have been Breeny Mór, on higher ground near the Kealkil stone circle. When the high priest lit the fire on this particular site, it was a sign to all the others to light their fires.

When the prayers and incantations of the priests were completed, the young men were purified by leaping back and forth over the flames three times. When the fires had subsided, it was the turn of the young women, then finally it was the turn of the older women, who walked through the embers in their bare feet. It is uncertain where these particular customs originated, but we do find similar practices amongst the early Aryan tribes of the Middle East, and later in the festivities of the early Minoans of Crete, *c.* 2800 BC. These rituals were then followed by singing, dancing and relating old tales of the might and valour of the gods. With dawn approaching, the festivities came to an end, and everybody took a burning sacred branch home with them for good luck.

The second half of the ancient year began with *La Samnah*, the first of November, otherwise known as the Season of the Moon. It was the beginning of that period of long, dark nights and short days when the spirits of evil were out and about. Belief in the power of evil was very strong amongst the primitive people, who lived in fear during the following months. It was a time when the dead were believed to wander about, and it was unsafe to leave one's house or abode. If someone ventured forth, there was always the fear that the risen dead would assault them and drink their blood. According to Mary Shelley, the idea of Dracula did not come from Transylvania, but from ancient Irish beliefs.

The powers of the sacred fire and the ash tree were the main sources of protection. The fires were lit, as during the other festivals, and the nearest ash tree was decorated in long ribbons of coloured cloth before the dancing and sacred music began.

Afterwards, pieces of the cloth were bound around the head, and also on the animals' horns, to protect them from evil spirits. When the festivities were over, everyone would carry home a burning branch from the sacred fire for protection against evil spirits.

The Sacred Wells

Water was another of the four elements held sacred by the early inhabitants, and the power of water and the sea-god Manannan were celebrated at Whitsuntide.

All over Ireland the sacred wells, surrounded by trees and usually in a sheltered location, were regarded as one of the most important places of worship. A stone circle, pillar stone, cromlech or some other ancient monument was nearly always to be found in the same locality.

Here in the Bantry region there are many such wells—at Kilmacomoge, St. Bartholomews, Beach, Kilnavanig and Colomane, to name but a few. Most of these have been converted to Christian usage since the advent of Christianity to the region, and still retain their attraction for the faithful. However, well-worship is one of the earliest rituals of humanity and was brought to our shores by travellers from the East, where it was first known to be practised by the Aryan race of northern India and Pakistan, around 5000 BC. This ritual of well-worshipping was practised throughout the eastern Mediterranean civilisations, but had special significance in the ancient Hindu religion, in relation to the sacred cow. The cattle were herded westwards, garlands were thrown on their horns and they were sprinkled with water from the holy well. Like the Hindus, those who were first to throw a tuft of grass into the well after midnight on May Eve considered themselves protected against evil.

The famous oracle of Delphi in Greek mythology was nothing more than a well of springwater shaded by trees, where the natives brought their offerings to the gods until the rulers of the ancient Greek kingdoms adopted it as the 'most sacred place'.

In Ireland, especially here in the south-west, the wells took on a very special significance due to the strength of the ancient religion. As water was the sign of life, and bubbling springs were held in great esteem by the high priests, these wells became one of the focal points of the ancient rituals, where the 'snake dance' was performed in honour of Manannan. This was an ancient ceremony rite, where the young people, with their heads garlanded with flowers and greenery, danced in a snake-like formation from west to east, and then, in rotations of three, six, twelve and so on, circled the sacred well, and threw small stones into the water for good luck. Others circled the well on hands and knees while calling on Manannan for protection. More often than not, the well was located near a whitethorn or an ash tree, which were revered as symbols of health, happiness and protection from evil spirits.

Many interpretations of these rituals were incorporated into the early Christian ceremonies. Where once there were 'pagan' rites, now there were Christian rituals, such as the Mass, reciting the Rosary while circling the well, doing the 'rounds'—where people walked through two parallel mounds of stones, picked up one pebble, and before depositing it on another mound said prayers and made the sign of the cross. This custom was subsequently modified and, until quite recent times, people still picked up the stones and blessed themselves three times before carrying on to the next. The best example of this is at St Colman's site at Colomane, where the wells and heaps of stones are still visible. Each pagan well was called after a particular local saint, and each person having partaken of the water hung a coloured ribbon or handkerchief on the nearby ash or whitethorn tree. Instead of throwing a pebble into the well, a coin subsequently became the norm.

It was never accepted by Christian teaching that the waters of the wells had any particular powers of healing, but that any medical cures were a result of intercession by the particular patron saint, and, likewise, any miraculous healing was a result of prayer rather than of an inherent power in the waters of the well.

In the context of the holy wells, it is interesting to note that the deposit of white shining stones, like quartz or barytes, was highly regarded, and some people made a point of collecting these, in the belief that they had a special power of intercession with the saints.

The Holy Wells

The holy wells—the living wells—the cool, the fresh, the pure,
A thousand ages rolled away, and still those fount endure,
As full and sparkling as they flowed ere slave or tyrant trod
The Emerald garden, set apart for Irishmen by God.
And while their stainless chastity and lasting life have birth
Amid the oozy cells and caves of gross material earth,
The Scripture of creation hold no fairer type than they—
That an immortal spirit can be linked with human clay.

How sweet of old the bubbling gush—no less to antlered race,
Than to the hunter and the hound that smote them in the chase!
In forest depths the water-fount beguiled the Druid's love
From that adored high fount of fire which sparkled far above;
Inspired apostles took it for a centre to the ring,
When sprinkling round baptismal fire—salvation—from the spring;
And in the sylvan solitude, or lonely mountain cave,
Beside it passed the hermit's life, as stainless as its wave.

The cottage hearth, the convent's wall, the battlemented tower,
Grew up around the crystal springs, as well as flag and flower;
Abiding in those basics, free to poverty and wealth;
The brooklime and the water-cress were evidence of health;
The city sent pale sufferers there the faded brow to dip,
And woo the water to depose some bloom upon the lip;
The wounded warrior dragged him towards the unforgotten tide,
And deemed the draught a heavenlier gift than triumph to his side.

The stag, the hunter, and the hound, the Druid, and the saint,
And anchorite are gone, and even the lineaments grown faint
Of those old ruins into which, for monuments, had sunk
The glorious home that held, like shrines, the monarch and the monk.
So far into the heights of God the mind of man has ranged,
It learned a lore to change the earth—its very self it changed
To more more bright intelligence; yet still the springs endure,
The same fresh fountains, but become more previous to the poor.

For knowledge has abused its powers, an empire to erect
For tyrants, on the rights the poor had given them to protect;
Till now the simple elements of nature are their all,
That for the cabin is not filched, and lavished in the hall—
And while night, noon, or morning meal no other plenty brings,
No beverage than the water-draught from old, spontaneous springs;
They, sure, may deem them holy wells, that yield from day to day,
Our blessing that no tyrant hand can taint or take away.

J. de Jean Fraser

— 9 —
Superstitions

Having examined the various ancient festivals in the preceding chapter, we will now consider the customs and superstitions which were closely related to this ancient culture. In fact, many of these, both good and bad, are slowly disappearing from daily life in the countryside, where they have existed up to the present generation. This means, of course, that Irish rural society is moving into a new phase of behaviour and beliefs. Yet, for some living in the countryside, there is still a strong regard for the ancient *piseoge*. These ancient superstitions were passed down from the earliest time by tradition, or by word-of-mouth, through the continuity of the Irish bards and storytellers.

We have already considered some of the religious beliefs and practices of ancient peoples and the fact that our own religious traditions were very similar. Combined with these worship practices was a deep superstitious fear of evil spirits, and from this grew a multitude of customs designed to ward off the spirits of evil. The sacred trees were not cut down or tampered with, the stone monuments were revered as signs of worship to the gods, and the holy wells were not interfered with. All of these were regarded as holy places, and the influence of the priestly sect of the pagan religions dominated the lives of the ordinary people.

Anything connected to the elements of fire, wind, earth and water were held as sacred, and to violate the rituals brought the evil spirits amongst the guilty. Baal's fire was the protector from evil, especially at Samhain when the dead were accustomed to walking around. Food was always left out for them before departing for the festivities of Samhain. Whitsuntide was the most unlucky time, as the god Manannan searched through the oceans, rivers and streams for a victim. Death was close at hand at Whitsuntide, and the evil spirits were always waiting to take a victim. Fires were kept burning, and no sick person was to be left alone. The priests made offerings of animal blood to the evil spirits and they were also able to tell the future by the flight of birds, by dreams, the motions of the wind, the drawing of lots and the cast of the dice.

Amongst the trees, the yew, the ash and the elder were held as sacred. The willow tree was believed to possess the music of the gods and was also not to be tampered with.

The Banshee

The subject of the banshee could not be omitted from any account of Irish superstition. In fact, when I started to research the banshee in Irish folklore I was under the misguided impression that this superstition commenced around the Middle Ages, but this I soon found to be completely incorrect. Superstition, or the belief in the unknown and unseen, the mysterious and the spiritual, has been with man from earliest times, when he first came to believe that both the material and spiritual worlds existed side by side. In fact, after the need for food, the fear of the unknown dominated the life of early man, and elements of these old pagan customs and traditions have filtered through the ages down to the present day.

This is true of the belief in the banshee, or beanshee, in Ireland. The word itself means 'the woman of the fairy race' and can be compared to Venus in Greek mythology. But, if we spell the name banshee as *ban-sidhe*, we find that it means 'the spirit of the dead', while its counterpart was called *leeanan-sidhe*, or 'the spirit of life'. In Irish mythology, both of these figures were one, i.e. a spirit who appears as a beautiful young woman during daylight, or as a witch at night. It is the latter that took hold in the ancient Irish traditions. She has been described as a shrouded, veiled old hag who emitted an unearthly wailing at night-time which indicated the certain death of some person living nearby. Although she was seldom seen, many people would testify on oath or on the Bible that they heard the wailing cry of the banshee before somebody close by died. In past times, when the banshee was heard, people would rush to get some ash tree branches, twigs or leaves and scatter them around the cattle in the pen, and then around everybody in the family, who would be seated in the middle of a room or hut.

When one speaks of the banshee, one automatically thinks of the fairies, as both are intertwined in Irish folklore and tradition. The fairy forts and caves and the music and dancing of the fairy folk come immediately to mind.

Many historians relate the fairies to the Tuatha-de-Danaan race who had mystical powers and who were permitted to live in the caves and forts by the invading Milesians. This idea cannot be based on historical fact or tradition, as the Tuatha-de-Danaan were supposed to have come to Ireland *c.* 1700 BC and were closely followed by the Milesians *c.* 1200 BC. The *lis*, or forts, which were supposed to be inhabited by the fairies were not, however, built until the eighth century BC at the earliest.

Yet, regard for the fairy folk, whatever its origins, grew almost into a cult in early times, especially at the time of the festivals. While the young people were enjoying themselves at the Midsummer festival, the fairies were also celebrating with song and dance in the fairy forts. The ancient tales relate how the people feared for their young girls, as the fairy king, Finvarra, and his followers were always on the prowl to carry away the prettiest girls to the fairy kingdom. Those they succeeded in entrapping were held for seven years, until they had lost their beauty, but in return were given the gift of the magic herbs. In order to capture the young girls, the fairies were supposed to approach the fires of Baal as a whirlwind, in order to extinguish them, thus leaving the place in darkness.

So, even today, we use the phrase 'the fairies will take you away' to a disobedient child.

— 10 —

The Gatherings

The two major festivals of the early inhabitants were *Lá Baal-Tinne* (day of the fires of Baal), or May day (day of the sun-god Baal), and *Lá Samhna* (the day/night of the moon), or November Eve. The festivities on these occasions were eventually called 'gatherings' *c.* 1000 BC. These traditional gatherings of the people centred around or adjacent to the sacred sites. These sites were nearly always situated on hilltops, or in locations which had a commanding view of the countryside. Here, in the Bantry region, three immediately come to mind: Curran, near Coomhola; Breeny Mór above the Kealkil stone circle; and the Colomane stone circle and holy well.

These old assemblies, or fairs, were celebrated in many of the ancient ballads and folklore for their games and horse riding. Held over a period of three days, they were called the 'gatherings', the 'fair day', and the 'scattering day'. The times of the major assemblies were on the first of May and on the first of November. At these gatherings, under the auspices of the tribal chief and his head priest, the division or allotment of land was given out or reclaimed back, the Brehon Laws were invoked for disputes, marriages were arranged, dues were paid to the chief and cattle raids were planned.

Besides these, it also seems that important marriages took place on these occasions. The event commenced with the arrival of both the bride and groom, first meeting by a decorated hawthorn tree situated near a stream. Young girls and boys surrounded the tree with burning lights. As the children led the way to the sacred site, they were joined by the musicians playing flutes, pipes and the goatskin drums in a steady rhythm, while others rattled bones and stones in their hands like Spanish castanets. A young boy holding a large burning torch led the bridal pair, who had a canopy of moss and leaves held over their heads and were followed by a crowd singing and dancing to the music.

As the pair passed through two fires, which symbolised protection from evil spirits, they approached the sacred stone altar, where the high priest sprinkled them with 'holy water' and pronounced them married under the sign of Baal. After the bride and groom had kissed, the wedding celebration commenced, and lasted into the following day, when the bride left to join the groom's family home.

With the advent of Christianity, the old sacred ceremonial sites were mostly taken over by the early missionaries, and converted to Christian use *c.* AD 450. However, the old customs were difficult to obliterate, and the gatherings and fairs continued. Nearly all vestiges of the old religion were suppressed, and the stone monuments were removed and replaced by rudely made churches of timber, mud and thatch.

In the Bantry region, we can find numerous ancient wells with stone monuments nearby, including those at Ardnatourish, Coomhola, Kilmacomoge, St. Bartholomew's well, Kilnavanig on Whiddy Island, Our Lady's well at Beach, and the Colomane well and stone circle. Right down to the present time, these sites and wells still have an attraction for the Christian faithful.

As to the significance of 'well worship', we have to return to its prehistoric usage. It is one of the earliest rituals of humanity, brought to our shores by the invaders, or travellers, from the East, where it was first practised by the Aryan race (of Northern India/Pakistan) *c.* 5000 BC. From here, the ritual spread across the eastern Mediterranean, North Africa and the Iberian peninsula to our shores. Here in Ireland, especially in the south-west, the wells took on a very special significance and all the priestly rites were conducted with springwater, which signified life. The symbolic dance to the snake (or water) god Manannan was of prime importance.

As the fairs (*aonach*) continued down from *c.* AD 500 to the 1850s, so too did the druidic rituals, festivals, games, dancing and debauchery. They were condemned by the Catholic Church as an example of devil worship, and were therefore believed to be unlucky. It was thought that God showed his scorn for them by always sending foul weather. Hence, we still have the custom of saying 'It always rains in Bantry on Fair Day'.

To prevent or inhibit the rowdiness and debauchery of these festivities, the Catholic clergy demanded that the faithful should hold them after confession, mass and rosary at the sacred sites, which had now been designated after some patron saint. The events then began to be called the 'pardons', either after the sacrament of penance or the patron saint. But, despite the presence of the clergy, the merriment, drinking, fighting and general debauchery continued. Finally, the festivities were banned during the period 1850–1860, and then they transferred to the crossroad 'patterns', or dances, where they flourished until the early 1950s, when the parochial dance halls were built all over the country. The local clergy strictly supervised the dancing and the merriment at these dance halls. No close dancing was allowed, as this constituted a "mortal sin", and if someone did not behave properly they were banned from the dance hall for the future.

— II —

The Race of Lughaidh, Son of Ith

On examination of the various manuscripts including the *Leabhair Gabhala*, Keating's *History of Ireland*, O'Flaherty's *Ogygia: The Book of Ballymote*, and others, the race of Lughaidh is not identified with any of the major 'seven invasions', but was reputed to have come from the north-western corner of Spain, now known as Galicia, and especially from the area around the river Breogan. Ith was killed in a battle with the Tuatha de Danaan and his son Lughaidh escaped back to Spain and informed his relations, amongst whom was Milidh or Milesius. A large force was brought together and sailed for Ireland to avenge the death of Ith and his followers. They engaged in various battles with the Tuatha de Danaan and finally defeated them. O'Flaherty gives *c.* 1450 BC as the date of the incursion of Milidh and his army. Ireland was divided into five kingdoms by the descendants of Ith and, in time, Lughaidh Laidhe, who was one of the sons of Daire Sirchreachtach, was the main progenitor of all the main tribes of Corca Laidhe (Carbery), and all the West Cork tribes claim their descent from him.

Corca Laighe was originally co-extensive with the diocese of Ross, and, within the western boundaries, comprised of the parishes of Milmoe, Scoole, Kilcrohane, Durrus, Kilmacomoge, Kilcaskan, Kilcatherine and Caheragh. According to E. Hogan in his *Onomasticon Goedelicum*, the territory of Corca Laidhe extended from Beann Fin to Traig Omna (Omhna). He quotes the *Annals of Innisfallen*, O'Curry's *Cath Muige Lena* and MacCurtain's *Antiquities of Ireland*, which state that the Caislean Dun-na-mBarc was built by Carunach, that Coomhola estuary was identified as *Benn Remar* (thick strand) and was situated north of the town of Bantry, that Bantry Bay was referred to as *Inmbear Sceine* and that Kilmacomoge 'within the lands of O'Brien and O'Cuanach was called "Cill na Muchoige"'. Corca Laidhe was, broadly speaking, that territory bounded by the Old Head of Kinsale and Dursey Island to the west.

According to the ancient sources of both bards and historians, the Milesians tried to make a landing at *Inmbear Slainge* (Wexford) but were repulsed by the Tuatha de Danaan. They then sailed down the coast and successfully came ashore at Inmbear Sceine (Bantry Bay) *c.* 1600 BC. According to the annals, the Milesians seem to have for the most part lived in peace, except for inter family rivalry for kingship.

Commencing *c.* AD 1600, the O'Mahony territory was invaded by the Barrys on the eastern side; the O'Sullivans occupied that portion of territory now called Bantry and Beara; the Cairbre Aebhdha or the O'Donovans and O'Collins who had occupied the land of Cois Maighe (Cosma) and the plains of the west side of the river Maigue were driven southwards by the FitzGeralds and claimed the northern section of Corca Laighe, from Glandore to Bandon to the northern boundaries. In 1232, Cormac Gott, son of MacCarthy Mór, acquired domination over all the minor septs and the entire Corca Laighe.

With particular reference to West Cork, the name Tighearnmhas is mentioned as having fought many battles, including one near the Old Head of Kinsale and the other at Beara. This latter battle might be identified as the battle of Cnocura (*c.* 1250 BC), which is mentioned in other earlier sources.

Of those early septs or tribes which inhabited the region of Corca Laighe, we find the following names mentioned: O'Driscoll, O'Falvey, O'Shea, O'Connell, O'Coffey, O'Cowhig, O'Flynn, O'Ceadagain, McAuliff, O'Dowling, O'Hogan, O'Doogan, MacKeady, O'Keevan, O'Mangan, O'Macken, O'Barr, O'Kennedy, O'Ruirce, O'Hennessy,

O'Downe, O'Dinneen, O'Downing, O'Cullen, O'Horan, O'Hyne, O'Hussey, O'Fehilly, O'Field, O'Corman, O'Nolan, O'Cronin, O'Hea, O'Haye, O'Donnelly, O'Lynch, O'Kelly, O'Murray, O'Gavan, O'Downey and O'Leahy.

Ith

Corca Laighe is described as extending from Beann-Fhinn to the strand at Traigh-Omna and then westwards to Frith-na-hImghona and from a fiord called Beal-Atha-Buidhe to the strand called Traigh-Clean. John O'Donovan, the noted historian, from his personal research limits the territory from Courtmacsherry Bay to the river Ilen and north to the parish of Drinagh. This is based on the supposition that these were the boundaries of the O'Driscolls and also on evidence suggested by local place names with reference to dubious boundary marks.

This opinion seems to be in contradiction to the *Book of Leinster*, Folio 3, to the *Book of Lecan*, Folio 272, and to *An Leabhair Gabhala* (*Book of Invasions*), where the landing of Cessair and the battle of Magh Leana are described, with the former being at the southern Iorrus of Corca Laidhe. Also, in the genealogy of the Corca Laidhe, we find that the descendants of Aedh Garbh (Hugh the Rough) were known as the Ua Eidersceoil of Beara, who were later driven out by the O'Sullivans, and that Beara itself was the western section of the diocese of Ross.

Some historians state that the Milesians were also called Goidels or Gaedheal (Gaels) and in fact were a branch of the Celts who had dwelt in Egypt at the time of Moses and who had befriended the Israelites. They were supposed to have travelled along the north coast of Africa and crossed over at Iberia and journeyed to the north-west corner of that country.

It is difficult to accept this description of a tribe wandering so far that they reached Ireland, but when the case of the Israelites wandering in the desert for forty years is considered the distance to north-west Iberia could easily be covered during the same period of time. Yet, these Milesian invaders are not to be confused with the European Celts who crossed over from the Continent (*c.* 350 BC) with their weapons of iron. In fact, the earlier Milesians had weapons of bronze similar to those used in the eastern Mediterranean.

As far as can be ascertained, the Milesians (Gaels) had their own language. This supposition is very interesting in that the ancient language of this country which is now called Gaeilge or Gaedhilge contained a high percentage of Hebrew words. In fact, according to linguistic experts, the language is made up of ten per cent Hebrew.

The majority of early historians who argued that all the prehistoric so-called invasions came from nearby England and western Europe seemed to have ignored this fact, which will be discussed later in the chapter on the Celts.

The next important episode in the history of the Milesian descendants in Corca Laidhe occurred *c.* AD 123, when Conn Cead Cathach (Con of the hundred battles) came on the scene as high king. During his period of kingship, Eoghan Mór (Mogh Nuadhat) was the powerful king of Munster who gave battle to Conn on many occasions and disputed his high kingship. Eventually, it was agreed that Conn would rule the northern half of the country while Eoghan Mór would rule the southern half. It was also agreed that Conn's daughter would marry the eldest son of Eoghan Mór, called Oilioll Olum. Sadhbh, Conn's daughter, was the young widow of Lughaidh Mac Niadh of the Corca Laighe clan and this marriage was intended to consolidate the friendship of the two kings, as well as being the foundation of the great Corca Laidhe dynasty which ruled West Cork—and, at times, Ireland—until AD 1152.

The peace between the two kings did not last long, despite the marriage connection. Eoghan Mór again took up arms against Conn, but after suffering two defeats fled to Spain to seek the assistance of his father-in-law's family—having previously been married to Beara, the daughter of the King of Castile. He returned with an army, but was defeated and killed.

Oilioll Olum, his son, now became the all-powerful king of Munster. His own stepson, Lughaidh MacCon, requested that he should have the portion of lands which he was entitled to by succession—the territory of Corca Laidhe. This was refused. Lughaidh sought the assistance of Beine of Britain, who landed in Galway with an army. This force was augmented by the troops of the High King Art. In the ensuing battle near Athenry, Art was killed, even though the forces of Oiloill were defeated.

The result of this battle was that Lughaidh MacCon became the chief of the Corca Laidhe and, a short time later, was enthroned as the High King of Ireland (AD 195–225). Being a wise man, he stipulated in his will that the descendants of his two sons, Eoghan Mór and Cormac Cas, should rule alternatively as kings of Munster.

The principal families of south Munster descended from Eoghan Mór were called the Eoghanachta, while those descended from Cormac Cas were referred to as the Dal Cais. Even though the descendants of Cormac tried to invoke the arrangement of alternative kingships, they were unsuccessful, and the Eoghanchta ruled until the time of Brian Boru.

After the death of Lughaidh MacCon in Corca Laidhe, Cormac Mac Airt came to power, but not without conflict. Another famous battle was fought on the Beara peninsula (*c.* AD 245) which ended in a pyrrhic victory for Cormac Mac Airt.

As with all the tribes of Ireland, the West Cork tribes were most careful in preserving their genealogies, as all the questions of ownership and rights depended on family connections, subject to the Brehon Laws. These genealogies were perfectly preserved in the poems of families or by the tribal bards or poets, like the O'Dalaigh of Kilcrohane. It was most important that those amongst the lower ranks of the tribes were able to trace and retain the whole line of their descent. In a word, each individual possessed a charter of his civil state, his right to property, where he was born, and to the soil which he tilled. No one toiled the tribal land unless he was of the same race as the chief, unless he was engaged as a dispossessed labourer or slave working for the tribal chief himself.

Part Two

From *c.* 1500 BC to AD 850

— 12 —

Tara

One might ask why a chapter dealing with the hill of Tara should be introduced into a history of Bantry Bay. The answer is that, as the local tribe leaders were subject to the high king of Ireland, they were obliged to make the journey to Tara every three years. The importance of Tara was accepted all over the country from earliest times, and especially from *c.* 1200 BC. However, it must be said that some of the powerful kings of Munster did not always pledge their allegiance to the high king, especially if they had previously waged war against him or if he was considered a usurper.

A great debt of gratitude is owed to Drs. Petrie, Keating and O'Flaherty for the information that has been passed down to date about the history and description of Tara. Much of this has been condensed into a novel called *The Last Monarch of Tara*, by Eblana (d. 1887).

From O'Flaherty's *Ogygia* we learn that the Milesians divided the island of Ireland between Heber-Fionn and Heremon, and the brothers and children of Milesius. Heber took possession of the southern part, afterwards called Munster, and built a 'palace' (possibly Cashel). Heremon was given Leinster and built a palace on the banks of the Nore. However, at the request of his wife Tea (or Thea), he built another palace at a location which became known as Tea-Mór. Their cousin Lughaidh, son of Ith, received the region known as Corca

Luidh (Laidhe), which was the south-west corner of Munster, extending from the Bandon river to Kenmare.

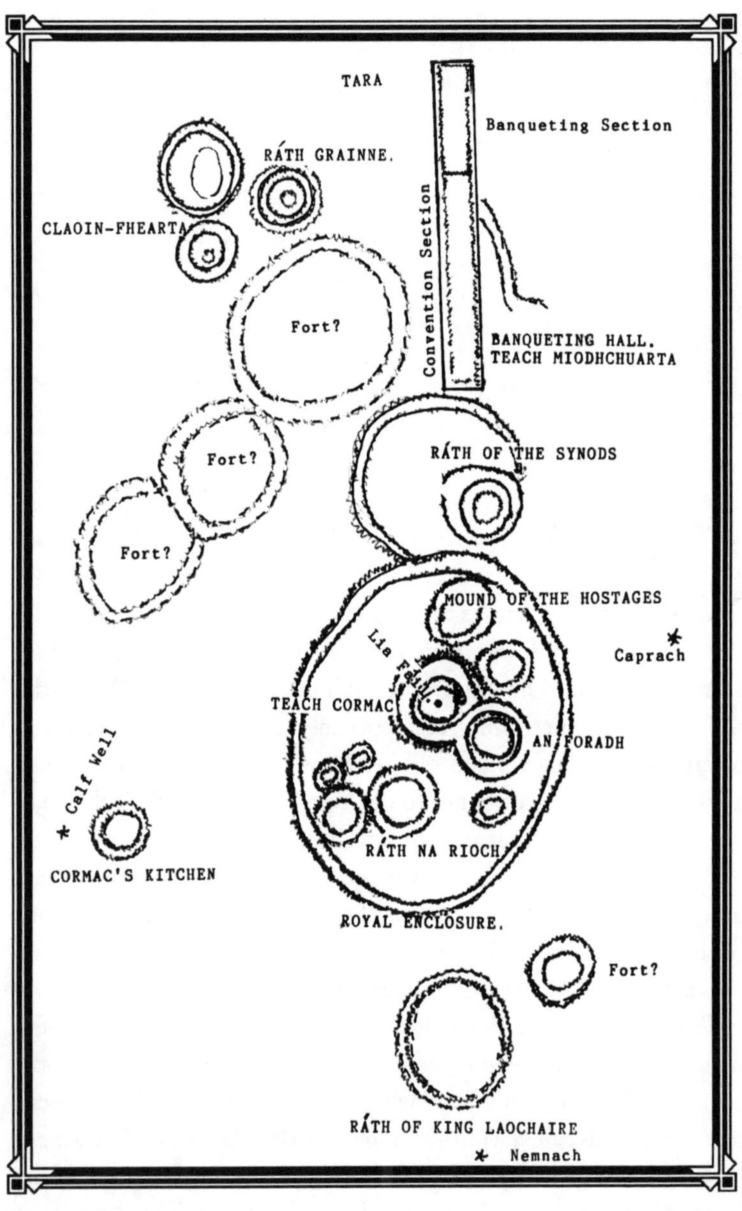

A map of Tara

After a few short years, Tea incited her husband, Heremon, to do battle with his brother Heber and gain control of both Leinster and Munster. Heber was killed in the ensuing battle and Heremon ruled the country afterwards for some thirteen years. His descendants, about fifty-eight in all, ruled the country until the coming of St. Patrick and retained their power until the time of Brian Boru.

Tara was also known in ancient times as *Temair Mairghe*—Tea, or Tara, of Sleibhe Mairghe. It was the main centre of the druid culture in early history and, as far as can be ascertained, Tea herself was recognised as a priestess. Her descendants included Carman, who gave her name to the 'Fair of Carman' which happened to be the most important event in the early calendar, held every third year on the first of August. In time, the name Tara became synonymous with the Fair of Carman, as the event brought together the high king, kings, princes, chieftains, and all their followers from all over the country, as well as people from western Europe and further afield. It seems to have been the major event of western civilisation from *c.* 1100 BC–AD 500. The royal city of Tara was called *Chatham Teamhrach* and consisted of palaces, duns, raths, forts, schools, places of worship and many houses.

It is difficult to imagine what Tara looked like in its prime. The early descriptions make it larger and more important than Troy, Knossos, Ephesus, Nineveh, or any of the major Middle Eastern cities of that period. Sources state that it was composed of seven 'duns', or large enclosures, each containing some one hundred and fifty houses and accommodation for seven hundred soldiers, i.e. one thousand houses and five thousand soldiers. The king and the nobility resided on the hill of Tara itself, within the duns and buildings. This central position was enclosed by a giant rath, which was approximately sixty feet wide and fifteen feet high. The interior, besides the main raths of the king and the nobility, comprised the Great Hall or the *Teach Miodchuarta* (House of Conventions), which was seven hundred and fifty-nine feet long by ninety feet wide (roughly half the size of Bantry Square). The banqueting section of this building was three hundred feet long, eighty feet wide and fifty feet high. The whole building was reputedly built of solid oak. As for the royal residence itself, it consisted of one hundred and fifty apartments, each capable of housing sixty persons. To feed the great masses who attended the convention, there were twenty-seven kitchens for the preparation of food.

Tara was described as the 'Tara of the Scribes', where the early annals of history were accumulated and written down. This knowledge comes down to us in the *Dinnchenchas*—a collection of early legends connected with place names which are written in both prose and verse form (with Middle Eastern influence). As the Dinnchenchas were written *c.* AD 1200, historians such as Petrie and Gwynn found it almost impossible to form a clear picture of the original Tara. In fact, the number of important sites on the hill mentioned in the Dinnchenchas is almost double what can be found today. Considering that nearly all the old landmarks and reference points have disappeared over time, it will take our modern historians and archaeologists many years to piece together the jigsaw puzzle of Tara.

The ancient ballads and poems furnish us with details of Tara. The following poem (probably fourth century) is an example.

Temor of Bregia, whence so called,
Relate to me, O learned sages,
When was it distinguished from the Brugh?
When was the place called Temor?

Was it in the time of Partholan of battles?
Or at the first arrival of Cessair?
Or in the time of Nemid, famed for valour?
Or with Ciocal of the bent knees?

Was it with the Firbolg of great achievements?
Or with the race of fairy elves?
Tell me in which of those invasions
Did the place obtain the name of Temor?

O Tuan! O generous Finnchadh!
O Bran! O active Cu-alladh!
O Dubhan! ye venerable five,
Whence was acquired the name of Temor?

Once it was a beauteous hazel wood,
In the time of the famed son of Olcan,
Until that dense wood was felled
By Liath, the son of Laighne, the large and blooming.

From thence it was called the Hill of Liath,
And it was fertile in crops of corn,
Until the coming of Cain the prosperous,
The son of Fiacha Ceannfionan.

From thence it was called Druim Cain,
This hill, where the great assembled,
Until the coming of Crofinn the fair,
Daughter of the far-famed Alloid.

The fortress of Crofinn, well applied,
Was its name among the Tuath da Danaan,
Until the coming of the agreeable Tea,
The wife of Heremon of noble aspect.

A rampart was raised around her house
For Tea the daughter of Lughaidh,
She was buried outside in her mound,
And from her it was named Temor.

The seat of the kings it was called,
The princes, descendants of the Milesians,
Five names it had ere that time—
That is from Fordruim to Temor.

I am Fintan, the Bard,
The historian of many tribes;
In latter times I have passed my days
At the earthen fort above Temor.

Finn Mac Cumhall, General of the Irish militia, had his palace at Almhain (Allwinn) in County Kildare.

A point worth noting is the reference to the early Irish naval force, which raided far and wide along the western coast of Europe. Furthermore, the practice of granting 'gifts' of warships by the high king to the noble princes of coastline tribes is also significant. In fact, the Irish kept a considerable naval force with which they raided and kept under submission other countries, such as the coastal areas of Britain and France, especially during the second and third centuries AD.

During the Fair of Carman and the Convention of the High Kings, the laws were enforced, feast days were appointed, history was recorded and the will of the high king was declared. The throne on which the high king sat during the exercise of his office was called the *Forud* and it has been suggested that this gave its name to the Forum of Rome. It is interesting to note that the early Estruscans (Romans) referred to Tara and the Feast of Carman, and more interesting still are the Middle Eastern references to Tara as the 'Palace of Ben Hedar'. All of this underlines the importance of Tara in Western civilisation during the period 1200 BC–AD 400.

The Phantom City

A story I heard on the cliffs of the west,
That oft, through the breakers dividing,
A city is seen on the ocean's wild breast,
In turreted majesty riding.
But brief is the glimpse of the phantom so bright,
Soon close the white waters to screen it,
And the bodement, they say, of the wonderful sight,
Is death to the eyes to have seen it.

I said, when they told me the wonderful tale,
My country, is this not thy story?
Thus oft, through the breakers of discord, we hail
A promise of peace and of glory.
Soon gulfed in those waters of hatred again
No longer our fancy can find it,
And woe to our hearts for the vision so vain;
For ruin and death come behind it.

Gerald Griffin

— 13 —
The Brehon Laws

When the Statutes of Kilkenny were passed in AD 1367, the Brehon Laws were denounced as 'wicked and damnable'. This opinion has been upheld by English writers and historians through the centuries. This has been mainly due to ignorance, prejudice and religious hatred, as well as hatred of all things Irish.

The Brehon Laws were the code by which the Irish race in both pagan and Christian times was been governed. The name brehon derives from the old Irish word for 'judge'—*breitheamh*—whose duty it was to explain the law and apply it to the cases which were presented before him for judgement. The office of the brehon was separate to that of the druids. To become a brehon, one had to study for a minimum of twelve years. The Irish word *breith* signifies to carry, seize, or to join. Applied to the functions of the mind, it means to grasp a thought, or a comparison, and form a judgement.

Brehons were reputedly introduced into this country by Amergin, brother of Heber and Heremon, and son of Milesius and Scota. Amergin was known as *An Ollamh Fodhla* (The Sage of Ireland) and reigned as Ardrigh (High King) of Ireland *c.* 1200 BC. The Laws themselves came into existence around the time of the destruction of the Assyrian empire and during the birth of the three kingdoms of Nineveh, Babylon and Media.

The Brehon Laws are often compared to the Roman Code (Etruscan)—the Twelve Tables—and is in fact its twin sister, being founded on the natural law and conforming in part to the written law of that period before the foundation of Rome itself. Both of these codes of law have the same Aryan roots and are not dissimilar to the ancient Hindu Law. The Brehon Laws, unlike the Roman which were transformed and modified to suit the advance of Roman culture, survived in a purer form, due to Ireland's isolation from the Roman and other conquests.

These laws were further expanded by the introduction of the 'Commentaries' by Ugoni the Great, who flourished *c.* 350 BC. However, during the following centuries, the laws became unmanageable due to the influence of some of the Irish druids whose incorrect interpretation—to their own advantage—caused much distress throughout the land. King Conor Mac Nessa of the kingdom of Ulladh produced a revised code of laws which were easily understood by all of the people. These were later known as the *Breatha-Nimhe* (the Judgement of the Heavens). Amongst these were the writings (interpretations) of Moran, son of Cabrie, King of Ireland, who was the Chief Brehon *c.* 85 BC.

In addition, King Cormac Mac Airt, when he was in power, assembled all the *ollamhain* (judges) of Ireland to collect together the chronicles of the country. These later became known as the 'Saltair of Teamhair'. He is also believed to have commissioned the *Teagasc-na-Ri* (Teachings of the King). The Saltair itself contains the list of dues or levies which were payable to the high king by everybody—from the poorest peasant to the provincial kings—as well as details of the exact boundaries of each kingdom and even each smallholding.

As to how this code of laws came to Ireland, we have only to travel its path westwards from the Far East (Hindustan). The Sumerians practised a code of law which found its way to Egypt—as identified on the Rosetta Stone—and then to Crete, where the Law Code of Gortys was discovered *c.* 1884. This Law Code, written in early Greek, is almost word for word in many passages as our Brehon Laws. The connection of the Brehon Laws of Ireland with the Middle East is further substantiated by ancient references to Tara as the Palace of Ben Hedar (Arabic for Heber). As the Phoenicians traded extensively with

Crete, these laws were probably adopted in many parts by these sea-traders and explorers.

Under the Brehon Laws, the early inhabitants of Ireland survived as an isolated civilisation where the men were truthful and brave, the women were free, honoured and devoted, learning was fostered and esteemed, the arts and sciences were practised without interference, and social and religious life were held in high regard.

Originally, the Brehon Laws were a collection of many volumes of writings, also containing the following:

- a Military Law
- b Philosophy
- c *Teacht-Bhreath*—Miscellaneous Law
- d *Fuigheal-Bhreath*—Supplement to Laws
- e *An Fotha Mór*—Office and duties of Judges (Brehons)
- f *An Fotha Beag*—Laws of Partition, such as *Aid-Bhreathe* (Treatise on Theft)
- g *An Corrasfinnes*—Rules of dynastal tribes or clans regarding disputes, etc.

The Brehon Laws in their present form have been handed down to us by the noted historians O'Donovan and O'Curry. The original pre-Christian laws were preserved in rude verse or in rhythmical prose, Sumerian style, as were the early myths and legends. If we compare the exploits of Gilamesh with those of Mael Duin, we can immediately see the relationship between the two odysseys. These verses and selected prose were collected at Tara by St. Patrick, with the aid of Benignus, Cairnech, three bishops, Laeghaire son of Niall Corc son of Lughaidh, and three poets. *Nofis* (knowledge of nine) was the name of the book they produced. Due to the Christian ardour of St. Patrick, many important changes and modifications were made to the original text, but these only conformed to Christian doctrines and basic Roman law with which it was originally connected. With St. Patrick came the introduction of the Roman alphabet and the rearrangement of the ancient Irish alphabet so that it conformed the Roman, even to the extent that the same characters were introduced.

The last important event at the Feast of Carman—or the Gathering of Tara—was the reading of the Brehon Laws by the Chief Ollabh. This was an abbreviated form and went thus:

> Éire is the birthright of all the children of the land; the king hath his portion, the princes, the nobles, each hath his portion thereof; the priest, the Ollamhan, the bards and the minstrels have their portion.
> And the Gael by their clans have their portion thereof. from the earth man derived sustenance, whereby to live. Hath any increased his store of cattle, or of stuff, or of arms? Let his words, as to these, and these like stand: Of his portion of the land none can have dominion longer than he doth abide thereon.
> His children and the mother of his children shalld well thereon till portion be made; then let not the woman who bore, nor the damsels who are to bring forth, be forgotten; are not all the race born of woman?
> Sons of Éire, honour and respect thy father. Love, honour, respect and tenderly cherish all the days of thy life the mother who bore and suckled and reared thee up.
> Let thy hands minister unto her in all her necessities; let thy eye never look upon thy mother but in thanks and gentleness.
> Sons of Éire. Let the strength of thy arms protect the weakness of the daughters of the land;
> Let none enter into the office of another.
> The minstrel to his harp.
> The bard to his measure.
> The ollamh to philosophy, to nourish the young mind with lessons of truth and wisdom, thereby to teach man to subdue his passions.
> The sage to wait on the moon, and mark the seasons, and note times, and watch the motions of Tarsnasc (Orion).
> The people to make laws.
> The judges to declare the words thereof.
> The king to see them observed.
> The high King to watch over Eire.

It must be remembered that the Brehon Laws were introduced into Ireland some 1,800 years before the English Parliament was founded—modelled on Tara—by Alfred the Great who had been educated in Ireland. He also modelled the judicial and legislative institutions on those of Ireland, and the division of England into shires, still in place today, with their governing bodies was also copied from the Irish. Any suggestion that the British Parliament is the basis of all others in the world is a fallacy.

The brehons alone had absolute power as to the interpretation of the laws and their application to individual cases. They were so esteemed that the chiefs gave them free land for their livelihood and this remained in their family for generation to generation, like the profession itself. Those brehons who did not have a chieftain's support lived on the fees charged, i.e. a fee (fola) which was either one-twelfth of the value of the property in dispute or of the fine charged for damages or injuries. The Brehon Laws were extremely difficult to understand—no third party could master the intricacies of interpretation, only the Brehons themselves. If they gave a wrong or unjust judgement, they would forfeit their fee and become liable for damages.

From earliest times, the brehon was regarded with awe as a person that the gods watched over. As a sign of his office he wore a *sin* (sheen) or collar of gold around his neck. Most brehons were also *file* or poets. Even the king or his immediate aides could not follow the intricate language of the brehons, with the result that when Concobar Mac Nessa came to power he introduced reforms enabling all intelligent people to understand the arguments and the ensuing judgements.

There were two kinds of Brehon Laws—the *Cain* Law, which applied to all Ireland, and the *Urradus* Law, which applied only to the province or region where it was in force. Of the four surviving volumes of the Brehon Laws, the *Seanchas Mór* and the *Book of Acaill* are the most important. The former deals with Irish civil law, while the latter is mainly concerned with criminal law and personal injuries. When St. Patrick, in AD 438, ordered that the collection of the old pagan laws be condensed into a workable format, it is believed that no great alterations were made, except where there was conflict with the Scriptures or early Canon Law. After all, the old Brehon Laws did nothing more than expound the Law of Nature. However, under the influence of St. Patrick, the Law of the Letter (Old and New Testament) and the canonical rules were included, or replaced certain aspects of law (i.e. 'an eye for an eye' was changed to a law of compensation).

St. Patrick's original version of the *Seanchas Mór* has been lost. However, many copies were made and these have been handed down to us, though often with many variations, commentaries and explanations. Cormac's Glossary—written about the ninth century—mostly deals with changes of terminology and gives up-to-date explanations. Also in this glossary we encounter another law text called the *Bhreatha Nemed*, which deals with the laws governing the privileged classes of Irish society at that time.

As mentioned earlier, all Irish laws were in verse, and this form is evident to some degree in surviving tracts, such as the *Seanchas Mór*. The ancient form of Irish was used, which was more closely associated with ancient Latin and Greek than with the spoken word. In fact the early brehons had to receive special instructions in this type of archaic language. Furthermore, the distinctive, truncated style of the *Seanchas Mór* indicates that it was intended as a guide to prick the memory of the brehon—in other words, they were brief notes based on an oral transmission of the full text.

It must be remembered that Ireland never had a legislative body or machinery to enact or to make laws, as no king had sufficient power to introduce or enforce new laws, up to the time of the Anglo-Norman invasion. From the *Feis* of Tara through the period of the *Aenochs*, the laws were proclaimed, promulgated or requoted so that the people could understand them to the best of their capabilities. In the early assemblies, only matters dealing with local or general interest were discussed, such as what we now refer to as civil works, redrawing boundaries and the rights of tribes or individuals. The only assembly which attempted to bring in a new law was that convened by St. Adamnan at Tara in AD 697, when he introduced a law exempting women from taking part in war as this was un-Christian. Women had taken a very active part in wars up to this time and were sometimes more feared than their male counterparts.

If the *Book of Acaill* (treatise on criminal law and personal injuries) is examined, it will be found that it consists of lists of precedents and legal pronouncements or statutes which have been copied by the British legal system. Likewise, the *Seanchas Mór* delivered judgements based on precedents and their interpretation by renowned earlier brehons. The Brehon Laws can be described as a collection of customs which, by long usage, hereditary habit and public opinion, attained the force of law.

In order to understand how comprehensive the *Book of Acaill* is in dealing with criminal and personal injuries law, the following is but a brief outline. It regulates the various ranks of society, from the king down to the slave, and enumerates their several rights and privileges. There are minute rules for the management of property, for the many industries—building, brewing, mills, water-courses, fishing-weirs, bees and honey—for distress or seizure of goods, for tithes, trespass, and for giving evidence. The relations of landlord and tenant, the fees of professional men—doctors, judges, teachers, builders, artisans—the mutual duties of father and son, of foster-parents and foster-children, of master and servant, are all carefully regulated. In the area corresponding to what is now known as criminal law, the various offences are minutely distinguished: murder, manslaughter, assaults, wounding, thefts, all kinds of wilful damage, accidental injuries from flails, sledgehammers, machines, and weapons of all kinds. The amount of compensation is laid down in detail for almost every possible variety of injury.

Contracts or covenants are regarded as peculiarly sacred and are treated in great detail.

There were several ways of striking a contract or ratifying a covenant—all very simple. One was by the two parties joining their right hands, which should be first ungloved if gloves were worn. Sometimes, one of the parties put his drinking horn into the hand of the other—also an ancient practice in England, especially in the transfer of lands. Certain legal formulae were commonly used: the conditions were to be observed 'while the sea surrounds Erin', 'so long as the sun and wind remain', etc. Important contracts were always witnessed, and it was usual for each side to name persons of standing as guarantors for the fulfilment of contracts or conditions. These persons became liable in case of default. A contract was denoted by the words *cor*, *cotach*, and *ernaidm*.

Ownership of Land

Under the Brehon Laws, the land was originally common property, as it was from prehistoric times. Only when the tribes took possession of certain parts did the tribal leaders grant portions to individual tribesmen who would have had no right of ownership *per se*. However, with the passing of time and the continuous occupation of certain tracts of land by individuals, private ownership came into existence. This was in contrast to land held in common ownership, which nowadays is referred to as 'commonage'.

Under the Brehon system there were five ways of holding land:

1 A tribal chief held a portion as long as he lived
2 Clan or sept leaders (noblemen), brehons and professional men received land from the chief, as well as all 'free members' of the tribe
3 Tenants of number 2 (above) who paid 'in kind' over a period of seven years
4 Tracts of tribal land could be held by the members in general for their own use for a period of one to four years
5 Waste land was common to all the tribe for personal grazing, timber or hunting

Payment for usage

Every person who held land shared the responsibilities of the tribe—military service, contributions to the support of old people, those who had no children, widows, orphans, etc. Besides this, the land owner had to pay his chief a subsidy, according to his means, while those who used commonage were obliged to pay a proportion of the value of each animal, yearly, for seven years.

The custom of giving and accepting animal stock for hire was widely practised, either under a method of security or else subject to a type of interest which was usually severe and subjected the tenant to a loss of his rights as a freeman.

Subsidies were paid in cows, pigs, bacon, malt, corn, etc., plus a number of days' work or army service. For those who took stock under security, one third of the value had to be paid yearly for a period of seven years until the stock officially changed hands. On the other hand, those who accepted stock on an interest basis had to pay twice yearly in cows, pigs, bacon, etc., and at the end of the seven years had either to hand back the stock or pay the equivalent.

In addition to the above, all tribal borrowers were obliged to give free hospitality to the chiefs, and those people of high rank within the tribe, together with those serving as military personnel. This practice was reflected in later years by the Anglo-Irish as the custom of Coyne and Livery (food for man and horse).

Bond-slaves

Another section of the tribal community which requires some mention is that of the bond-slave (*daer-fudir*), who was a tenant without rights. They belonged to the land and could not leave it and mostly consisted of people from outside the tribe who had been forced to move from their previous abode for one reason or another. With the advance of the Norman conquest, many of the tribes had to move to other locations and became bond-tribes to some other powerful chieftain, As a result of such moves, many of the lesser tribes and septs lost their identity.

Inheritance of Land

Land was passed on in three ways:

1. Private land—for those who held land in their own right, it would be passed on to the heirs, usually the sons, while the daughters received stock in lieu of property.
2. The land held by a chieftain or tribal sept leader passed on to his successor and not to his heirs, i.e. descent by Tanistry.
3. When a tenant who held a section of tribal land died, his land did not pass on to his heirs but was divided amongst the male adults of the tribe, which included the male offsprings of the deceased. There was no difference between the rights of the legitimate and illegitimate adults in such a division.

These last two were abolished in Ireland during the reign of James I, when the first son became the heir to his father's property.

Laws of Compensation

The Brehon Laws also contained a detailed section dealing with the laws of compensation and the administration of justice. As previously stated, the high king had insufficient power to bring any action against those who opposed him or his government, so therefore there was no 'offence against the state', as such. Every offence was against an individual—what is now referred to as 'tort'. Even though there was no policing force, lawlessness—if the term can be used in this instance—was contained by the society of that time by bringing the offence to the attention of the tribal leader, provincial king, or high king. During the earliest times the Law of Retaliation prevailed (i.e. 'an eye for an eye'). However, in order to uphold peace within each community or settlement, the Law of Compensation gradually took over. This law of compensation for a wrong-doing was exercised by the local brehon and took the form of a type of fine for the offender, his family or his tribe.

The procedures of the Brehon Laws in these cases is somewhat complicated, legalistic and 'foreign' to our present way of thinking, and shall be explained as briefly as possible.

Distress

Distress does not mean here what is understood by the word today, but rather translates to distrain or seize assets of the offender.

1 If the offender refused to acknowledge the fine, or withheld payment, the injured party had the right to seize the offender's cattle or assets. This was done with due notice and with the presence of a tribal agent and seven witnesses.

2 In most instances, there was a 'stay' (or *anad*) before the cattle were removed—usually a few days. If the offender had to give a pledge of payment but was unable to release his cattle, he had to hand over his son or another family member until the cattle formally changed hands. In a case where the offender totally refused to pay the fine, the goods or person given in

lieu became the property of the injured party who had the right to dispose of these as he liked, i.e. he could sell the family member into slavery. If all the cattle were taken on the spot, it was referred to as immediate seizure. They were then kept in a 'pound' until the debt was agreed or paid in full. If the debt was not paid or agreed after a certain period of time, the cattle were sold.

One of the most unusual customs of claiming distress was when the plaintiff 'fasted on' the offender. The process was referred to as *troscad* (fasting), and was used only when the plaintiff was of a lower grade than the offender. Having given due notice to the offender, the plaintiff sat before his door and remained there without food. This process was intended to compel the offender to do justice. The fasting was regarded as a type of superstitious curse, which obliged the offender and his family to also fast or to pay the fine.

Murder (homicide or bodily injury of any kind) was paid for by a fine (*eric*) in two parts:

a Payment for the injury (set by the brehon)

b Honour-price—the amount depended on the rank of the offended or injured party and varied from three to seven and a half cows.

In all cases, if the fine was not paid by the offending individual, his family or tribe either had to pay, or to be placed in slavery, or forfeit their life. Capital punishment was not widely tolerated in early Ireland. In fact, nobody was put to death (by judicial sentence) for intentional murder, as long as the eric (fine) was obtained, but, if it was not, his life was forfeited.

It is interesting to note that, according to the Brehon Laws, it was customary to burn women for adultery. The word *druth* (harlot), which derives from the two words *dir* (right) and *aod* (fire), frequently occurs. According to the law, any woman who had violated her contract of marriage could be burned to death. This particular custom was followed in the earliest days, according to the Commentaries.

When the court was held for the trial of a legal case, it was commonly referred to as the *dal*, and other times as the *oirecht* or *airecht* (meaning meeting of representatives). One may note the derivation of the terms used for our present government system. Courts were mostly held in the open air, with a chieftain and the privileged classes officiating. A brehon sat in judgement and the profession lawyers and pleaders represented the parties involved in an action. There were many rules to be followed, especially in regard to a case of conflict between husband and wife. If a husband gave evidence against his wife, she was entitled to give evidence in her defence, but the daughters were not allowed to give evidence against the father. The rights of the woman were equal to that of the man and, in the case of divorce, the woman was allowed to take with her her dowry or equivalent plus a percentage of family gains (profits) accrued during the period of her marriage.

There were many more interesting facets of law contained in the ancient Brehon Laws, but space prohibits the author from expanding further.

— 14 —
Ogham Script

In addition to the Beith-Luis-Nion alphabet, there was a also a script called *Ogham* or *Orhum-coll*, a type of writing which represented the branches of a hazel tree. Ware, in his *Antiquities*, wrote that he had a book of parchment full of these characters. Unfortunately, this has now vanished. This type of script is peculiar to the south-west of Ireland, where about three hundred and sixty examples out of a total of three hundred and eighty still exist on these western islands.

Some historians say that Ogham script was introduced to Ireland *c.* 500 BC, at about the same time as the arrival of the Celts. However, no discoveries have so far been found in Europe to justify any connection with the Celtic tribes. On the contrary, it appears to be indigenous to the early inhabitants of Cornwall and the south-west coast of Ireland. Even the date of usage given by historians is questionable, as it appears to be inscribed on existing standing stones as an afterthought. The fact that it is based on the early Latin alphabet does not mean that it actually followed it in time and is dated accordingly. Early Latin derives from the Greek and Etruscan dialects, which in turn are based on the alphabet of the Phoenicians. On examination of all the early types of hieroglyphics, scripts and writings of the prehistoric period in the Mediterranean and Middle Eastern regions, there appears to be only one type of script that is in any way similar, and that is part of the Middle Cycladic (Northern Aegean Sea) script of 1900–1500 BC, in which a basic line for consonants and vowels is used. A number of examples are set out on the opposite page to give an idea of the similarity between the two types of writing.

It is strange that this Cycladic script is peculiar to one region only, not being found elsewhere in the Mediterranean. So, we encounter two almost similar scripts used in two regions which are thousands of miles apart, and are left wondering how this could be possible!

Even the early antiquarians and historians were unable to explain the origins of either the Beith-Luis-Nion or the Ogham script without referring to the early Mediterranean civilisations. This placed them in a quandary, as they refused to accept that any historic facts were contained in the *Leabhair Gabhala*. The elements of the above scripts are either completely original or else are derived from some other similar type of writing. If we are to accept the former, then we must automatically conclude that our ancient ancestors were as highly gifted in intelligence as the Phoenicians, who are regarded as the first great explorers. If, however, we accept the latter, we must ask by whom and for what purpose these two scripts were introduced to Ireland; by which tribe of invaders?

It is possible that the Phoenician traders themselves brought the script and languages to our shores as a means of communication between themselves and the native Irish, as well as those Phoenicians who happened to settle here on a trade basis. On the other hand, we must not forget that the legendary supreme god of the Tuatha de Danaan was called *Dagda* or *Og*, and the divine writing of the priestly cast was referred to as *Ogam*. We would have been much better informed about these scripts if St. Patrick had not burned over one hundred and eighty volumes of druidic doctrine and knowledge at the hill of Tara.

If we refer to the writing of Caesar, we find that 'the druids never committed their mysteries to writing, except in their public acts in which they made use of a type of Greek characters'. This part of the druids' behaviour is akin to the customs of the ancient Egyptian priests, where the ceremonies and hieroglyphics were held in the same esteem and secrecy.

The use of letters was very important to the early Irish, as it helped in the retention of the genealogical lines of the chief families for the purposes of heredity and the right to fill important posts in society.

The Beith-Luis-Nion alphabet was mainly used on the bark of trees, while the Ogham script was preserved on thin square lengths of preserved oak. The former was mainly used to record history and genealogy, while the latter was reserved for ceremonial rites such as funerals and marriages.

The Ollam Fodla, who lived and reigned *c.* 500 BC, founded the triennial assembly at Tara. He established the seats of antiquity in each of the provinces where the records were to be preserved. Each and every record had to be examined at the gatherings at Tara, and copies were made of everything recorded, under his supervision. This copy was called the Psalter of Tara, which was written in verse in the manner of the ancient Egyptians, using the Beith-Luis-Nion alphabet. In fact, as O'Curry states in his *Manuscript Materials* (pp. 463, 472), 'the pre-Christian Gaels possessed a practice, a system of writing and keeping records quite different from, and independent of, both the Greek and Roman form and characters, which gained currency in the country after the introduction of Christianity in the first part of the fifth century'. This is amply verified by the composition of the *Saltair of Tara*, compiled in the third century by Cormac Mac Airt, who died in AD 266, and by the manuscript called *Cin Droma Sneacta*.

As for the Beith-Luis-Nion itself, it had only seventeen letters. Ancient Greek also had seventeen letters, but lost one, namely *F*, during the early period. The alphabet was originally called Phoinika, having derived from the Phoenicians, and also because the letters were written on leaves or tablets of the palm-tree (phoinix), and consisted of twelve consonants and five vowels. With each consonant and vowel having a short and long sound, the ancient Irish tongue had no equal in the world as a complete language, either then or now.

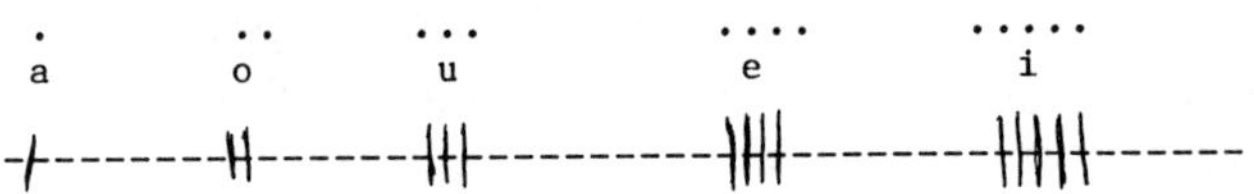

B L F S N H D T C QU

M N NG ST R P.

EARLY CYCLADIC SCRIPT.

X = P.

NUMBERS - LINEAR B.

I	= One Unit.	III II	= 5.
-	= Tens.	- - - - -	= 50
0	= Hundreds.	0 0 0 0	= 400
0	= Thousands.	0 0 0	= 3000
0	= Tens of Thousands.	0 0 0 0	= 40,000.

Samples of Ogham and Cycladic scripts

BEITH-LUIS-NION.

B	Beithe	Birch.
L	Luis	Wild Ash.
F	Fearn	Alder.
S	Suil	Willow.
N	Nion	Ash.
H	Huath	Wild thorn.
D	Duir	Oak.
T	Timne	
C	Coll	Hazel.
M	Muin	Vine
G	Gort	Ivy.
P	Peth-boc.	
R	Ruis	Elder
A	Ailm	Fir tree.
O	Onn	Broom.
U	Ur	Heath
E	Egdhadh	Aspen
I	Idho	Yew.

THE RUNIC ALPHABET.

F	ᚠ
U	ᚢ
b	ᚦ
A	ᚨ
R	ᚱ
K	ᚲ
G	ᚷ
W	ᚹ
H	ᚺ
N	ᚾ
I	ᛁ
J	ᛃ
P	ᛈ
E	ᛇ
R	ᛉ
S	ᛊ
T	ᛏ
B	ᛒ
E	ᛖ
M.	ᛗ
L	ᛚ
ng	ᛜ
D	ᛞ
O	ᛟ

Samples of Beith-Luis-Nion and Runic alphabets

The Celts

Long, long ago, beyond the misty space
Of twice a thousand years,
In Erin old there dwelt a mighty race
Taller than Roman spears;
Like oaks and towers, they had a giant grace,
Were fleet as deers:
With wind and waves they made their biding place
The western shepherd seers.

Their ocean-god was *Manannan Mac Lir*
Whose angry lips
In their white foam full often would inter
Whole fleets of ships;
Crom was their day-god, and their thunderer,
Made morning and eclipse;
Bride was their queen of song, and unto her
They pray'd with fire-touch'd lips.

Great were their acts, their passions, and their sports;
With clay and stone
They piled on strath and shore those mystic forts,
Not yet undone;
On cairn-crown's hills they held their council courts;
While youths alone
With giant-dogs, explored the eld's resorts,
And brought them down.

Of these was Finn, the father of the bard
Whose ancient song
Over the clamour of all change is heard,
Sweet-voiced and strong.
Finn had as spouse Granu, the golden hair'd
The fleet and young;
From her, the lovely, and from him, they feared
The primal poet sprung.

Ossian—two thousand years of mist and change
Surround thy name;
Thy Finnian heroes now no longer range
The hills of Fame.

The very name of Finn and Gael sound strange;
Yet thine the same
By miscall's lake and deserted grange
Remains, and shall remain!

The Druid's altar and the Druid's creed
We scarce can trace;
There is not left an undisputed deed
Of all your race—
Save your majestic Song, which hath their speed
And strength, and grace;
In that sole song they live, and love, and bleed—
It bears them on through space.

Inspired giant, shall we ever behold
In our own time,
One fit to speak your spirit on the world,
Or seize your rhyme?
One pupil of the past, as might-soul'd
As in the prime
Were the fond, fair and beautiful, and bold—
They of your song sublime?

Thomas D'Arcy McGee

— 15 —

The Celts

In the context of Irish or local history, mention has to be made of the Celts, who are said to have originated in the upper region of the Danube. They were not in fact a race, but a band of several warlike tribes who found it necessary to move on, due to the invasions of other more powerful tribes from the north-east (Russia). They split up into various groups, one going south into northern Greece, and another which headed west and divided into two further sections—one going into France and the other heading further south into northern Spain and southern France.

A part of the latter group stayed in northern Switzerland and became known as the La Tiene culture, which historians have accepted as the major influence in western European civilisation. But, for the reader, the most interesting section is that which invaded northern Greece—as related by Hecataeus, Aristotle, Hellanicus and Ephories (*c.* 500–350 BC). Their attributes were rather varied, as they were said to 'practise justice and righteousness and at the same time to be frenzied warriors imbued with potent drink when going into battle'.

Having conquered the Illyrians of northern Greece, they marched south and then sacked the city of Delphi *c.* 273 BC. They made a truce and then an alliance with the Greeks in which they agreed to protect the northern borders and to assist the Greeks in their struggle against the Carthagenians and the Persians. In fact, they played no small part in the preservation of Greek civilisation and culture, and there was a certain similarity between both their customs.

When Philip of Macedonia was attacked by the Thracians and the Illyrians, the Celts came to his rescue and defeated the enemy. Afterwards a strong bond grew between both races and when Alexander the Great, Philip's son, moved east into Asia Minor (Turkey, etc.) *c.* 330 BC to conquer the Persians his best soldiers were the Celts, who by their appearance—being covered from head to toe in white powder or chalk, wild shouting, hammering of swords on shields and roar of battle—plus their disregard for their own lives, often throwing away their shield, was guaranteed to put the enemy to flight.

Their battle chant, taken from the early Greek, to the rhythm of beating on shields, was:

> We fear no man; there is but one thing we fear, namely
> That the sky should fall on us and crush us.
> May the earth gape and swallow us up
> May the sea burst out and overwhelm us.

If the *Táin Bó Cuailnge* is consulted, as related in the Book of Ulster, the scenes described are almost the same. As they gathered speed on their horses and chariots they shouted:

> Heaven is above us, the earth beneath us and the sea around us, we shall never retreat and death shall only defeat us.

Even the custom of covering their bodies in white powder is identical. However, these particular customs do not seem to appear in any other western European sources of that time.

For anyone who has seen the film *Zulu*, the scenes portrayed will give an idea of those early Celtic warriors going into battle.

When the exploits of the northern band of Celts which invaded France and then England are considered, no documented record that they actually crossed the Irish Sea and invaded Ireland with an army can be found, although it could be that they crossed in small groups *c.* 350 BC and slowly subdued the existing Irish inhabitants by the force of their stronger and more powerful weapons (iron versus bronze). Another possibility is that the southern tribe (eastern Mediterranean) found its way by land and sea to the south of Ireland.

However, the similarity between the Irish Celts and those who were the allies of the Greeks requires more detailed comment, and this is discussed later in this chapter.

In all their invasions and conquests throughout Europe, the Celts were noted as fearless warriors, but they did not exterminate their defeated foe. Instead, they spared the former enemy and became the dominant class, by imposing their customs, art forms, traditions and way of life while adopting or integrating that part of the religion and customs of the original subdued inhabitants which they found compatible with their own.

The presence in Ireland of Celts before any incursions from La Tiene or from the Hallstatt via France or Britain (*c.* 300 BC) presented some major problems for early historians. The place names preserved by the poet Festus Avienus, and said to be derived from the Greek Pytheas who sailed the Atlantic in 400 BC, give an indication that these names are in fact a type of Illyrian or eastern Celtic, i.e. Hierni (Ireland), Orcades (Orkney), Albu (Britain), Orcas.

It is, therefore, obvious that one of the most important facts in ancient Ireland is the existence of a unique and well-structured language. A language, in fact, which has no similarity with the existing western European tongues of that period and which cannot be defined as Teutonic or Middle European, but which is similar in its alphabet and construction to Phoenician and early Greek. It was called the Beith-Luis-Nion, an alphabet which had its own particular order, but which was later changed by the early scribes or monks to correspond with the Latin alphabet.

The early Milesians used birchen boards to inscribe the characters—*Feadha*—so that events and history could be recorded. Even though this language preceded the Celts to Ireland, they readily adopted it due to the fact that it was similar to their own southern dialect.

Finally, it should be pointed out that the term 'Celt' is a misnomer. There was no such thing as a Celtic race, but rather a number of tribes which shared the same original homeland, customs, beliefs, art, military strength, dialects, and the desire to fight to conquer.

The word 'Celtic' is a mixture of Latin and Greek and is a quasi-ethnic term. It identifies a certain group of people who are devoid of any geographical location or homeland.

In the regions which the Celts are supposed to have originally occupied, there was a type of language spoken which had certain distinctive peculiarities, such as lacking the *P* sound. It was more by the identification of these particular language and warlike characteristics than any other feature that the Celtic tribes were known. Besides their languages, there was a certain type of culture associated with these Celtic tribes which infiltrated the structures of various other European civilisations through military domination at that time.

Even though Ireland, south-western Britain and France were areas occupied by the Celts during the Roman conquests, these regions were never identified by Roman historians as Celtic. Ireland itself was a 'Goidelic' speaking nation and had been influenced somewhat by the 'iron culture' of the Celts, who in small groups dominated the existing authoritative power, language, religion and civilisation. In fact, they were now transformed from their earlier distinction of being the feared nomadic fighters who had established a kingdom in north-eastern modern Turkey (called Galitia), sacked Rome, and dominated western Europe.

Finally, it must be deduced that the Celtic invaders came in groups mostly made up of men who intermarried with the local inhabitants (Goedils) and, in time, the predominant earlier language survived with very minor alterations. Any useful knowledge on culture, metalwork and science that had been brought by these Celtic invaders was integrated into the civilisation that they encountered in Ireland.

— 16 —

Early Christianity

The exact date of the arrival of Christianity in the south-west of Ireland is a very much debated subject. Those records that do exist concerning this period of AD 400–AD 600 differ in many respects. It is hotly contested amongst historians whether there was more than one St. Patrick, without trying to ascertain who introduced Christianity into the south-west. Before we examine such records as do exist, let us first briefly refer to Ireland as a whole, in relation to the introduction of Christianity.

It is generally accepted that there were Christian congregations in Ireland prior to the mission of Palladius in AD 431. His chronicles state that he was sent to the 'Scots living in Ireland who believed in Christ'.

As most writers do not refer to the earlier life of Palladius, it is worth noting that he was a follower of the holy hermits who lived in the upper regions of Palestine, probably amongst those who did penance, prayed and fasted at Mount Carmel. It is said that Palladius, who had been under the direction of a holy monk from his early years, embraced hermit life at the age of twenty years. Having spent some time in Jerusalem, he journeyed to Rome, where he was eventually selected by Pope Celestine to go to Ireland and preach the Gospel. If we refer to Tacitus, the Roman historian and writer of that time, we find that he states that 'the ports of Ireland were better known to the Romans than those of Britain'. The persecution of Christians by both Diocletian and Maximian in all parts of the Roman empire caused many believers to flee from Gall (France) and England, and to seek safety in Ireland. Sedulius refers to Scotus Hyberniensis and the southern part of Ireland in this regard (*c.* AD 430). Even Prosper, who was widely respected as a historian, states that Palladius was sent to Ireland before Patrick. Prosper goes on to state that Palladius arrived as Bishop of Ireland, landing somewhere near Wexford, and in time established a number of churches where he kept the relics of St. Peter and St. Paul with his 'tablets'. We do not know what exactly is meant by the word tablets—possibly tables of doctrinal teaching or sections of an altar top.

One of the churches built by Palladius was referred to as *Teach-na-Romanaig*. This may have possible connections with Kilnaruane, near Bantry (see Lanigan's *Ecclesiastical History of Ireland*), or else it was so-called due to its adherence to the new Roman calendar introduced *c.* 633 in the south-west of Munster.

As to Prosper's assertion that paganism had disappeared from Ireland around the sixth century, this conflicts with other writers about early Christianity. It appears that Prosper's judgement was influenced by the erroneous reports arriving in Rome that Palladius had converted the whole of Ireland. This, however, was not true, as the powerful druids had influenced the tribal leaders to expel Palladius from Ireland. Before he departed, he charged a number of his followers, unknown to the pagan priests, to remain and preach to the people. A year after his expulsion, *c.* AD 432, Palladius died. When St. Patrick arrived, he found an infant church, based on the Eastern monastic form, which he considered it wise to follow, rather than to introduce any major changes as dictated by Rome.

If we look at Usher's *Third Order of Saints*, we find that he states that 'there were those holy priests and a few bishops who dwelt in deserts and lived on herbs, water and alms. They had divers rules and masses and divers tonsures, some having the corona and others with their hair. They differed also in the Pascual Celebration in that they honoured the Resurrection from the fourteenth day of the moon and others from the sixteenth.'

Amongst those mentioned are a Colman, a Carthagh (Kerry) and two St. Mochoemogs, one of whom was son of Cuaith, a disciple of

St. Carthagh and a bishop, whilst the other was the illegitimate son of Vairt, also a disciple of St. Carthagh (AD 540–AD 580). He also gives details of three brothers, Gobban, Graphan and Laseran, the sons of Nescainn. Gobban is mentioned later as a bishop and as a saint by Colgan the historian.

The Mochoemogs were placed in a monastery, which had been built on a small island called Inispict (AD 620) by St. Carthagh, where they remained for a year under the bishop Domangen, together with twelve other monks. Inispict was described as lying near Inishirkan in Roaring Water Bay. It is interesting to note that Colgan, the historian, refers to the Acts of St. Gobban and places his feast on the seventeenth of March. There is some confusion as to where the Island of Inispict was located in Roaring Water Bay. It is widely accepted that the island of Inis Ceim (Skeams Island West), called after Cein of the Ivagha sept, is the same island.

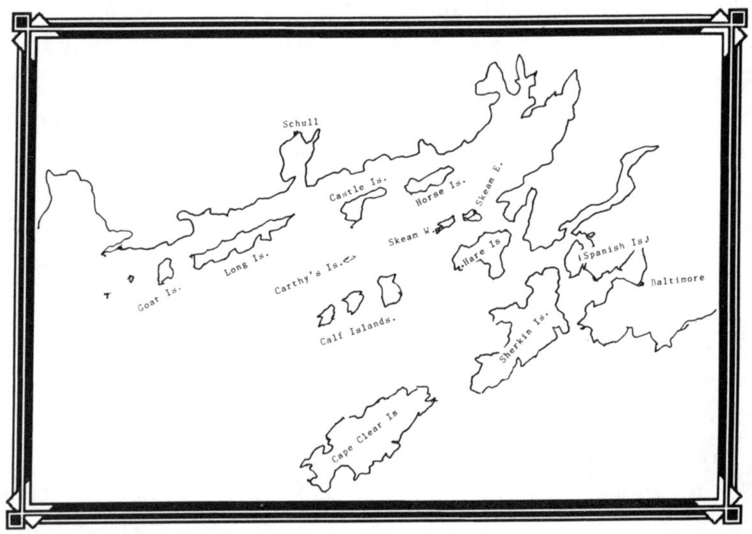

Map of ecclesiastical sites in Roaring Water Bay

When we consider early Christian practices, we find that they used the old (Jewish) Paschal system, which was introduced by St. Patrick, until after the arrival of Roman missionaries in Britain and Ireland. They also used the old Alexandrine method of cycles of nineteen years in computing movable feasts.

It does seem strange that, even though St. Patrick was trained by the Church of Rome, he adhered to the Eastern (i.e. Coptic) computation of the major Christian feast of Easter. Why, we may ask? Was it because it coincided with the pagan festival? I shall not enter into the dispute regarding the Edict of Nantes concerning this matter, except to state that it is interesting that those who continued to follow the oldest calculations for Easter were deemed to be 'heretics, schismatics, and disturbers of public tranquillity'.

Usher makes a vague reference to the local custom of 'Skelligs', which is mentioned here in a later chapter. He also mentions that the new Roman Cycle and rules were generally accepted in Munster from about AD 633. As for St. Gobban, we find that he was located at Leighlin (Old Leighlin), where he governed a monastery and was visited by St. Laserian on his return from Pope Gregory in Rome. St. Colman (or St. Comman) is described as having died in AD 677.

Evidence of Early Settlements

Tradition has it that a St. Colman and a St. Cieran, having converted the tribal leaders and peoples around Cape Clear and Baltimore, came to Colomane in the Bantry area and, with their followers, established a Christian settlement. We must not get mixed up with various other early saints with the same name, such as Colman (Comman). As for St. Cieran, we find that he is also associated with Ossory, as Osraige at that time was ruled by a section of the Corca Leidge (Laidhe) until the middle of the sixth century.

St. Colman is believed to have set up his settlement high on the northern hill overlooking Colomane and Dromore. The large site itself is rather a puzzle, as on the one hand there is evidence of an early megalithic site with standing stones, a stone circle and a possible dolmen, while on the other hand there is a (possibly ceremonial) holy well, an avenue of penitential stone heaps, a graveyard, a stone burial site (where the saint is reputed to have been buried), the remains of a settlement and a circular stone enclosure. We are therefore led to believe that this was a very important religious site in early times, and even up to recent times it was a place of religious visitation for the local rural population.

Kilmacomoge

Local tradition holds that the church site at Kilmacomoge near Kealkil was an ancient religious location, prior to the advent of Christianity, with an arrangement of stones and a sacred well. And if certain interpretations of the name Kilmacomoge—such as Kil-na-Commoge—are considered, they would translate into the 'afflicted of the gathering' or the 'gathering of the afflicted'—meaning taking solace from the sacred well. So it is not known whether the name Kilmacomoge has Christian or pagan roots.

As to which of the Mochoemogs settled in the Kealkil region, this is now only a matter of guesswork. However, it must be accepted that there was a Mochoemog, a Gobban, and a Gobnait. All saints who have a past link with this region.

Other references state that the local chieftains of the area were the O'Briens, while E. Hogan in the *Onomasticon Goedelicum* (1910) calls the place 'Cil-na-Muchoige'. The *Annals of Inishfallen* also state that the local tribe was the O'Briens.

There is a very strong local legend in this area around Kealkil that Fionn Mac Comhuil stayed at the large fort at Breeny Mór and went hunting in the area, and it is also believed that there existed an ancient burial ground, known as a 'tumulos'. The O'Crowley clan occupied na Lisina (Lisheens) and there is a reference to Brien Boiroimhe coming south to the Kealkil region to mediate amongst the clan leaders and their subjects about their obligations to give military service under the Brehon Laws. Another early tradition linked Cathair-Mac-Ith (son of Lughaigh) with the townland of Ahil (*aichil, ahill, aguila*—meaning 'place of eagles'). There was also an Ogham Stone called Cloc hInhle or Cloc Gur (loadstone) at Ahil, and Cahirmuckee, which was called Cill-na-gCropog, has the ruins of an early church.

There were other Christian settlements in the area, but little evidence remains today. Taking site names, local tradition and documented information, the following emerge as strong possibilities: Kil-na-Ruane, Kil-atha-Fineen, Kil-More, Reen-a-Disert, Kil-namBan-Oige, Kil-Macomoge, Reen-na-mBan-Oige, Ard-na-Monaig, Maulavanaig.

Taking each of these in turn, we shall examine what little information we have which may be of some relevance.

Kil-na-Ruane 'St. Ruan's church'.
There are no indications of any ruins in the immediate vicinity of the site of the Kilnaruane Stone. It was not until an aerial photograph of the area was taken by Dr. P. Mould that the existence of some type of enclosure was revealed. The photograph showed the outline of a square enclosure which was approximately 50m square, which, in those times, was a substantial settlement. A square Christian enclosure was a new departure from the customary circular type of those times. It is difficult to connect any local saint to this location, except to say that St. Gobnat is reputed to have established a monastery in this region.

The following is a detailed description of the Kilnaruane Stone.

The cross in the top panel represents both the symbol of the supreme sun-god of the ancient civilisation, and the sign of Christianity. The strand of interlacing would suggest the influence of the ancient sea-god Manannan, as he was usually portrayed by the sign of the sea serpent or snake. Thus we have the conflict of the old religion and Christianity—and good and evil.

The lower panel depicts an *orans,* or praying figure, wearing a simple ankle-length garment. The two feet clearly represented a holy one sent by God in early Christianity. Before that, the symbol represented the feet of the Egyptian sun-god Osiris. The figure is therefore praying, or instructing his audience on the liberation from past beliefs.

The next panel is of a Greek-style cross of the early Church and represents the introduction of the converted to the new Christianity.

The lower panel displays two seated figures, each with one hand extended to a wafer-shaped bread on the top of a pedestal or altar, having just been dropped by a bird. This represents a passage about St. Paul, written by St. Jerome, and is here interpreted as the reception of the Bread of Life after conversion.

On the bottom panel, the symbol of the boat derives from the ancient Eastern religions, especially Egyptian, representing the ship of Isis transferring the 'beatified dead' to the Other World. Here the ship equates to the Christian Church by having crosses around it.

The central panel shows four animals, symbolising the four Evangelists in the early Church, or, more accurately, as in Revelations 4 (4: 8), signifying the throne of Heaven. The twin interlacing spirals in the top panel are believed to represent the spiral of life. Thus we have the intertwining of God and man in perfect and eternal harmony.

The Kilnaruane Stone

Kil-atha-Fineen

The name means the 'church of Fineen's Bridge'. This site is situated on the high field to the south of Bantry town. There is little evidence of any settlement in this location, except that the outline of the ditches, or mud walls, indicate some sort of ancient rectangle enclosure.

Kil-More

Kil-More, meaning 'large church', is situated on Whiddy Island. Today, all that can be seen are the ruins of a large church and graveyard. These are not the ruins of the early settlement, but date back to *c.* AD 1500. It is believed that the original location was first a druid ceremonial site and then became a Christian settlement *c.* AD 600–700.

Reen-a-Disert

At Ballylickey (*Bealac Leachta, Bealac-a-Lice, Beal-atha-na-Lice*), on the small isthmus to the north of the entrance to the inlet, St. Canera was reputed to have established a priory. She is referred to as a nun from Bentraighe by Colgan and Smith's *History of Cork*. Her feast day is 29 January. She died a year after leaving Bantry, in a monastery on the Shannon. Little or nothing remains of the priory, but close examination of the site reveals hewed building stones in an old retaining wall on the east side of the beach. Besides this priory, there were a number of others in the region, including one on Whiddy Island, north-east of the castle ruins in the hollow near the holy well.

Kil-na-mBan-Oige

The priory at Kilnavanig (meaning 'church of the young women'), near Gearhies, was located to the north-west of the present church building.

B. O'Donogue, in his *Parish History of West Cork*, refers to a St. Mineog—Cill Mhineog Oiche—as being connected with this site. He does not define exactly where the site was located, except 'to the west of Bantry', so it is doubtful whether there is any connection between Mineog and this priory. However, there is a strong tradition regarding the existence of a priory to the north side of the existing disused Church of Ireland, as well as the existence of a burial ground and souterrains on the hillock to the south. As souterrains and graveyards do not exist simultaneously, the southern site must have an unknown history. Only a professional archaeological survey will answer the questions. As to the aforementioned location, it has been handed down by tradition that this was the location of the priory which was sacked by the Vikings, and is recalled in the old poem 'Caoine na mBan Oige'.

Reen-na-mBan-Oige

This name means 'knoll of the young women'. It is believed that, to the north-east of the O'Sullivan castle remains on Whiddy Island, there existed a priory of holy women. This site was commemorated up to recent times, both by the island and shore folk and by visitation to the nearby holy well. Whether there was any relationship or connection between this priory and that of St. Canera's at Reen-a-Disert is open to conjecture, as they were only 1.5 miles apart by water.

Ard-na-Monaig

This means 'height of the monks' and is situated near Ardnagashel. There is little, if any, evidence of a monastic settlement in this area, except for what appears to be the remains of some walls in the small valley between the two hillocks by the sea. Nearby is located Ardnaturrish, 'height of the pilgrimage', which, up to recent times, was a place of visitation and worship, due to the presence of a holy well and ancient burial ground.

There are also a number of other locations where there were possible early Christian settlements, such as Farranamanagh (monk's land), Kilnaknappoge (church of the hillocks), Maulavanaig (knoll of the monks) and Reenaveig (monk's point—as in 'headland').

A Standing Stone at Scart, Bantry

— 17 —
The Vikings in Bantry Bay

The Viking invaders and their exploits in Ireland are related in the book known as *The War between the Gael and the Gaill.* These Vikings or Norsemen were either from Norway or Denmark. Those who came from Norway were of fair or blond hair (Fionn Gaill) and those who came from Denmark were of dark hair (Dubh Gaill). The historical records of Ireland and West Cork make no reference to the conquest of Bantry Bay by the Vikings.

The Vikings first made their appearance in Ireland when they raided Lambay Island off the coast of Dublin in AD 795, and from that first lucrative raid they commenced a general conquest of the coast of Ireland during the following two centuries. For the most part they were pagan warlike tribes, goaded on by their chiefs whom they regarded as demi-gods. Their raids at first were for precious metals—such as gold and silver—women and slaves. Ireland at this time offered rich pickings, with its many important monasteries and religious settlements which were adorned with articles of gold, silver and precious stones.

The first wave of Viking raiders arrived at the north coast of Scotland and proceeded to plunder along the whole of the east coast of Ireland. Their first appearance around the south coast was an attack on Cork (*c.* AD 822) and then in AD 827 they entered Kinsale harbour and also attacked Timoleague Abbey, as well as all those monasteries and settlements within twenty miles of the coast. In AD 837 they moved further southwards and raided the monasteries at Cape Clear and Sherkin Island, as well as all other religious settlements and native hamlets in the Baltimore and Skibbereen area.

It was not until *c.* AD 882 that references were again made to the raiders, when Donnchadh, King of Eoghanacht, gave battle to the Danes near Glandore harbour, ending in the utter defeat of the local tribes and the death of the local king.

During the next one hundred years they sought to entrench themselves in Carbery (Corca Laidhe), against the will of the local tribes. In 916 they were defeated, then in 960 another battle was fought, and during 1012 they laid waste the countryside. Finally, they were heavily defeated by the local tribes of Corca Laidhe at a place called Oneachach.

Meanwhile, during those decades and centuries of war on the east and south coasts of Ireland between the Danes and the Irish tribes, further forces of the Norsemen had moved down the west coast. In 807 they ravaged Innishmury off Sligo and plundered inland from Sligo. Four years later, in 811, they moved further south and attacked Valentia Island, the Skelligs and the Kerry coastline. During that same year, a sea battle took place off the Kerry coast, and the local tribes defeated the Danes. Despite this, they returned to the Kerry coast in greater numbers and, while the local tribes fought amongst themselves, set up a base on Dursey Island. It is would appear that the name Dursey derives from the Norse *Thor Iy*, or the Island of Thor (the Norse god of war). Having established themselves in this island stronghold, they ventured up Bantry Bay. A monastic settlement near Blackball Head was first sacked before they entered Castletown harbour, where they attacked and plundered two monastic settlements on the mainland—one west of Dunboy Castle and another near the native settlement. Moving across to Bere Island, they sacked and plundered a number of religious settlements and then built another stronghold for themselves near the sheltered harbour of Lonehart, where they built a breakwater so that their longships would be protected in all weather.

As there is no reference to the destruction of the many other Christian settlements around Bantry Bay during the continuous strife between the local tribes, it is assumed that the Norsesmen were responsible for the destruction of the small hermitage at Adrigole, the monastic settlement on Garnish Island, the monastery near the present Eccles Hotel, and the other hermitages in Glengarriff harbour. It is assumed that the other monastic settlements in the Bantry area also suffered the same fate. These would have included the settlements at Ardnamonagh, Reendisert, Kilmacomoge, Whiddy Island and Kilnaruane. All of these were totally destroyed and almost no trace of their existence remains today.

One of the strongest local traditions which supports the above premise is the story concerning the sack of the priory at Kilnavanig near Gearhies. It relates that after landing at Gearhies the Norsemen made their way east to the priory, which they sacked and plundered. The older women were raped and then killed, while the young novices were raped and then taken as slaves or bounty to the stronghold on Dursey Island. The ancient poem called 'Caoine na mBan Oige' relates the event.

It is understood that the Norsemen, having taken the old fort at Donemark, eventually made their own settlement there. The dykes were deepened and two large timber sluice gates were built on the river's edge to retain the waters within the dyke and thus prevent easy access for the Irish enemy. Within the large fort there are many souterrains and deep holes which were probably used to store food and arms. To the west of the fort itself, one can see the outline of a cultivated half-acre of ground which no doubt was used to grow vegetables.

The Norsemen's stay at Donemark seems to have been short-lived—possibly about sixty years—as the local tribes, instead of fighting amongst themselves, finally came together to drive the enemy out of the region. Based on local tradition and the few vague references by O'Curry the historian, the battle was more like a protracted skirmish.

Having attacked the fort, the Irish withdrew as if in flight and allowed the Norsemen to follow them up along the Mealagh river into the wooded interior, then across into Kealkil and, finally, into the Coomhola valley near Curran, where the now depleted forces of Norsemen were defeated. The 'battle' is said to have lasted about two weeks and the last of the fallen Norsemen were buried near the stone cairn at the top of Curran on the Priest's Leap road.

When the Vikings decided to sail westwards on their voyages of discovery to the Faroe Islands and Iceland, they found that they had been preceded by Irish anchorites who lived in beehive structures. These the Norsemen referred to as *Papor* and their settlements as *Papey*.

Between AD 930 and 984 there was a general migration of Norse people westwards to these newly discovered islands. In AD 984, the Norsemen were in southern Greenland where they built a number of settlements. They are believed to have reached the coast of Labrador (*c.* 992), but the fact that no trace of Viking settlements has been found there makes this doubtful. There is only a brief reference in the Viking's history of exploration which mentions that they visited the shoreline to the west to cut timber for building their houses and settlements in Greenland. However, the whole story is now being re-examined, since the discovery of a complete Viking village near the southern shore of Lake Michigan, which is 1,600 miles from the Gulf of St. Lawrence. Whether the discovery of megalithic stone monuments in Maine, similar to the standing stones found in Ireland, will indicate early Irish migration is another matter.

In this context, little can be said about the voyages of St. Brendan, who is recorded as having reached the eastern seaboard of North America, as there are many versions and it is difficult to separate fact from fiction. Most of these texts were written in the ancient style, imbued with myths and legends, although the English translation of the *Navigatio Santi Brendani,* dated *c.* AD 945, reveals an account which is devoid of bardic style.

To discover more about St. Brendan's voyage, one has to examine other details which related to seafaring at that time—for instance, the existence of an ancient seafaring people who lived on the Kerry coast and who were referred to as the *Ciarraige*. They are reputed to have made regular voyages to Scotland, the Shetlands, Hebrides and even further, long before the time of St. Brendan.

Amongst the Ciarraige was the renowned Mael Duin, whose sea exploits are famed in legend and history. The voyages of both St. Brendan and Mael Duin were referred to as the *Immrama*, which denotes a physical sea voyage and not a spiritual voyage of the mind. These voyages were also pilgrimages to find other lands where the monks might set up their settlements.

If the date *c.* AD 525 is accepted as the commencement of Mael Duin's voyage, then St. Brendan followed him twenty years later *c.* AD 545, using the same seafaring knowledge. Even the Greek Pytheus refers to Iceland *c.* AD 370 and there are other references by Greek historians in AD 795 and AD 800.

The detailed topography of Ireland mentioned in these accounts gives an indication of the reality of those voyages. Furthermore, they were not recorded to prove that these islands existed to the north and west, nor were they a means to claim ownership. They were but a documented history of inter-island journeying by the seafarers and monks.

The voyage of Mael Duin is related in the *Book of the Dun Cow*. The copy consulted here was written *c.* AD 1100 and probably originated in the ninth century. It is written in the style of the old Irish legends and is intertwined with early Christian beliefs. Although much of the content has to be accepted as pure myth, certain aspects merit further examination.

Leaving the obvious mythical content aside, the sea journey was up the west coast of Ireland, across to Scotland's west coast, on to the Shetlands and then to the Faroe Islands. From the Faroes, the route was westwards to Iceland, Greenland and then to the coast of North America. Various aspects of the journey are fascinating, such as the volcanic eruptions in Iceland, the spouting waters—or geysers—of Iceland, the silver pillars (icebergs) in the sea, the silver islands of Greenland and Iceland, the large birds (wandering albatrosses or large falcons), giant trees (Canadian cedars and conifers), beast-like oxen (bears or caribou), and hairy people (wearing animal heads and skin) who blackened themselves in time of mourning.

For anybody interested in further research into the voyages of Mael Duin, this last reference is the most remarkable, as it proves that Mael Duin reached North America and encountered some of the native people (Inuit or Eskimos).

There were many small tribes of Inuit in north-east Canada at that time, including the Labrador Inuit, the Ungava and the Western Territory Inuit. They mostly spoke a common language called Inuktitut, which was divided into six different dialects. The Inuits had a very strong culture, which could be described as pure Shamanism.

Their elaborate 'feast of the dead' (*Potlach)* has not been properly researched by scholars investigating the voyages of Mael Duin or St. Brendan. For the celebration of the 'feast of the dead', or mourning, presents were exchanged around a funeral pyre and the men painted their faces and bodies and, having smeared themselves with fish oil, coated their bodies with ashes from the pyre or celebration flames. This is the type of ritual, in the author's opinion, that Mael Duin related in his account of the latter stages of his voyage.

Part Three

From *c.* AD 850 to 1670

— 18 —

The Granting of Ireland by Pope Adrian

The struggle against English dominance in Ireland commenced in AD 1115 when the then English Pope Adrian IV granted Ireland to the English monarch, Henry II. Adrian was in fact responsible for laying the foundation of the destruction of independent Ireland by this action. Soon after Henry II took the throne of England, Adrian was elected to the Chair of St. Peter. Henry communicated his congratulations and so began a strong friendship with Pope Adrian. In the year AD 1115, Henry, by the intercession of John of Salisbury, the then Chaplain to the Archbishop of Canterbury, requested permission from the Pope to take possession of Ireland for the purpose of 'extending the boundaries of the Church and thereby announcing to the unlearned and rude people the truth of the Christian faith and extricating the weeds of vice from the field of the Lord'.

Such a statement would give the impression that Ireland, instead of being the 'island of saints and scholars' had somehow returned to the depths of paganism and that the Church had degenerated into such a state that a so-called pious Englishman had to intervene with the Pope's authority.

Nothing was further from the truth. The Irish Church had many excellent bishops, and the various synods held in the country around that time were in accordance with the directives from Rome. Adrian's predecessor, Eugienius III, and Cardinal Paparo had held the Irish Church in high esteem.

Adrian, however, felt otherwise and, driven on by his love for his own country and his wish to please Henry, decided to hand over Ireland to the English monarch and immediately had a letter, or Papal Bull, drawn up to this effect. His premise for such an action was that Ireland undoubtedly belonged to the Chair of St. Peter and the whole Roman Church. In other words, the successor of St. Peter laid claim to, and regarded as rightfully his, all those lands converted to Christianity. This attitude is no better exemplified than in the conquest of the New World for the holy Roman Catholic Church by the Spanish Queen Isabella. The notion that the Pope was the owner of all Christian islands had been denounced by a Bull of Urban II in 1091, when he renounced the Papal claim on Corsica.

Adrian, in issuing this Bull, requested Henry to preserve inviolate the rights of the existing Church and that, in recompense for such an undertaking, Henry should levy the sum of one denarius per annum from every household in Ireland. (N.B. a denarius was a Roman gold coin equivalent to the value of twelve donkeys, which in those days was a substantial amount of money.) Adrian sent a gold ring to Henry as a sign of his investiture to govern Ireland.

It appears that this all stemmed from the idea of the Holy Roman Empire—that all those lands which were governed by Rome also belonged to the Church of Rome. However, the power of Rome never extended into Ireland, so this reason could not be defended, nor is it true that any Irish king ever transferred the jurisdiction of all Ireland to a Roman pontiff.

Adrian's Bull has been shown to exist, despite many claims to the contrary. It was kept secret until a suitable time arose for its use. At the great Synod of Bishops held in Mellifont in 1157, which was attended by the Pope's emissary, those attending were ignorant of the famous Bull. In fact, it was kept secret until *c*. AD 1316, when the Irish chieftains complained to Pope John XXII of the atrocities and cruelty perpetrated by the English on the Irish nation.

Wars between the Irish chieftains and provincial kingdoms had reached a new height in the early twelfth century and when Dermot

MacMorogh requested military assistance from Henry II he was playing into the hands of the English king. With the Papal Bull, and now a request from an Irish king, he was at liberty to invade and conquer Ireland for his own benefit.

In 1169, the first Anglo-Saxon army arrived at Bannow in the County of Wexford. Strongbow himself arrived with his army in Waterford the following year. Strongbow, by his victorious attacks and subsequent massacres and desecration of the churches—from Waterford to the city of Dublin—became so powerful that Henry decided to come to Ireland himself. Arriving at Waterford on 18 October 1171, he sought the obedience of all the Irish chieftains and provincial rulers.

In 1175 the Council of Windsor was held. This Council constituted the commencement of the English domination of Ireland. Two years later, Henry obtained from the then Pope Alexander III permission to declare his son John as king of Ireland. He also at this time granted the kingdom of Cork to Robert FitzStephens and Mile de Cogan for their loyalty and efforts in the just cause of conquering Ireland for the Throne of England. The next one hundred years was one of the most bloody periods of Irish history. Munster did not escape—in fact it was probably the most badly hit. It took the local chiefs until 1183 to realise that they had a common enemy, namely the Anglo-Saxons. Even in Church matters there was conflict, especially in the Diocese of Ross, where there were two consecrated bishops claiming the position—one a secular priest consecrated in Rome *c.* 1197 by the order of Pope Celestine III, and the other, called Florence, consecrated by the Archbishop of Cashel in 1198 on the instruction of Innocent III. With the Anglo-Saxons attempting to get a stranglehold on West Cork, the events leading up to the battle of Callan followed.

— 19 —

The Battle of Callan

Having negotiated the winding road through the valley of Borlin, gone over the pass and descended into the wooded valley to the north, one has arrived at the location of the famous battle of Callan in 1261. Despite its importance, it received very little mention by historians in the many versions of the history of Ireland, especially those writing about the province of Munster. In fact, only the *Annals of Loch Ce* gives it the prominence that it deserves as one of the most decisive defeats of the Norman forces in Ireland during the thirteenth century.

It was the time when the Normans were trying to get a foothold in Desmond by conquering and dispossessing the indigenous tribes—such as the McCarthys—of their lands and power. One of the means used was the building of fortified stone castles on each parcel of conquered land. The Irish tribes had no experience of attacking these Norman bastions and could do little against the gradual encroachment of their territory by the enemy. The Irish could not engage in battle with the Norman forces on open land, as the iron-clad horsemen and soldiers in a well-organised battle formation were almost impossible to defeat, especially as the Irish forces mainly consisted of footsoldiers clad in ordinary clothes and armed with pikes, swords and bows. Only the bravery and valour of the Irish was feared by the Normans.

During the time of Domhnall Mór (son of Dermot) McCarthy *c.* 1185, the Normans advanced southward, even as far as Durrus, but were beaten back. From 1192 the Normans began to build castles, many of which were sacked by Domhnall Mór. Yet, the Normans rebuilt them. While the McCarthy clan was divided by strife during the period 1211 to 1219, the Normans, as well as the 'friendly Irish', built many castles in West Cork, including the rebuilding of Donemark Castle, near Bantry. Again, during the period 1232 to 1233, the McCarthys were at war with each other and the Normans availed of this strife by gaining more territory in Cork and Kerry.

The Geraldines were the most prominent of the Norman families and they sought complete control of the Desmond kingdom, with or without the king's agreement.

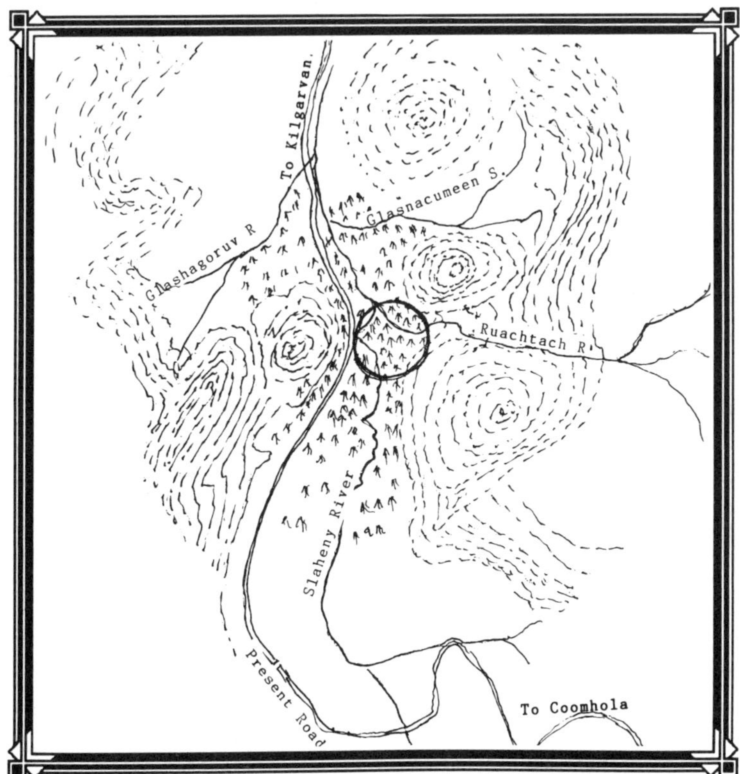

Map showing location of the Battle of Callan

However, a new McCarthy leader emerged on the scene (*c.* 1253) called Finghin, who was Domhnall's eldest son. He attacked and killed those who had declared themselves allied to the Normans. These included some of the O'Mahonys and the O'Donoghues. FitzThomas, who was the head of the Geraldines, realised that he had to suppress the McCarthys before he could claim Desmond for himself. He mustered a large force and marched southwards to engage Finghin and his allies. John FitzThomas had with him his son, Maurice FitzJohn, the son of Walter de Burgo, many knights, and also his Irish allies amongst, whom was Domhnall Ruadh McCarthy, a claimant to the kingship of Desmond, with a large Irish force.

Finghin, through his spies, knew that a large Norman and Irish force was heading south to meet him in battle. His experience, gained during the past year battling with the Normans, enabled him to pick out the most advantageous battleground that he knew. This was a place called Callan, to the south of Kilgarvan, where the fast mountain river Slaheny joins the Ruachtach river in a wooded and rough terrain.

Here both forces met in battle, and the heavily armed knights on horseback and the heavily armed footsoldiers were at a serious disadvantage in this rough terrain bounded by two fast-flowing rivers, where there was little means of arranging their forces in battle formation. In fact, there was little means of escape, as the two fast-flowing rivers formed a natural trap.

Finghin and his forces completely routed the Normans. Amongst the dead were FitzThomas himself, his son, the son of de Burgo, fifteen noble knights, eight barons, Barry Mór and over three hundred soldiers. There is no mention of Finghin's losses. The battle site is commemorated by a stone monument erected about five hundred metres off the main Coomhola–Kilgarvan road.

The death of the head of the Munster Geraldines and his heir was a serious blow to the Normans, but the defeat itself, being so comprehensive, gave the Irish courage and an insight into the ways and means to defeat the Norman forces. The immediate result was that Finghin and his forces swept everything before them both north and eastwards throughout Desmond, burning castles, strongholds and laying waste the land. Finghin was determined to drive every Norman out of the McCarthy kingdom.

However, he over-stretched his forces by marching towards Kinsale and de Courcey's Castle at Ringrone and, having refused peace terms, he encamped at Bearnach Reanna Roin. Seizing the opportunity, Miles de Cogan, grandson of Milo de Cogan, assembled his troops and made a surprise night attack from the castle on Finghin's encampment, wiping out the Irish forces, as well as killing Finghin himself. There is no record of those who fought on the side of Finghin McCarthy or those who died with him at Reanna Roin.

In the brief references to that period, it is interesting to note the mention of the 'castle at Dun na mBarc', which was the local stronghold of the Normans which Carew is supposed to have built AD 1214. However, some minor sources state that the castle was built at an earlier date by the McCarthys. The castle was utterly destroyed by Finghin McCarthy during the year prior to the battle of Callan. Nothing remains today of either castle or site, except for a few cut stones among the dense foliage. It is said that the stones from the ruins were used to build the old bridge and the mills at Donemark.

Donemark Falls

— 20 —

Local Clans or Septs

As a result of the Norman conquest of north Munster, the O'Sullivans left their native lands around Knockgraffan in Limerick, and moved southwards to West Cork and South Kerry. There were two main branches of this powerful sept: O'Sullivan Mór who settled in Kerry, and O'Sullivan Beare who settled around Bantry and Kenmare.

In 1531, Dermod the Elder married into the McCarthy clan when he took Sheena, the daughter of Donal McCarthy Reagh of Kilbrittain Castle, as his wife. Their son Donal succeeded him as chieftain of the O'Sullivan Beare, and was in turn succeeded by his brother Owen. Donal had a son, also called Donal, born in 1560. Meanwhile, Donal McCarthy of Kilbrittain Castle submitted to the English Crown in 1565 and was made the Earl of Glencar. Owen O'Sullivan also submitted and became Sir Owen, Lord of Beare. This entitled him to hand down his title and property to his firstborn, in contradiction of the old Irish custom.

However, when the younger Donal came of age, he disputed the rights of Sir Owen his uncle to the O'Sullivan Beare title and all that it encompassed, and his younger brother Philip also claimed a share in this inheritance. Sir Owen was now the dominant power in the region and a period of inter-tribal feuding began.

Eventually, all three agreed to place their individual cases before the English Commissioners in 1587. Finally, after six long years, in 1593 the Crown gave its verdict, by which it ordained:

That Donal the son of Dermod was 'the O'Sullivan Beare', entitling him to the area of Beara and Bantry, consisting of sixty quarters, each of three ploughlands. (Of these quarters, the Bishop of Cork had eight, thirty-three belonged to various minor clans, and the O'Sullivan sept had nineteen.)

The Crown divided these nineteen amongst the three contenders as follows:

Donal, son of Donal, received eight quarters and two townlands in Beara, which included the Castle of Dunboy. Sir Owen received seven quarters and two townlands in Bantry, including the Castle at Carriganass. Philip received the castle at Ardnagashel with one and a half quarters.

We can see from the above division that, in the space of some six years, the O'Sullivans had already lost two and a half quarters to the English settlers. The English policy of divide and conquer was beginning to take effect.

Donal, son of Dermod, was the famous Donal O'Sullivan Beare, otherwise known in history as Donal Cam, who became famous at both the battle of Kinsale and afterwards. We cannot leave the O'Sullivan Beare sept without mentioning that Dermod, father of Donal Cam, had another, younger brother also called Dermod, who had lands outside those disputed. This younger Dermod had a son called Philip, who, having accompanied his cousin Donal Cam to Leitrim, also left for Spain. Philip became well known for his *History of Ireland* and the *Zoilomastrix*, both of which were written in Latin.

When Sir Owen O'Sullivan of Carriganass died in 1594, his family, who were bitter enemies of Donal Cam, fought with the English before and after the battle of Kinsale. The family was held in such high regard by the English that Sir Owen's son, also called Owen, received the lordship of the whole county by special grant (ninth of James I) after Donal's flight to Spain. However, Owen and his family lost almost everything in the upheavals of 1641, and thus ended their lordship of Beara.

Early Tribes

If we revert for a moment to the early period of Bantry Bay, we find that the first tribe to inhabit the area were the Corca Leidhe (Corcalee). Later, the area was passed on to the Uibh Eachac tribe of the O'Mahonys, and was incorporated into the Diocese of Cork. From the O'Mahonys it passed to the O'Sullivans (*c.* 1169).

The harbour of Bantry was called *Ineer na mBarc* (Harbour of Ships) from earliest times. The south channel was referred to as the Fiord from the time of the Vikings (*c.* AD 900).

Bantry is situated in the ancient parish of Kilmacomoge and, in its infancy, was referred to as Ballygobban. The name Bantry only came into usage at the end of Elizabeth's reign, around 1601.

From the *Annals of the Four Masters* we learn, in connection with the Desmond rebellion, that a Captain Zouch and his English forces set out from Cork with the O'Donovans and McSweeneys and attacked the monastery at the Abbey in 1581. Donal Cam, then only eighteen, gathered a section of his clan and attacked the English forces near Bantry, killing some three hundred men. This event is also recorded by Philip O'Sullivan, who mentions the death of Dermot O'Donovan at Lathach-na-nDamh, but places the battle at Rossmacowen near Adrigole. It is unlikely that the English forces had ventured that far west into enemy-held territory, especially as Carew and his army of six thousand men were blocking any move west to Dunboy. After the above battle, the O'Donovans and the McSweeneys sided with Donal Cam against both Sir Owen and the English.

With the defeat of Donal Cam and the fall of Dunboy Castle on 18 June 1602, the 'torched earth' policy of Carew, and the Cromwellian confiscations that followed, ended Irish influence in the town of Bantry, or Ballygobban, and its environs.

Sir Owen O'Sullivan sent a petition to the English Crown—then Charles II—for the restoration of his estates in recognition of his loyalty to the Crown during the preceding period of upheaval. However, Sir William Petty had great influence at the royal court, and Sir Owen's petition was ignored. In fact, he never recuperated a single acre of his territory. This ended the supremacy of the O'Sullivan clan. Sir William Petty, being Cromwell's Surveyor General, amassed the O'Sullivan territories to himself and thus claimed the greater part of

Beara and Glaneroughty. With the marriage of his daughter into the Fitzmaurice family of Kenmare (Marquis of Landsdowne), the whole peninsula passed into his hands.

However, he did not have everything his own way, as Arthur, Earl of Anglesey, secured for himself some ninety-four thousand acres of forfeited estates between Beara and Bantry in 1679.

By royal charter, 'these lands were erected into the Manors of Bantry and Altham [Beara] each with two thousand acres in demesne with the power to hold courts, 'leet and Baron'. Permission was also granted to hold two markets each week and three fairs annually at Ballygobban in the 'Manor of Bantry'.

The O'Donovans

One of the most important clans in the area from around AD 1100 were the O'Donovans, who had one of their castle strongholds east of Bantry.

They are supposed to have been descended from Fiacha Fidhgeinte and also the families of the Cairbre Aehbda and Ui Connaill Gabhra, at Cochma in County Limerick. The head of the O'Donovan clan came from one or other of the two families above, until the tenth century, when Brian O'Donovan came on the scene.

It is generally understood that, fed up with the raids of the Dalcassian tribes from across the Shannon, Brian led his clan in arms and, with the assistance of Maolmuadh of the Uibh Eachac, defeated the Dalcassians at Bearna Dearg (Red Gap) in AD 976, resulting in the death of Mahon, son of Cinneidi, brother of Brian Boru.

Incensed at his brother's death, Brian Boru raised an army and invaded the territory of Ui Fidhgeinte in AD 977, defeating the O'Donovans and their allies. Brian O'Donovan and his Danish ally Amhlaff were killed.

Not satisfied with this victory, Brian Boru engaged the forces of the Eoghanacht and defeated them in AD 978, a few miles east of Macroom. The Eoghanacht gave up their ancestral rights to the kingdom of Munster after this defeat, and peace ensued for the next thirty-six years. In 1014, Cathal O'Donovan, the grandson of Brian O'Donovan, and Cian Uibh Eachac fought beside Brian Boru against the Danes at the battle of Clontarf.

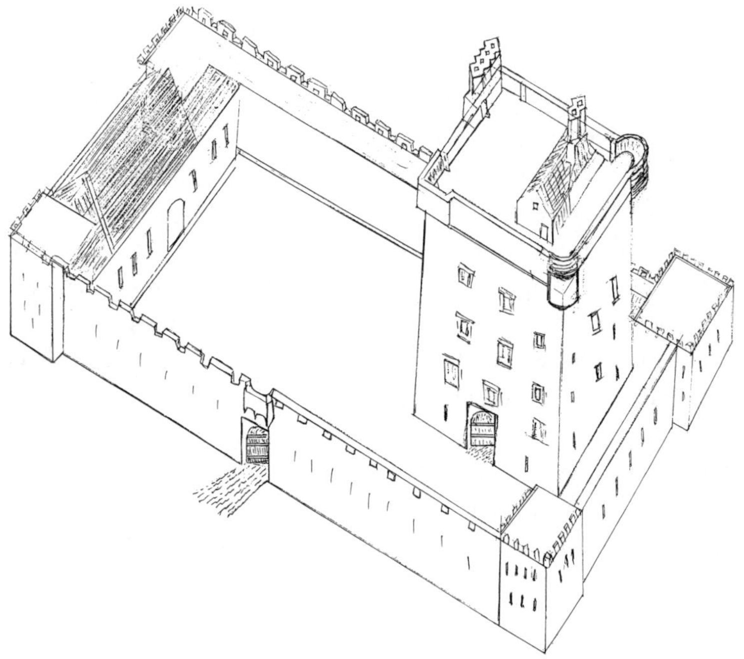

Carriganass Castle

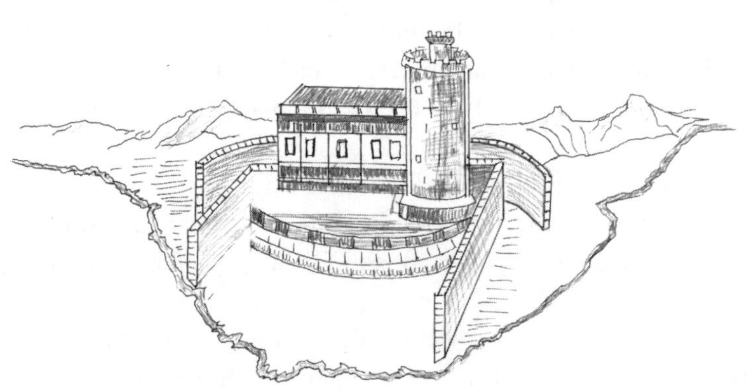

Artist's impression of Dunboy Castle, Castletownbere

The following century and a half provide us with little information on the O'Donovan clan until the arrival of Crom O'Donovan, who is reputed to be the ancestral leader of the O'Donovans of West Cork. His son Cathal founded the O'Donovans of Clancahill, Aineslis and Lochlann.

As to exactly when the O'Donovans moved south into West Cork, there are many different opinions. To quote but a few: Dr. O'Donovan states that 'the O'Donovans were driven from the plains of Ui Fidhgeinte and were forced to flee beyond the Mangerton mountains as a consequence of the Norman Invasion'. The year 1178 is quoted by the Revd. Canon O'Mahony in *West Cork and its Story* This date is quoted in the *Annals of Innisfallen*. However, Sean O'Cullane of Myross quotes the later year of 1229, without giving his source.

However, if we consult the *Annals of Innisfallen*, we note that Crom O'Donovan died in battle against the O'Mahonys in 1224 at Innis a'Bheil near Enniskeane. From this, we are led to deduce that Cathal was in fact his son, not his grandson.

The relevant point here is that the O'Donovans moved south early in the 1200s and immersed themselves in the almost continuous rivalry of the other clans of West Cork (McCarthys,O'Mahonys, O'Briens, O'Donoghues, O'Driscolls and the recently arrived O'Sullivans) to hold whatever lands they could by force. Soon after the battle of Innis a'Bheil, as the O'Mahonys were returning home victorious, they were attacked at an opportune moment by Finn McCarthy of Ringrone and his forces. Macraith O'Mahony (son of Dermod) and many of his able followers and allies were killed.

From the thirteenth century onwards, the O'Donovans were the lords of a large expanse of territory in West Cork, which previously was held by either the O'Mahonys or the O'Driscolls. This area stretched from Castledonovan in the north to the coastal castles of Rahine (near Castletownsend) and Glandore (Clocha Tra Bhaile).

The Inquisition of October 1607 at Cork gave the boundaries of Clan Cahill O'Donovan as: 'A parcel of the country of Carbery, containing three score and seven ploughlands, extending from the sea on the south to the river Mealagh on the north, bounded on the west by the lands of Clan Teighroe and by the lands of Clan Dermodie, on the north by the lands of Clan Donnell Roe and on the north and east by the lands of Glanicrime and the Clan Loughlen and consisting of the manors of Castledonovan and Rahine'.

In the Inquisition of 1636, we note that the O'Donovan territory of Clan Cahill consisted of thirty-eight townlands, including Castledonovan and Carrowkeale. A yearly tribute of £5 6s od was paid by the O'Donovans to the O'Driscolls for this territory. As it is this area which concerns us in the present history of Bantry, we shall but note that there were two other sections of the O'Donovan clan occupying lands at Leap, Kilmeen and the Courcies near the Old Head of Kinsale. Much has been written about the O'Donovans and their exploits around Rahine and Rosscarbery, and so we shall not dwell on these historical events, which have been well covered in the *History of West Cork* by Revd. Holland.

The O'Donovans, headed by Dermot the eldest son of Donal a'Croiceann, the chieftain, joined with the English forces of Captain Zouch in their attacks on the Bantry region (especially the monastery at the Abbey). There were repeated skirmishes with the O'Sullivans as he sought a way of getting revenge and regaining some of the lands he had lost to them. However, he was killed in the battle of Lathach-na-nDamh. Donal II, another son, succeeded Donal a'Croiceann in 1585. Just one year into his chieftaincy the news came from Dublin that John Perrott had summoned all those who had taken part in the Desmond rebellion to be present before his Parliament. Sir Owen McCarthy Reagh, Sir Fineen O'Driscoll and the O'Mahonys of Ivagh attended, but there is no record of Donal O'Donovan being present. He continued his fight against the English, while at the same time joining with them against his old enemies the O'Sullivans and the McCarthys. Two battles are mentioned around this time—one at Beal-atha-an-Daimhin near Caheragh and the other at the pass near Castledonovan called Bearn-na-Fola, meaning Bloody Gap.

With the arrival of the Cromwellian forces in West Cork (Cromwell himself did not pass beyond Bandon Bridge), the raids on all the strongholds of the Irish clans commenced in earnest. The O'Donovan castles at Castledonovan and Clan Cahill were amongst those that suffered serious damage. With Cromwell's regime of confiscation and forfeiture, the O'Donovans suffered like everyone else. With the succession of Charles II to the throne, they sought restoration of their lands. However, Donal IV was only successful in securing the demesne of Rahine, whilst the lands and castle of Castle-donovan passed into the hands of a Lieutenant Evanson, one of the Cromwellian officers.

After the battle of Kinsale, the O'Donovans became small landowners, with a few portions of land which they had managed to hold onto, and some even changed their religion to preserve what little land they still owned.

The McCarthy Scairteens

Bantry has a townland named Scairt, and in this context we know that the clan of Tadg Ruadh na Scairt occupied Ardragh, where there was a fort and possibly a castle. The fort was originally three ringed, which indicates that it was occupied by a clan leader.

Tadg Ruadh na Scairt was a descendant of Tadg Ruadh, grandson of Cormac Liabthanach, son of Dermod, who was killed in 1185.

The Woman of Three Cows

O, Woman of Three Cows, agragh! don't let your tongue thus rattle!
O, don't be saucy, don't be stiff, because you may have cattle,
I have seen—and, here's my hand to you, I only say what's true—
A many a one with twice your stock not half so proud as you.

Good luck to you, don't scorn the poor, and don't be their despiser;
For worldly wealth soon melts away, and cheats the very miser;
And death soon strips the proudest wreath from haughty, human brows;
Then don't be stiff, and don't be proud, good Woman of Three Cows!

See where Momonias heroes lies, proud Owne More's descendants,
'Tis they that won the glorious name, and had the grand attendants!
If they were forced to bow to Fate, as every mortal bows,
Can *you* be proud, can you be stiff, my Woman of Three Cows?

The brave sons of the Lord of Clare, they left the land to mourning;
Movrone, for they were banished, with no hope of their returning—
Who knows in what abodes of want those youths were driven to house?
Yet, you can give yourself these airs, O, Woman of Three Cows?

O, think of Donnel of the Ships, the Chief whom nothing daunted—
See how he fell in distant Spain, unchronicled, unchanted!
He sleeps, the great O'Sullivan, where thunder cannot rouse—
Then ask yourself, should you be proud, good Woman of Three Cows?

O'Ruark, Maguire, those souls of fire, whose names are shrined in story—
Think how their achievements once made Erin's greatest glory—
Yet now their bones lie mouldering under weeds and cypress boughs,
And so, for all your pride, will yours, O, Woman of Three Cows!

Th' O'Carrolls also, fames when Fame was only for the boldest,
Rest in forgotten sepulchres with Erin's best and oldest;
Yet who so great as they of yore in battle or carouse?
Just think of that, and hide your head, good Woman of Three Cows!

Your neighbour's poor, and you, it seems, are big with vain ideas,
Because, forsooth, you've got three cows, one more, I see, than she has;
That tongue of yours wags more at times than Charity allows,
But, if you're strong, be merciful, great Woman of Three Cows.

James Clarence Mangan

— 21 —

The English Plantation

Sir Owen O'Sullivan of Carriganass had many Irish peasants thrown off their smallholdings in favour of the English settlers, but, long before the 1600s—since *c* AD 1150 in fact—the English, or Anglo-Normans, had gradually established a hold on the land by building castles and fortifications, while the local tribes fought amongst themselves.

Before discussing the major confiscation and occupation of the land by the English in the 1600s, we will examine how the land was held and divided before this time. Within the tribes or clans, the land was let on the basis of a *gneeve*, which equalled a twelfth of a townland, by the chief to his subjects. The term of the lease was usually for a period either of three lives, one life or for thirty-one years, or for twenty-one years and a life. The latter was mainly used in letting to a minor local chieftain—see also chapter on The Brehon Laws.

The lowly peasants only obtained about half an acre on which to survive by growing food and grazing an animal. They could not even eat what they grew as this was required to pay their rent to the landlord or chieftain. They also had to dedicate themselves for a certain number of days each month to work for the benefit of the landlord. It is interesting to note that the same system operated with both black and white slaves in the colonies of the West Indies and the Americas.

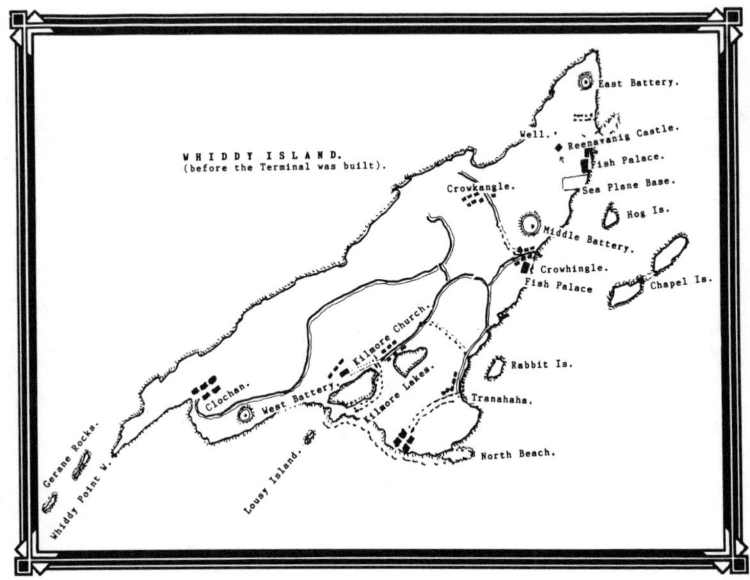

Map of Whiddy Island

As far as the author is aware, there are no records of the early English settlers in the area from *c.* 1150–1605, except for the mention of a John Galwey of Kinsale having a fish palace at the estuary of Dunna-mBarc *c.* 1410 and those who had Norman names—Barry, Carey, Roche, Barrett, Goggin, Arundel, Hodnett—and those mentioned in other chapters referring to this period.

It is on record that Sir Owen O'Sullivan gave leases to two English settlers named Derbyshire and Broigley on Whiddy Island *c.* 1605. These leases were later transferred to Walters and Davies, who established a pilchard industry on the island and were already exporting to the Continent before the 1640s. During the 1641 rising, the English settlers on the island had their houses wrecked and their cattle driven into the sea, while those on the mainland suffered a worse fate by having their cattle and goods taken away, as well as their houses burned down. During the rising, the rebel forces had taken possession of O'Sullivan's Castle at Carriganass and it was not until May 1642 that the castle was recaptured.

Turning to the general scene in Ireland, Ireton, Cromwell's son-in-law, became Lord Deputy of Ireland for the period 1650 to 1651.

During his term of office, the fort at Newtown came into existence. When Ireton died at the end of 1651, he was succeeded as Lord Deputy by Ludlow, who took up residence in Limerick. After ten years of wrangling the Adventurers' claim for repayment (of monies donated to Cromwell for raising and sustaining an army in Ireland) was finally considered by Parliament and, in August 1651, the Act of Settlement of Ireland was passed. A total of £336,000 had been subscribed by the Adventurers and they, as well as the unpaid soldiers, were to be compensated by the allocation of parcels of land to them in Ireland. A body called the Irish Commissioners was set up to oversee the 'plantation' of 'forfeited lands'.

The members of this body were Ludlow, Corbett and Jones, under the guidance of the Earl of Fleetwood, who happened also to be a son-in-law of Cromwell.

The division of the country into counties in 1562 was used as the basis of allotments, and the county of Cork was reserved for the Parliamentarians themselves.

The seven baronies of County Cork, including the tithes to church property, were allocated to both Adventurers and soldiers. In theory, half of each barony was given to both Adventurers and soldiers, but in practice it was the Adventurers who obtained the best land. The awarding of land always favoured the favourites and friends of the Parliamentarians.

The allotments were made in sections of one thousand acres to the Adventurers and high-ranking officers of Cromwell's army. The 'going rate' in Cork was £450 per thousand acres of good land. Bogs, woods and mountains were included without any additional charge but always in proportion to the good land allocated. It should be pointed out that the allotment of land was made regardless of who occupied it—whether royalist sympathisers, early English unaffiliated settlers or the native Irish.

Broadly speaking, the lands bounded by Glengarriff on the north side, by Gearhies on the south side and extending east for about twenty-five miles were those confiscated in this region.

In addition to the conditions of the Act of Settlement, whereby it was forbidden for any Irish or Catholic to live within the boundaries of garrison towns, an edict was passed in October 1653 to lay waste the lands, including those of County Cork, which were not confiscated, or in the hands of the English.

During the Cromwellian period of confiscation, a Major George Walters occupied the lands on Whiddy Island. This Major Walters appears to have been connected to the Bristol slave traders and to the planters in Barbados and All Saints Island in the West Indies. He became known, in English circles and locally, as Walters of Whiddy Island. It is recorded that he (Walters) 'permitted' a Daniel Skinner, merchant of London, to 'use' his lands on Whiddy Island and on the mainland. In turn, this Mr. Skinner, sold the 'use' of the lands on Whiddy Island to a Mr. John Davies of Middle Temple, London, who happened to be a friend of William Petty at that time.

Again, the leases for the 'use' of these lands were, at the time of the Act of Settlement, yielded to Annesley, Viscount Valentia and Earl of Anglesey, and then rented back over a period of ninety-nine years. To complicate the matter further, the leases were then taken up by Hutchinson, Depard and White.

It is, therefore, obvious from the above-mentioned transactions that ways and means were found by the English settlers to hold onto their lands in this region, regardless of who held power in England.

As far as can be ascertained, the Hutchinson family held extensive plots of land in and around Bantry. These included the land south of the town (Bantry House, etc.), Reenrour on the north side of the town, and parts of Ardnagashel. Depard also held some land on the mainland, principally the section east of the town.

White made his home on Whiddy Island and, through diligent hard work in the pilchard fisheries and the use of the land, amassed sufficient funds to buy out Depard's leases (and lands). This left Hutchinson and White holding most of the land in and around the town of Bantry. Hutchinson, meanwhile, had built a fine house on the south side of the harbour (not far from the present Bathing Box site), which he called Blackrock House—probably named after the Blackrock where vessels moored in those early days.

It is related that *c* 1652 over seven thousand members of the Irish forces were exiled to the Continent (principally France and Spain) from the port of Bantry. A certain Don Ricardo White (Sir Richard White) was involved in the shipping of the disbanded Irish army to

Spain, for which payment was to made by the Spanish King. Despite many visits to Spain by the aforementioned Don Ricardo White, payment was never forthcoming. There is no evidence to suggest that the above-mentioned Don Ricardo White was in any way connected to the White family of Whiddy Island around that time.

Walters, on the other hand, was involved with the colonisation of the West Indies and a saying that survives from that time—'to live under England's slavery or be treated as Barbados merchandise'—suggests that it is possible that some of the Irish went to the colonies (see chapter on Transportation).

In April 1679, the first Bantry Charter came into existence—whereby the Earl of Anglesey received some ninety-four thousand acres in and around Bantry Bay (see Charter in Appendix), which included those held by the Cromwelliam settlers (Adventurers and soldiers). Walters and some of the other settlers had, with good foresight, already handed back their lands to the Earl of Anglesey and leased them back. However, the lands leased by Walters were soon under the control of Richard White, whether by rent, purchase or claim.

Towards the end of the seventeenth century—from the 1680s onwards—there was general unrest in this part of the county. There were isolated uprisings, and bands of dispossessed Irishmen roamed the countryside plundering and robbing the English settlers.

The arrival of a French fleet in 1689 gave fresh impetus in the fight against the English. A Colonel Beacher was sent to the Bantry region in 1691 to quell the Irish insurgents. During that year there was a battle between Beacher's troops and the local Irish (location unknown) where over seventy were killed and a number taken prisoner.

Meanwhile, a Colonel Townshend also had a force of troops in the area and, in two skirmishes with the Irish insurgents, killed over a hundred (the precise locations are unknown, except that one was near Bantry and the other was somewhere on the Muintir mBaire peninsula). An important event occurred in 1697—which receives very little mention in any source—the arrival of a fleet of Dutch battleships and transporters from Flanders to disembark land troops for William of Orange.

Before 1712, the Whites took possession of the Hutchinson estate around the town of Bantry. This included the demesne of Blackrock

House, which was demolished, and a new house called Seafield House. The transactions involved in the take-over of the Hutchinson estate were very complicated and resulted in much ill-feeling amongst both families at that time. As the Whites moved into Seafield House, the Hutchinsons moved to Reenrour House and to the Ardnagashel property which they still retained.

Digressing slightly, it appears that the Earl of Anglesey had an appointee—a Revd. Davies—to look after his interests in this region. Using the Earl's influence, Davies received a charter from the Crown for the Bantry region. In 1712, Davies appears to have been operating on his own initiative, separate from the Protestant Diocese of Cork, as the then bishop, Dives Downes, who visited Bantry regularly, had a Minister called Homes appointed to the locality. The Revd. Davies was only the Minister to the major landowners of the area—the Whites and Lord Bandon. At this time, the islands of Chapel, Hog, Horse and Rabbit were leased by a Mr. Beamish of Bandon from the Revd. Davies. In order to strengthen his position in Bantry, Richard, the son of the first Richard White, married Martha, the daughter of the Revd. Davies, thus consolidating the possessions of both families—which included, as a result of the charters, the rights of all markets and fairs. It should be recalled that, since about 1652, all Catholic Church property was in the hands either of the English landowners or the Established Church (Protestant). In this regard, it is clear that the ancient Catholic Church at Kilmacomoge had also passed into Protestant hands, as there is a reference in 1665 to the church, rectory and demesne at Kilmacamoge.

Regardless of differences in the religions, the Protestants and Catholics in the Bantry area supported and helped each other.

As already mentioned, one of the early Catholic (English) settlers to arrive in the area was the Galwey family from Kinsale. Two centuries later, one of them—a Henry Galwey—is mentioned as having 'renounced Popery' at the Church of Kilmacomoge, yet the same family was also assisting the Catholic Church—as well as the Meades, Caseys, Morrows, Skiddys, Sextons, Goolds and Leahys.

Between 1720 and 1730, the town of Bantry began to prosper and grow. Messrs. Galwey, Davies, Young and others were actively engaged in the export of pilchards to the Continent, while the Whites continued to amass their fortune in the fisheries, timber and bark exports, in land returns and as smelters. By 1751 they had sufficient monies saved to purchase outright all the lands that were leased by them—all of the lands on the north side of Muintir mBaire, around Bantry, Glengarriff and the south side of the Beara peninsula (almost all the lands included in the charter to the Earl of Anglesey). The Whites were now in full control of the Bantry Bay region and were the first official landlords.

— 22 —

The Spanish Armada

Nowadays, there is much interest in the wreck of the *Lusitania*, and conflict over rights to some of the wreck sites of the various Spanish Armada vessels on the west coast of Ireland. Because of this, we are bound to witness a growing interest in underwater exploration of our coastline. There will, no doubt, be many teams of divers around the south-west and west coasts of Ireland in coming years, searching for the lost ships of the Spanish Armada of 1588.

A complete lack of leadership led to the disasters in the Channel. What remained of the Armada sought a safe passage home, around the north of Scotland and down along the west coast of Ireland. However, the most atrocious winter storm for centuries descended upon the various flotillas. With violent storms, and hurricanes reaching wind force twelve (equivalent to between seventy to one hundred mph), some of the fleet's ships sought shelter on the inhospitable west coast, with its sheer cliffs, reefs, hidden rocks and shoals, and difficult harbour entrances.

After proceeding across the North Sea, the greater part of the Armada fleet passed through the channel between the Orkneys and the Scottish mainland. There they encountered Scottish and English fishing boats, and traded with them for salted fish, food and water.

They commandeered the English boats as tenders and used them to ferry crews ashore to barter with the native Scots for food and supplies, as there was a serious shortage of food aboard many of the fleet's vessels.

The total fleet which sailed westwards through the channel consisted of almost three hundred sails. The majority of these sailed about two hundred and fifty miles westward in order to avoid the west coast of Ireland on their way home. However, some sections of the fleet took a more easterly route, and perished off the west coast, from north Donegal right down to Loop Head. The map of Ireland used by the navigators and pilots aboard the Armada vessels was that of Abraham Orelius, dated 1558, and was far from accurate, especially as far as the south-west coast was concerned.

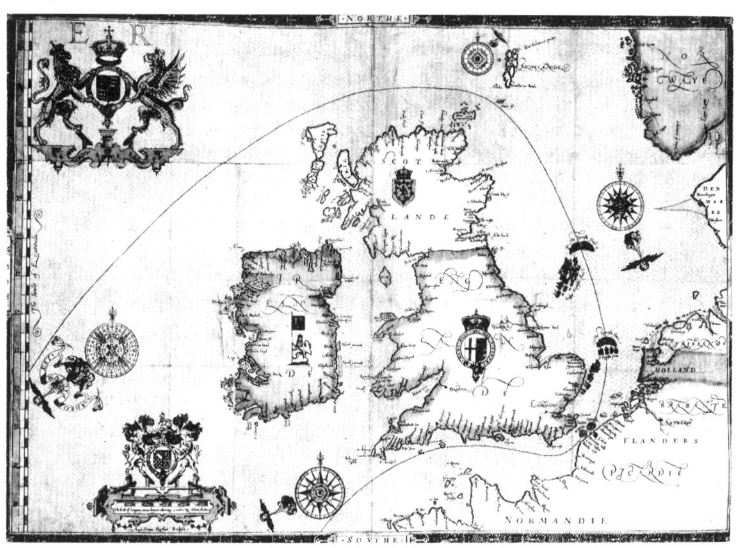

The map of Ireland used by the Spanish Armada

The map was so inaccurate that the captains mistook the Blasket Islands for those of the Ox, Cow and Dursey. Prior to the vessels anchoring off the beach at the Great Blasket, the pilots on the *San Juan Bautista* became confused when they first sighted islands to the leeward, early on the morning of 11 September. It was only when the vessels came close to 'the harbour of Vicey' that the Blaskets were identified by either Recalde or Marco de Arumburu. While anchored to the west-south-west of the islands on the night of 15 September, during another storm, two unidentified vessels passed them, running south-east, which would bring them to Valentia Island in a matter of hours. When Recalde and the others finally anchored near the Blaskets the following morning, they did not see any sails proceeding southwards, or sunken vessels to the west. Only one vessel perished off Cape Clear between the Blaskets and Cape Clear Island. From study of detailed records, including those in Spain, there is no mention of any Armada vessel entering, seeking shelter or sinking in this vast expanse of coastline.

Considering that many of the pilots were Irish, probably from West Cork and Kerry with surnames such as O'Leary, McSweeney, O'Donovan, O'Driscoll, it is strange that they did not instruct their captains to seek shelter in waters known to them personally. In addition, there was a lucrative sea trade at the time between the south-west ports of Kinsale, Baltimore, Castletownbere, Bantry, Valentia and Dingle and Santander, Ferrol, La Coruna and Vigo, so this section of the coastline must have been known to some of those aboard the Spanish ships.

On 7 September, as Recalde was shepherding a small flotilla of twenty-seven vessels southwards off the Blasket Islands, a severe storm commenced. He immediately headed for shelter in the Blasket Sound, which he knew fairly well, with a number of ships. However, with the fading light, he was unable to make contact or give instructions to the remaining flotilla. So, during the period, between 7 and 21 September, there were at least twenty-four vessels in difficulties, some eighty miles west-south-west off the Blasket Islands. With the wind coming from that same direction, the options of these vessels were limited to either tacking west-north-west, or north-west, or to try to run east before the storm and hope to avoid the south-west coastline of the Skelligs, Bull Rock, Mizen and Cape Clear Island.

It is almost impossible to give an accurate account of the number of Armada ships lost. This is mainly due to the absence of records of all those vessels which finally sailed northwards—after their many scatterings due to gales—and returned to Spanish ports up to the end of October 1558.

It is generally agreed by the majority of Armada historians that:

33 small pinnaces sailed, of which approximately 20 were listed as missing.

10 Andalucian hulks sailed—2 were definitely listed as missing.

13 Guipuszcoans sailed—*Santa Maria de la Rosa* sank at Blaskets and *San Estaban* went down on 20 September, location unknown.

13 Biscayans sailed—all accounted for, including wrecks and sinkings (*Maria Juan*, *San Juan* [location unknown] and *Gran Grin* at Clare Island).

13 Portuguese sailed—3 galleons lost, including the *San Marcos* which foundered on 20 September on the west coast, location unknown.

A number of Castilians sailed—exact number unknown, but all galleons accounted for, including *Juan Menor*, lost at Streedagh strand; *San Juan Bautista* at Blaskets; and *Trinidad* off Valentia Island.

From the above, omitting the *Doncella* and the *Santa Ana*, eleven of the great galleons were believed to have been lost. However, on examination of the Mediterranean and Baltic built ships which made up the rest of the squadrons, we find another story. Of the great levanters, only two returned to Spain. Two of the four galleasses were lost, and nine of the twenty-two vessels which accompanied the squadron of levanters failed to reach any Spanish port.

So, out of the great ships (hulks and levanters), thirty of the fifty-four failed to return to home ports. In total, therefore, we see that approximately fifty-five large warships did not return to Spain, and of these some thirty foundered in waters unknown.

According to Armada sources and tradition, the list of unknown Armada ships lost off the west coast is as follows:

2 wrecks on the Donegal coast; 2 wrecks off Blacksod Bay; 1 wreck off Killary Bay; 1 wreck off Rossaveal; 3 wrecks off the Clare coast; 1 wreck south side of Shannon estuary; 1 wreck north of Fenit; 1 wreck off Brandon Head; 1 wreck off Cape Clear

This gives us roughly thirteen wreck sites along the western seaboard, requiring identification and examination, and also approximately twenty ships which either foundered at sea or went down along the coastline. When we consider the area between Cape Clear and the Blaskets, most of the known wrecks have been identified. There may also be wrecks in deep water off Bantry and Dunmanus Bays. Local records tell us very little about this period, except for odd details of reported sightings of lantern lights disappearing amidst storm and high seas in certain locations.

Maybe someday, with the use of modern underwater technology, we may be lucky enough to witness the discovery of a lost galleon near our coast.

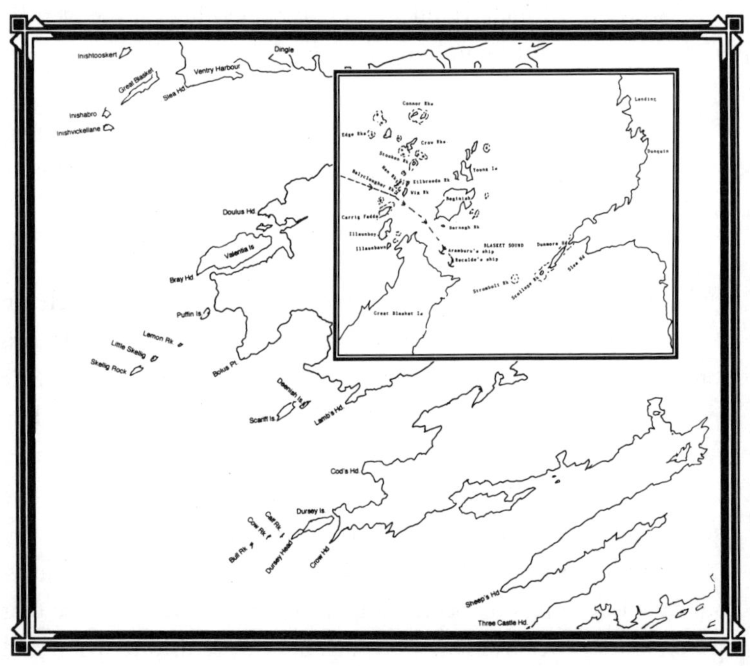

Vessels of the Spanish Armada sheltering in the Blasket Sound

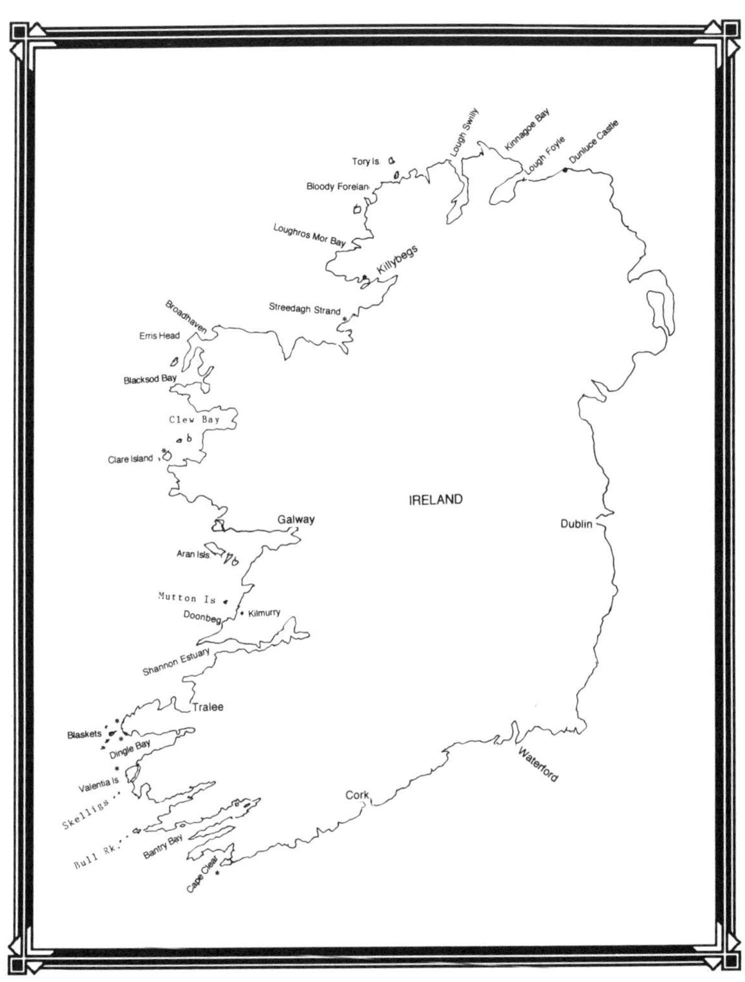

Map of the west coast of Ireland

— 23 —
The Fishing Industry

In the ancient accounts of the first people to set foot in Ireland, mention is made of three Iberian fishermen who were shipwrecked on the south-west coast. This event was supposed to have taken place many millenniums before Christ. From the earliest times, the inhabitants who lived by the shore gathered edible shellfish such as clams, mussels, periwinkles and urchins to supplement their diet of berries and meat. Later, they began to fish for pollock, cod, ling, hake and mackerel, using animal bones as hooks, eventually perfecting the system of long-lining, i.e. a length of line with some twenty hooks anchored by stones. This method became one of the main supports for the population involved in fishing.

The early history of West Cork contains accounts of Iberian fishing boats fishing off Cape Clear and the south-west coast with long lines. The kingdom of the O'Driscolls seems to have carried out a lucrative trade with these foreign fishermen from *c.* 500 BC onwards. It was not, however, until the arrival of the O'Sullivan clan in the area that any evaluation of the local fishing industry was made, as they levied dues on all fishing boats, generally a percentage (one tenth) of the catch. Also, on certain days, the total catch was dedicated to their chieftain. When the Anglo-Saxons became established in certain areas of West Cork, their main income was from the fisheries.

Chapter 23

When Sir Owen O'Sullivan of Reendisert and Carriganass Castles granted Whiddy Island to the two Englishmen called Broigley and Derbyshire, they immediately perceived that the main income for those who lived on the island was from fishing, especially the pilchard fisheries. They were impressed by the local development of that fishery, which had been of economic importance from *c.* 1587. An English settler who joined Broigley and Derbyshire was a man called Edward Davenport, a brother of John Davenport, Bishop of Salisbury. During his early period in Ireland, he borrowed too much money from his friends in England and made some rash decisions, but further assistance from his friends and his brother abled him to establish himself in the pilchard industry by building a fish palace (palais de pesc) on Whiddy Island. As there were two fish palaces on Whiddy Island—at Croangle and at Tobin's slipway—it is not known which of these was originally built by Davenport.

Pilchard fishing usually commenced in July and lasted until December. During the first three months the pilchards were large and full of oil, but they were also soft and brittle which made them extremely difficult to catch and handle. Despite this, their yield of oil was high, which increased their value. Pilchards were caught either during the day or at night. Watchers took their place on high ground around the Bay and, as soon as a shoal of pilchards was seen to school at the surface of the water, word was quickly passed down the line to the fishermen waiting in their boats just off the shore. The nets used were called 'purse seines', which were from one hundred to one hundred and forty fathoms long and from six to nine fathoms deep. As soon as the net was shot, or dropped, into the sea surrounding the bank of fish, the two boats—one called the seine boat and the other the follower—brought the two ends together and the crews began to haul up the footrope, thus closing the net at the bottom. The 'wings' of the net were then brought aboard until the net resembled a deep funnel in the water with the fish inside. By means of large baskets dipped into the middle of the net, the crews loaded the boats to capacity with the trapped fish. If there were still fish left in the net, one boat remained while the other transported its load of fish ashore.

To cope with the handling and packing into barrels of the fish, large fish palaces were built. It is not known for certain how many of these processing establishments there were in the area, but the following have been documented.

There was one on the north side of the present Square (from the church wall to the next street); two at Newtown; one at Ballylickey (south side at near entrance); two—possibly three—on Whiddy Island (at Croangle and Tobins). By far the largest was the one located in town, which had been built using some of the building material from the Abbey ruins. This was a stone-walled enclosure with a number of buildings in the interior used for the preparation and the storage of barrels. On the outside was a gently inclining cobbled pavement where the workers first covered the fish with salt and then laid them out with the heads facing downwards on the slope so that the brine would run off. Then more layers of both salt and fish were added until the heaps reached three or more feet in height. After about twenty days, the fish were removed, the salt was brushed off and they were dipped into fresh water a number of times until they were completely clean. The fish were then carried in basketloads to the yard and emptied into casks (large barrels), where they were closely packed. These casks were pierced with holes to let out the water, blood and oil that remained in the fish.

As soon as a sufficient number of the casks were full, they were lined up against the press-wall on timber stands. Using a long plank witha round piece of timber attached, which was hinged to the wall, the workers squeezed the fish down into the casks by applying pressure on the artificial top covers. As the fish were compressed, the casks were repeatedly topped up until they were completely full and ready for market.

Under the casks were placed sealed containers to catch the water, blood and oil. When this reached a certain level, the oil was skimmed off the top and poured into small barrels, and the remainder of the liquid was run off into the sea.

It was mainly women and older girls who worked in these fish palaces, the ratio being ten women to one man. The women did most of the work—laying out the fish and salt, carrying the baskets of fish to the casks and collecting the oil—while the men handled the presses, and the casks and barrels. With over six hundred barrels of fish being caught in some hauls, large amounts of labour were needed—as many as one thousand workers in the Bantry Fish Palace on some occasions.

Bantry grew rapidly during those years of the pilchard industry. In fact, the saying that 'Bantry was built on the pilchard fisheries' is fairly accurate. No figures are available as to how many people were affected either directly or indirectly by the industry, but there must have been several thousand.

With exports of some fifteen to twenty thousand barrels of fish per annum, transported by luggers to the port of Cork or direct to England or the Continent, there must have been huge employment for carpenters and coopers. It is on record that there were twenty-two timber yards in the town at the height of the fishing industry.

Towards the end of the 1600s, the shoals of pilchards disappeared from the Bay. While this coincided with the arrival of French boats—with very large nets—fishing at the entrance of the bay for a period of three years or more, it is unlikely that this was the main reason for the disappearance of the pilchards from the bay. It is more likely to have been a combination of over-fishing, a change in the water temperature and a change in the migration of the pilchard. However, the pilchard fisheries did not collapse altogether, as a Sir Richard Meade of Bantry obtained a premium after he had caught and cured some 380,000 fish (equivalent to one thousand medium-sized barrels) in 1749.

Meanwhile, some twenty years later, there was a serious complaint sent to British naval authorities in Cork that over fifty large French boats were fishing for mackerel off Bantry Bay. Most of the cured fish up to this time was exported to Spain, Portugal and Italy, but with the demand from the colonies in the West Indies and the Americas there was a quick change in the direction of the exports. During the year 1778, a total of eighty-eight transporters departed the from the port of Cork (Cobh) in two convoys with foodstuffs, including a substantial quantity of barrelled fish from the south-west ports of Kinsale, Baltimore and Bantry Bay.

Various efforts were made to revive the fisheries during the next hundred years by changing to other species such as sprat and herrings. Long-lining for cod, ling, and hake had continued, but this was not sufficient to sustain the large numbers fishing on the shore side. The local yawls and small-sailed fishing boats began to fish well outside of the Bay, in some cases up to twenty miles offshore.

During the 1780s there was a gradual changeover to herring fishing, where the same type of seine netting was used. In one haul in 1785, over 200,000 herrings were taken—this is the equivalent to about 1,300 of today's size fish boxes. It is not known exactly how many seine boats and crews were engaged in this type of fishing during the next one hundred years, but a rough estimate would be twelve to fifteen seine boats and their followers, employing over one hundred men. In addition to these, in the 1830s, there were eight half-deckers, five decked, fifty-nine sail and six hundred and forty-one small rowing boats, giving employment to 3,075 men.

The history of the fishing industry during the famine years is vague, to say the least. It does appear that the industry was in a phase of decline again, due to the absence of the herring shoals. However, the fishing of mackerel and long-lining continued, with the mackerel being cured in barrels and the other species being salted and dried both for local consumption and export.

But, prior to the outbreak of the famine, these fisheries had also been in decline, and the fish palaces had closed down and deteriorated into ruins. Over the years, most of the stonework was removed and used for building houses, so that little, if any, trace of that bygone era remains today. Some of the buildings on the north side of the Square were built *c.* 1848–49, retaining some of the old walls.

During this time the gathering of shellfish from the shores of the Bay continued and proved a cheap means of keeping a family household fed. In addition, there was the seasonal fishing of salmon and trout at the mouths of the rivers. What happened to the gathering of shellfish during the famine years is a mystery, but there is a report in local folklore that during those years shellfish were not gathered due to a 'disease' in the waters. Was this the first reported 'red tide', which now seems so common in our local bays, especially during the summer months?

After the famine there was a return to the sea for a livelihood, but the numbers had decreased drastically to about four hundred men, who were mainly engaged in long-lining, trammel netting and line fishing for mackerel, cod, pollock and hake, as well as a lesser number on the seine boats. With the advent of steam there were now steam-driven trawlers from England and France fishing up to the coastline, to the detriment of the local fishermen. Where trammel nets were anchored on good fishing grounds the trawlers would often tow right through, thus destroying the nets. On one occasion (*c.* 1861), when a number of fishermen—C. McCarthy, two O'Mahony brothers and a Denis Bohane from Muintir mBaire—set out in bad weather to try to recover their nets, they were all lost.

It was also during that year (1861) that the building of a pier for Bantry was first mooted, as a means to promote sea traffic and fishing in the locality. This proposal was delayed for some six years by the objection of the Castletownbere ratepayers, who would have had to foot some of the costs. They saw no advantage to them in subscribing to a project which would be in competition with their own home port. Finally, with a government grant of £3,000 and an interest-free loan of another £1,600 over six years, work was started by W. M. Murphy, a local contractor, using stone from Scart and from the quarry field at the Hospital Cross.

During the next twenty years the fishing industry revived, with the introduction of a number of steam trawlers to the local fleet. However, there was sometimes bitter antagonism between the traditional fishermen who used fixed nets and the trawlermen when nets were destroyed. This especially occurred along the south shore, where the traditional spawning grounds of herring, sprat and pilchard were located.

The fishing industry continued on a small scale during the next decades of civil unrest and struggle. Catches were small and no great increase in the number of fishing boats took place.

It is difficult to ascertain when exactly the English settlers got involved in the fisheries of Bantry Bay, but it is generally agreed that it was during the latter half of the seventeenth century. However, there are references in Tuckey's *History of Cork* that a Marquis Caro (Carew) had a yearly income of £2,200 from local fisheries, excepting those of 'Dorzey' and other creeks, and that a certain Lord Barnewale of Berehaven had an income of £1,600 from creeks in the Bay. This was during the period 1406 to 1410. There is also mention of a John Galwey of Kinsale building a fish palace in the area now known as Newtown.

Fishing was always a contentious matter in the Bay, with trammel-net users, long-liners, pot users and gill-net operators arguing their rights, and with the arrival of the trawlers. Temporary arrangements were made, in an attempt to address the problem, whereby certain areas were designated to certain types of fishing, but these ad hoc rules were never obeyed. The arrival of trawlers from Cornwall, Milford Haven and France fishing at the mouth of the Bay forced the local trawlers to fish inside, which further disrupted the status quo.

It is impossible to estimate how many were engaged in fishing towards the end of the last century, as most were part time and only fished during particular seasons (herring and mackerel fishing occurred in the winter and other types—including shellfish—in the summer months.

With the conversion from sail to steam, there was a revolution in fishing methods. Boats became bigger and were able to fish in most types of weather, and the distance fished from port depended on the quantity of water and coal aboard. English steam trawlers began to visit Bantry and Castletown ports, either for water or for coal.

Seeing these developments, those involved in fishing here began to take notice. A Mr. Pike, together with Tisdall and Murphy, introduced a few steam trawlers, while those who could not afford the cost of change continued fishing with luggers and half-deckers. Yet still more had relied on oar-driven boats, like the large eight-man seine boats, of which only some four or five remained working. These, as far as the author can recall, belonged to the Downeys and O'Driscolls of Whiddy Island, the O'Donovans of Bantry and two in Gearhies were under joint ownership amongst the crews. These continued fishing up to the late 1940s.

A number of half-deckers were converted to diesel engines during the 1930s and, with the setting up of the Fastnet Fisheries Company Ltd. by Messrs. Biggs and Company, a number of larger fifty-five-foot diesel trawlers were purchased. These included the *Mary Audrey*, which was built by Skinners of Baltimore in the 1920s, the *Theresa*, the *Angela*, the *E.D.J.* (built of iron) and the *Connie*. Of these, the *Mary Audrey*, the *Theresa* and the *Connie* doubled as coral-sand boats during the quiet fishing seasons. The m/v *Donemark* (45 ft) and the m/v *Togo* (40 ft) are also from this period.

Later, in the 1940s, a number of large diesel trawlers were introduced. These included the *Deirdre*, the *Johanna Mary*, the *Star of*

Maeve and the *Hidden Treasure*, and these continued fishing until the late 1950s.

With a decline in fishing catches during the late 1950s, the local fishing boats were tied up or sold, and only the seine and herring boats continued fishing, during the winter months, while the shellfish fishermen continued their seasonal occupation.

In 1966, the herring shoals returned to Bantry Bay and there was a fishing boom in the Gearhies fishing grounds. Small thirty-footers came from all over the south coast to join the small number of local boats—which included rowing boats. Tempers flared as the locals were 'pushed off' the spawning grounds and rows occurred at sea, with nets and other fishing gear being cut, destroyed or lost. Eventually things quietened down, as some of the 'outside' boats departed, while those remaining used Glengarriff pier as their base.

With the eventual fall in prices, the herring fishing gradually decreased. The arrival of large pair trawlers entering and fishing the herring grounds caused local fishermen to finally abandon the fishery.

Meanwhile, in the past and even up to the late 1950s, there were those who dredged coral sand from the seabed and others who cropped seaweed off the rocks to be used as fertiliser for the land. The dredging of coral sand in Bantry Bay was a minor industry, with boats working out of Bere Island, Castletown, Adrigole, Glengarriff, Snave and Bantry. The early English settlers on Whiddy quickly realised the value of coral sand as a benefit to the land and, from the seventeenth century, it became the major occupation of a number of men and boys. During the eighteenth century, there were in total about fifty boats employed in this occupation. Even though the work was a type of slavery and the pay just a pittance, it helped many a family survive. The main areas where coral sand was to be found were at the eastern end of Bere Island, the mouth of Glengarriff harbour, and the eastern end of Whiddy Island. A boat load of about four ton was worth about 8s (40p) in the 1870s. The *Mary Audrey* was the last boat to be involved in this type of work, continuing until *c.* 1955.

Song of the Boatman (Duan an Bhadora)

Bark that bears me through foam and squall,
You in the storm are my castle-wall;
Though the sea should redden from bottom to top,
From tiller to mast she takes no drop.

She dresses herself and goes gliding on,
Like a dame in her robes of the Indian law;
For God has blessed her, gunnel and wale—
And O! if you saw her stretch out to the gale,
On the tide-top, the tide-top
Wherry aroon, my land and store,
On the tide-top, the tide-top,
She is the boat can sail go-leor.

God of the air! the seamen shout,
When they see us tossing the bring about;
Give us the shelter of strand or rock,
Or through and through us she goes with a shock!

Samuel Ferguson

— 24 —

Donal Cam O'Sullivan Beare

After the disastrous rout of the Irish forces at Kinsale, Donal O'Sullivan Beare retreated with his depleted army to his stronghold at Dunboy Castle, west of Castletownbere. This castle was considered impregnable, due to its location and double bastion walls.

He still had plenty of Spanish gold at his disposal and with this he was able to entice local chieftains to join him, as well as hiring mercenaries. In fact, he managed to raise a sizeable force of over two thousand men. Early in 1602 he marched up the Beara peninsula and sacked the castle of Carriganass, near Kealkil. This was the stronghold of his cousin, Sir Owen O'Sullivan, whose family had sided with the British forces in the events leading up to the battle of Kinsale and who had been instrumental in inviting the first British settlers to the Bantry region. He then focused his attention on local chieftains who had not sided with him during the advance on Kinsale, and commenced a 'scorched earth' policy and cattle raids on the O'Donovans, McCarthys and others.

As the O'Sullivan raids began to spread through West Cork and the outlying districts, Sir George Carew, the then President of Munster, began to take notice. He summoned his allies to join him and, with the combined force of over two thousand troops, he placed the Earl of Thomond in charge for the march south.

Meanwhile, Sir Richard Pierce and Captain George Flower, commanding a large force, laid waste the territory between Kinsale and Ross. And at the same time Harvie, Slingsby, Stafford and Lord Barry did likewise to the lands between Ross and Bantry.

When the Earl of Thomond arrived at the ruins of Bantry Abbey, he was informed that O'Sullivan and his forces had retreated to Dunboy Castle, while his first-in-command, a Captain Tyrell, was defending the route west to Dunboy through the wooded area of the Beara peninsula.

At Bantry, the Earl of Thomond billeted his forces in various locations near the ruins of Bantry Abbey, Dunamark Castle (in ruins) and O'Sullivan's castle on Whiddy Island. Meanwhile, Carew remained in Cork raising more troops and supplies.

O'Sullivan was kept informed of the movement of the English troops by his spy network in the Bantry locality and decided on a sudden attack. Seeing that the large force billeted on Whiddy Island was isolated and difficult to reinforce, he summoned his leaders together and planned an attack.

Having gathered a dedicated force of about five hundred experienced troops, he sailed from Castletown as evening was falling and headed towards Whiddy Island. Arriving unnoticed in darkness at the north side of the island, the troops disembarked silently at Traclonna and made a surprise attack on the English forces. Were it not for the timely arrival of English cutters in the harbour and the fact that Carew himself had brought additional forces the previous day, the O'Sullivan attack would have resulted in a massacre. Yet the rout was such that the English troops were obliged to leave everything behind—guns, ammunition, baggage, etc.—as they swam or waded to the boats moored off the beach. It is not recorded how many were killed or wounded in this attack. Carew was enraged at this near disaster and became even more determined to finish off O'Sullivan and his allies. Seeing that his task was not going to be easy, he again returned to Cork. He raised an additional force of over three thousand men and set off in April, arriving at Donemark, outside Bantry, a week later. Here he set up camp in the area of the present Bantry golf course.

During the following weeks many attempts were made to march west to Dunboy through the thick woods and forests, but on each occasion he was severely hampered by the guerrilla tactics of Captain Tyrell and his forces, who picked off the English troops at random. Carew received additional assistance when Captain Wilmot came from Limerick, through the Borlin valley, with about two thousand troops. On his way through Kerry, Wilmot had defeated O'Sullivan Mór and Tyrell at the battle of Mangerton.

Realising that he could not reach Dunboy by land, Carew summoned a number of ships to come from Cobh to Gearhies and adjoining beaches on the south coastline. His troops embarked and made the passage to Bere Island, landing at Lonehart harbour on 5 June. The following day, he shipped his forces to Dinish Island and from there to the mainland, opposite Dunboy Castle. The siege of Dunboy began on 6 June and lasted until 18 June. An attempt on 13 June by Captain Tyrell to lift the siege was unsuccessful, due to the strength of the enemy forces. The small garrison of one hundred and forty-three men made a heroic defence of the castle, against a force well in excess of three thousand troops aided by two batteries of artillery. The castle was reduced to rubble and a final assault was made just prior to the few remaining defenders blowing themselves up—and the English troops who were storming the castle.

Those who survived the siege of the castle, some fifty-eight, were executed in the market place at Castletownbere. Finding no booty in the remains of the castle, or in the vicinity, the English troops ran amok, setting fire to houses in the area, and shooting, spearing and hacking down anyone they encountered.

There was no question of quarter being given by the English officers, under the instructions of Captain Blundell. While this siege and slaughter was taking place, Carew had sent a number of small ships with over one hundred and sixty experienced soldiers to capture the other stronghold of O'Sullivan on Dursey Island. The island defences were quickly overrun and the small number of defenders were killed, the only survivor being one man who hid in a concealed cave near the cliff edge. It is estimated that over six hundred innocent people were killed, between the Castletown and Dursey encounters.

After the fall of Dunboy and Dursey Island, Carew and his forces departed across the harbour to Bere Island and then by sea to Whiddy Island and Bantry harbour. Carew, himself, stayed in Reenavanig Castle for a night before returning to the mainland, but not before torching the castle which had almost been the scene of his downfall some months previously.

On the last day of June he left Bantry for Cork, thinking that the rebellion in West Cork was at an end. He was gravely mistaken, as the following events will reveal.

Where was Donal O'Sullivan while Dunboy and Dursey were being sacked and his kinfolk, allies and people being slaughtered? While Carew was sailing down Bantry Bay with his forces, O'Sullivan was north in Kenmare Bay awaiting the arrival of reinforcements from Spain. He was dismayed when only one ship arrived and anchored off Ardea Castle. On boarding, he found only Owen MacEgan, Bishop elect of Ross, a Father Nealon and Donal McCarthy. However, instead of troops and arms, it brought a substantial amount of gold and provisions and a letter promising large troop reinforcements.

Unable to break the siege of Dunboy or assist in the defence of Dursey, he retreated to the north side of the peninsula to await the Spanish reinforcements which never materialised. As Tyrell felt that no further resistance was possible, he departed and marched with his troops to his friends the O'Carrolls in Offaly.

While waiting for Spanish assistance, O'Sullivan Beare, now incensed with anger and sworn never to give up the struggle, began again to seek help from the other chieftains of the region, using the Spanish gold as an inducement.

With a small army he again took revenge on those who had assisted the enemy, by raiding their cattle and burning their houses, barns and crops. Always travelling by night and over rough terrain, he managed to avoid the British forces, except for the odd skirmish. However, with the vast numbers of British troops now on his trail, his forces were gradually depleted from various encounters and battles.

Seeing that there was no hope of reinforcements coming from Spain, or from his distant allies, he decided to withdraw from his ravaged kingdom, where his people were now suffering from severe hunger and deprivation, and march to the territory of O'Rourke in Leitrim.

Gathering his little band of some one thousand followers, of whom only four hundred were fighting men, he made his encampment on the high hillside of Comarkane valley. With little or no food the group started their long and perilous journey on 31 December 1602, in a driving snowstorm and freezing conditions. Before departing, Donal entrusted his wife and newborn son to his foster-brother, MacSwiney, until he was able to return and take them to a safe country.

Since various battalions of British troops were searching for him, Donal and his band kept to the high ground to avoid the enemy. As O'Sullivan's famous march has been well documented by many other writers, it is only necessary here to give a brief outline.

As they entered the outskirts of Muskerry by the Pass of Keimaneagh, the O'Sullivan band were set upon by the troops of Teg Mac Owen Carthy, who had once been a friend but was now an enemy. Many of O'Sullivan's men were killed or seriously wounded in a number of encounters, and O'Sullivan had lost almost his whole wagon train before he escaped from McCarthy territory. At Liscarrol, they were attacked from the rear by John Barry, brother to the Viscount, and suffered many losses as they attempted to cross the ford at Balaghan. When they arrived at the river Shannon they found that the river was in flood and no boats were available to carry them across, so they had no alternative but to kill most of their horses and make curraghs of horse skin as a means of transport. When approximately half of the force had reached the opposite bank, the remainder were surprised by a sudden attack by the sheriff of Tipperary in which about forty men were slain.

The greatly depleted band of O'Sullivan's followers passed in safety through the county of Galway, but, as soon as they entered O'Kelly territory, they were attacked by a superior force led by Sir Thomas Burke and Captain Henry Malby. In the skirmish Captain Malby was killed as well as many of his officers and troops before the remainder took flight. O'Sullivan collected the enemy's arms and colours and force-marched his exhausted men into O'Rourke country, where they were welcomed with open arms by their loyal ally. Of the one thousand followers who had left Comarkane in Glengarriff, only eighteen fighting men, sixteen helpers and one woman survived the terrible journey.

Dirge of O'Sullivan Beare

The sun on Ivera
No longer shines brightly;
The voice of her music
No longer is sprintly;
No more to her maidens
The light dance is dear
Since the death of our darling
O'Sullivan Bear.

Scully! Thou false one,
You basely betrayed him,
In his strong hour of need,
When thy right hand should aid him;
He fed thee—he clad thee—
You had all could delight thee:
You left him—you sold him—
May heaven requite thee!

Scully! may all kings
Of evil attend thee!
On thy dark road of life
May no kind one befriend thee!
May the strong hand of God
In his red anger seize thee!

Had he died calmly,
I would not deplore him;
Or if the wild strife
Of the sea war closed o'er him:
But with ropes round his white limbs
Through ocean to trail him,
Like a fish after slaughter—
'Tis therefore I wail him.

Long may the curse
Of his people pursue them;
Scully, that sold him,
And soldiers that slew him!
One glimpse of heaven's light
May they see never!
May the hearthstone of hell
Be their bed for ever!

In the hold which the vile hands
Of soldiers had made thee,
Unhonour'd unshrouded,
And headless they laid thee;
No sigh to regret thee,
No eye to rain o'er thee,
No dirge to lament thee,
No friend to deplore thee!

Dear head of my darling,
How gory and pale,
These aged eyes see thee,
High spiked on their gaol!
That cheek in the summer sun
Ne'er shall grow warm;
Nor that eye e'er catch light,
But the flash of the storm.

A curse, blessed ocean
Is on thy green water,
From the haven of Cork,
To Iver of slaughter;
Since thy billows were dyed
With the red wounds of fear
Of Muirteach Oge,
Our O'Sullivan Bear!

J. J. Callanan

— 25 —

Early Bantry

The question of land division was a most important issue to the local tribes, especially the rights of pathways, country routes and river crossings, where more often than not a toll was levied. River crossings became very important as the population and trade increased. Soon small clusters of mud huts (clochāns) were built at these vantage points. With the passing of time these crossings grew in importance, especially as they developed into trading places and the location for minor markets and fairs.

Taking into consideration the physical layout of the land in and around the present town, the main crossing of the mill river and the tidal creek was situated approximately halfway up present Bridge Street. On the right-hand side—up the present alleyway adjoining Michael Hurley's house—a cluster of mud huts existed between the rock and the river bank, together with a clearance which was known as the Fair Field (Carrig Aonach), where the ancient fairs were held.

In time, this little hamlet grew and extended along the river bank from the present Tig Osta an Droichead down to the Credit Union building. Meanwhile, further expansion occurred on the north bank of the river, with rows of huts running north-east along the present Pound Lane and along the river bank from the entrance of Hurley's garage to the corner of Main Street.

Up to the time that the present Bridge Street and the upper part of New Street were covered over, local folklore relates that the original river was crossed by means of large stepping-stones. There is also a reference to a very tall and well-built woman who carried people across the swollen river on her back for a small payment, until a timber bridge was eventually constructed.

Bantry Creek

It is not known when exactly the hamlet of Bantry Creek became important, but various sources indicate that it was during the period AD 1150 to AD 1250, as early references to the parish of Cuinge mention the 'souls of the inhabitants of Bantry Creek'. The earliest physical attributes of Bantry Creek are worth examining, as they give a good idea of the outline of the original village and surrounding area, with the river and streams, the long shingle beaches, the little island at the entrance to the 'slob' and the first laneways and bridge.

Parish of Cuinge

It is important at this point to return to the parish of Cuinge. There are very few references in the old manuscripts or in early writings concerning the establishment of this isolated parish. It is generally accepted that the McCarthy clan made a raid into Connaught *c.* AD 1125 and, contrary to Irish custom, they raided the famous monastery of Cong for booty, cattle and slaves. When this raid was brought to the attention of the high king, he demanded that restitution be made and a fine was imposed. This consisted of the handing over of one of the most lucrative sections of the McCarthy domain—Bantry, its harbour and islands. This included the mainland from Gearhies to Ardnagashel Point, the islands of Whiddy, Chapel, Hog, Rabbit and Horse, the fishing rights and, most important of all, the collection of all dues and tariffs from vessels entering or leaving the harbour.

From the evidence of early maps, it appears that the monks built a small monastery and church on Chapel Island. This site was chosen, due to the existence of an excellent freshwater spring. It is not known how long the monks remained in occupation, but, afer the arrival of the O'Sullivan clan (*c.* AD 1179), there is no further mention of this religious settlement. Finally, the derivation of the name

'Cuinge' is uncertain. It could indicate its relationship with the abbey of Cong, or it could be a translation of the old Irish word for 'narrows'—indicating the southern entrance to the harbour—or it could be a reference to the name 'Cing', which is associated with the early Milesians.

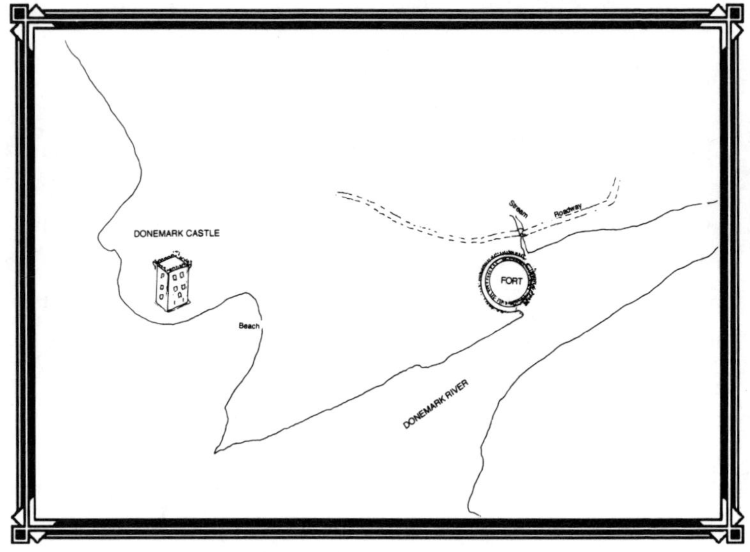

Donemark Castle and Fort

The only other cluster of mud huts worth mentioning in the area was that near and under the protection of Donemark Castle. However, it is not known when exactly this castle was built and by whom. On examining the records, it is mentioned that c. ad 1120 the McCarthys were in control of this region and there are some vague references to a McCarthy Castle at Dun-na-mBarc. This was taken over by the Norman Marquis de Caro and later totally destroyed by the Irish after the battle of Callan.

Ireton's Fort at Newtown

During the following centuries little if any reference is made to Bantry Creek until about 1658, when various references were made to the town of Ballygobban (Baile Gobhan) or the town of St. Gobhan. It was only with the abandonment of Ireton's fort at Newtown and the movement of that population back to Ballygobban that Bantry town as such came into existence.

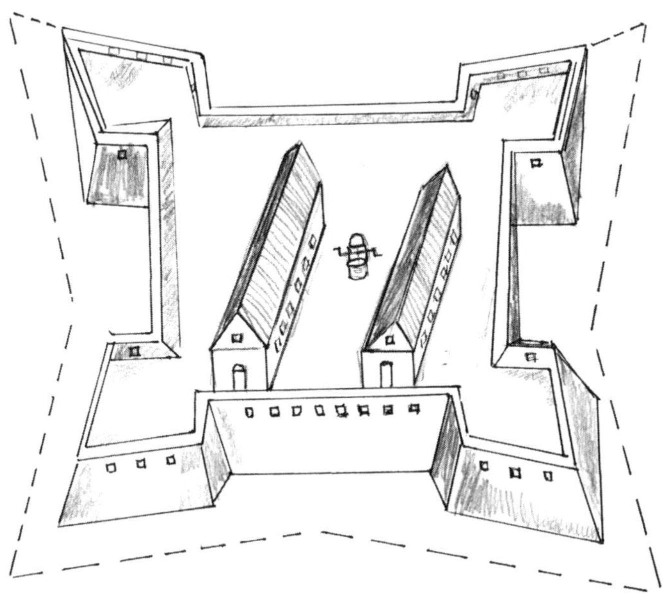

Ireton's Fort, Newtown

Prior to this migration, Ballygobban is described as a small hamlet, where seventy-four people lived, consisting of four houses worthy of note and a collection of mud hovels. This number was broken down into fifty-eight natives and sixteen English settlers. On the other hand, there were sixteen houses around the fort, with inhabitants numbering one hundred and nineteen.

As the fort played an important part in the establishment of Bantry town, it is worth sketching an brief history. During the 1500s, on one of his many visits to the area, the poet Edmund Spenser recommended to the Crown that Bantry would be an ideal outpost to build a fort to defend the harbour (as the south-west of Ireland was only forty-eight hours sailing from France). Cork, at this time, was the most southerly stronghold of the English forces. The English were preoccupied at this time with the fear that France would eventually invade Ireland and, once they established a stronghold there, that they would proceed to conquer England. Finally, some one hundred years later (*c.* 1650), Spenser's recommendation that Bantry was 'a most fit place to defend all the country (Ireland) from invasion' was acted upon.

During his short term as Viceroy, Ireton, Cromwell's son-in-law, set in motion the plans and building. The exact location of the building was rather strange, as it did not command a strategic position over the harbour. If it had been called into action it is very difficult to imagine that a canon shot would even reach the water's edge. However, the work commenced on the star-shaped fort with its deep ditches. Within the fort's boundaries were two long timber buildings running east–west with entrances on the long axis. A deep well was sunk in the centre for drinking water. Ireton's report when he visited the location in May 1666 gives a good description of the fort and its condition after just twelve months—'it is a small fort but regular and consists of four small bastions, the faces of which are but forty-eight feet long. All the stockades, which are on the inside of the brick of the Gaff, and placed there in the nature of a false bray, are rotten away, the guns unmounted, the drawbridge broken, and but one company of sixty men in it, commanded by a Captain Manley'. He goes on to state in his report that 'it stands over against Whiddy Island in the bottom of the Bay. The place must have one hundred men immediately sent to it, the drawbridge and palisades mended, the guns mounted, more ammunition sent to it and one month's food for one hundred and sixty men. This is the furthest west garrison of this country and we have no garrison between it and Cork'.

The Duke of Ormond replied that 'this fort must be put in repair and in it put eight guns costing £56, make a new platform (drawbridge £15), and repairing the magazine £80'. However, despite the repairs and the reinforcements, the fort fell into disrepair and plans to rebuild it never materialised. It is understood that the fort was demolished before the French landed in 1669, and the guns, which could not be taken away, were dropped into the deep well.

From the details shown in the relevant map of the fort, one can also make out the general outline of a gun battery on the edge of Reenbeg Point. As this map is of French origin, it is not known if this fortification actually existed or was included in the plans for the fort.

Bantry Woollen Mills.

Irish Tweeds,

Serges, Friezes,

Homespuns,

UNEXCELLED FOR PURITY, DURABILITY, CHEAPNESS, AND FASTNESS OF COLOUR.

Supplied direct from the Mills.
Any Length Cut.
Carriage Paid on Suit or Costume Length.

PATTERNS FREE, on receipt of Post Card, from

THOMAS COPITHORNE,
Woollen Mills,
BANTRY, CO. CORK.

Visitors to Bantry are invited to visit the Mills, where they can inspect the Goods in every stage of progress (in actual Manufacture), from the Fleece to the Finished Cloth.

Advertisement for Bantry Woollen Mills

The small town that grew up around the fort had a very short life, possibly some seventeen years in total, until the inhabitants were obliged to move back to the old location of Bantry Creek. The Down Survey of 1655–7 carried out by Petty shows that Newtown had one hundred and nineteen inhabitants, of which thirty-four were English settlers or colonists. It is interesting to note that both Newtown and Ballygobban had their own fairs and markets, even though they were only about one mile apart. There appear to be no records of how these two 'towns' obtained permission from the Crown to hold fairs, or whether special charters were given.

The White Boys

The second decade of the nineteenth century saw the emergence of the 'White Boys' as a marauding force in the countryside whose primary objective was to loot and burn everything English. Initially, the bands of White Boys were made up of the dispossessed Irish. However, in time they were nothing more than bands of renegades who preyed on their own as much as the English gentry and settlers.

Up to 1822 there had been little trouble with the White Boys in the locality. However, in January of that year, a band of armed men estimated at about five hundred attacked on horseback the outlying English houses. When the alarm was raised, the then Earl of Bantry pursued them with five companies and, as they reached the Pass of Keimaneagh, a skirmish ensued. When reinforcements arrived to assist the Earl a battle was fought and a number were killed on both sides. This incident is recalled in popular song as 'Cath Céim-an-Fhia'.

Industry in Bantry

In 1822, in the potato crop failed, which in a way heralded the calamity of the Great Famine which was to occur some twenty-three years later. With the population of the town increasing by leaps and bounds, people lived in squalor and, with severe unemployment, the ravages of hunger and fever began to appear. To combat this a relief fund was organised and subscriptions were made locally by the well-off. This was augmented by government funds from Dublin and London. These funds were used to purchase seed, to construct piers and to build the English Market at the end of Main Street. Until this time Main Street had been an open market with stalls selling everything from meat to eggs and fish. There was a section for each type of food or goods with stalls from the present Kelly and Company to Hegarty's, with farm goods on the upper half of Main Street and fish sold from Wiseman's to the corner. Meanwhile, Pound Lane contained many small shops, including saddlers, shoemakers and tailors.

Fishing and fish curing continued to be the main industry which sustained the town. However, at the instigation of Lord Bantry, the growing of flax and the making of cotton (vitries—coarse linen for making sacks) was introduced. When this proved successful, the linen trade became restricted to a few of the well-established merchants, including Vickery, Kingston, Clarke, O'Connell, Young, Murphy and Bird (for the Earl of Bantry).

Also, during this decade, plans were put in order for the building of a Bridewell (jail) by Lord Bantry. The mills at Donemark were taken over by Michael Murphy for scuthing machinery for linen, and the existing mills in Bantry town, which were originally built by the Galwey family, were leased by John Kingston and Richard Clarke from the Earl of Bantry to crush corn for export.

There was a dyeing mill at Donemark, three tannery yards in town, a number of flour and grain yards off the present Main Street and the Square, as well as salt and coal yards down towards the present docks.

Churches of Bantry

The present Protestant church was built in 1818, when the old church at Garryvurcha was abandoned. The Methodist church was built in 1822 and the Catholic church in 1826—with a two-storey boys' school in front. Also, during this period, there were a number of private schools which were mainly for girls. The early schools of Bantry are well covered by Jennie McCarthy in the *Bantry Journal* (Volume One).

Cholera

In 1832, Bantry was visited by a cholera epidemic which had spread down the country from the north. It is not known how many died, but it is estimated that out of a population in excess of five thousand about five hundred died. Various meetings were held in the Bantry courthouse to discuss the action being taken to combat the spread of the disease. When the cholera finally disappeared from the town and its environs the 'old hospital' and dispensary were torn down.

A map of pre-Famine Bantry

During the early 1840s there was a general decline in local industry. The thriving export of grain and bagged flour had fallen dramatically, so none of the mills were working to capacity, in fact they were almost shut down. The fishing industry which gave employment to about five hundred men and boys as well as an equal number ashore also declined due to the poor catches of hake, ling and cod by long-lining while the shoals of mackerel, herrings and sprat were becoming very irregular. Due to English tariffs, the linen industry had almost disappeared and as less cattle were being slaughtered the tanneries remained almost idle.

The Great Famine

With this substantial decline in the industry, commerce and general trade of the town, the forerunner of the Great Famine arrived in 1842 with the sudden appearance of potato blight on the land. In 1843 and 1844 the people had just recovered from the effects of lack of proper food when the blight struck again, casting the country into the abyss of hunger and despair. Bantry was fortunate in that the building of its workhouse had commenced in 1842, under the direction of the Poor Law Union. It was built on land purchased from Lord Bantry which overlooked the town from the east. With a capacity for about nine hundred inmates, it was designated to serve the baronies of Bantry and Beara.

Even though the worst of the famine and fever had finally declined late in 1847, it took some considerable time for the town to return to normality. The workhouse began to empty and people were able to return to the land. It was a time when emphasis was put on the raising of livestock, in preference to small crop growing.

Conditions in the town were far from good, with open sewers and heaps of dung and ashes thrown onto the roadsides.

Employment increased and there was an improvement in fishing. With this recovery in the 1850s after the famine years, a number of societies had been established in Bantry, from which many members emerged into the political arena. These included O'Donovan Rossa, from the folds of the Phoenix Society, A. M. and T. D. O'Sullivan of the Young Ireland Movement, and those involved in the Bantry Union.

Flood

A major disaster recorded at that time was the flooding of the town of Bantry and the surrounding countryside in September 1858, after weeks of torrential rain. The arched waterway under the town from the mill to the Square was unable to cope with the flood waters, and the river in full spate descended on the town from the bottom of the mill, making the existing streets into rivers of mud and silt.

Artist's impression of Bantry town from the pier, c. *1860*

Bantry Prospers

With the increase in commerce during the early 1860s, Bantry got its first bank—the Munster. Shipping traffic increased in the port, with importation of Indian corn, timber and general goods. After some six years of wrangling, Bantry's stone pier was completed in 1868, using local stone from the quarry field and elsewhere.

Work was undertaken to provide a supply of fresh water to the town. This was accomplished by using the substantial supply of spring-water from a well in the quarry above the town which gravity-fed a reservoir tank, from which a supply ran down to the Market and the Square by lead piping. Parts of the waterworks can still be seen.

With a major increase in livestock, the important Bantry Fairs became known all over the country. All the major houses which can be seen in the town today were built from this period onwards. Among these are the various hotels, such as Kingston's of Main Street, the Bantry Arms Hotel, Lannin's, and McCarthy's of the Square.

The growing of flax was reintroduced, with the mills at Donemark being converted for its preparation. The industry failed, however, due to the lack of an export market. Mining in the area commenced on a large scale and this is covered in a separate chapter.

There was a substantial economic depression after the 1870s and relief funds were set up to assist the poor. There was a general state of unrest in political circles. The Fenian movement was very active and the promotion of nationalism by Parnell and Davitt gave new impetus to the fight for independence. Bantry and Berehaven men were at the forefront in this struggle and emerged in the British Parliament as a force to be reckoned with.

During the latter half of the 1880s the economic depression began to lift. William Warner opened a Butter Exchange in William Street, which handled over £2,000-worth of butter each week. William Biggs built a steam mill at the quay for crushing grain and Murphy's timber yard imported large quantities of wood from North America and Canada for building purposes (this included deal, which no doubt gives its name to the present timber yard). Large quantities of coal were also imported for distribution throughout the region by Biggs. A dye-works was installed at the old mills at Donemark by Copithorne, where wool was spun, dyed and woven into tweed, although this venture failed after a number of years when cheap wool began to be imported from Australia. Next to the dye-works at Donemark was a paint works, which used the local mined barytes as raw material.

During the last decade of the nineteenth century there was a revival in the economic activities of the town and surrounding area. Many English tourists began to visit the region, with the new railroad providing easier access. Barytes, butter, fish and other products were sent to the markets in Cork and also exported from there to the UK and other countries. During this period a system of oil-fired street lamps was introduced to illuminate the town at night, while the mills used their own water-driven generators to produce electric lighting. And so the town entered the new century—with the British Atlantic Fleet in the Bay.

As a town Bantry had progressed faster than any other town in West Cork after the famine and the bleak 1880's. Around the turn of the century the population was given at about three thousand which was less than fifty per cent of that before the famine. Yet the majority of the people lived in base accommodation, with no sanitation facilities. Main Street, Marino Street, Blackrock Road and Barrack Street were then considered to be bad, but the worst example was Tower Street—'it is in a filthy and disgraceful state. There are heaps of dung and manure deposited there and other dangerous filth. The street is one of the beastliest in Bantry' (Medical Officer's Report at that time).

The Bantry Town Commissioners had formed and had nine members—B. O'Connor, D. Donovan, W. O'Sullivan, J. Gilhooly MP, J. O'Brien, R. Swanton, W. Warner, W. Biggs and J. Cullinane. The most pressing problem for the Town Commissioners was raising funds for the town's improvements. Approaches were made to the Bantry estate (Bantry House) to see if the tolls for fairs and the pier could be transferred to the Commissioners, but the request fell on deaf ears. In response to this rebuff, the Commissioners had the name of the Town Square officially changed from Egerton Square (in honour of the incumbent of Bantry House) to Wolfe Tone Square.

During this time Bantry House was the scene of lavish parties for visiting English aristocracy, including heirs to the throne and senior naval officers of the anchored fleet. Glengarriff was adopted by the English as their favourite resort (together with the South of France) during the summer months. Poets and writers such as Thackeray, Shaw and Davis found peace and tranquillity here—Shaw wrote his *St. Joan* in Glengarriff, while Thomas Davis wrote most of his poetry sitting on the 'Bakeen' field overlooking the harbour.

A photograph was taken of the Prince of Wales shaking hands with the German Kaiser on Bantry Pier, having toured around the countryside together. This was the last time they both met before the commencement of the First World War.

The Kaiser and the Prince of Wales walking on Bantry Pier

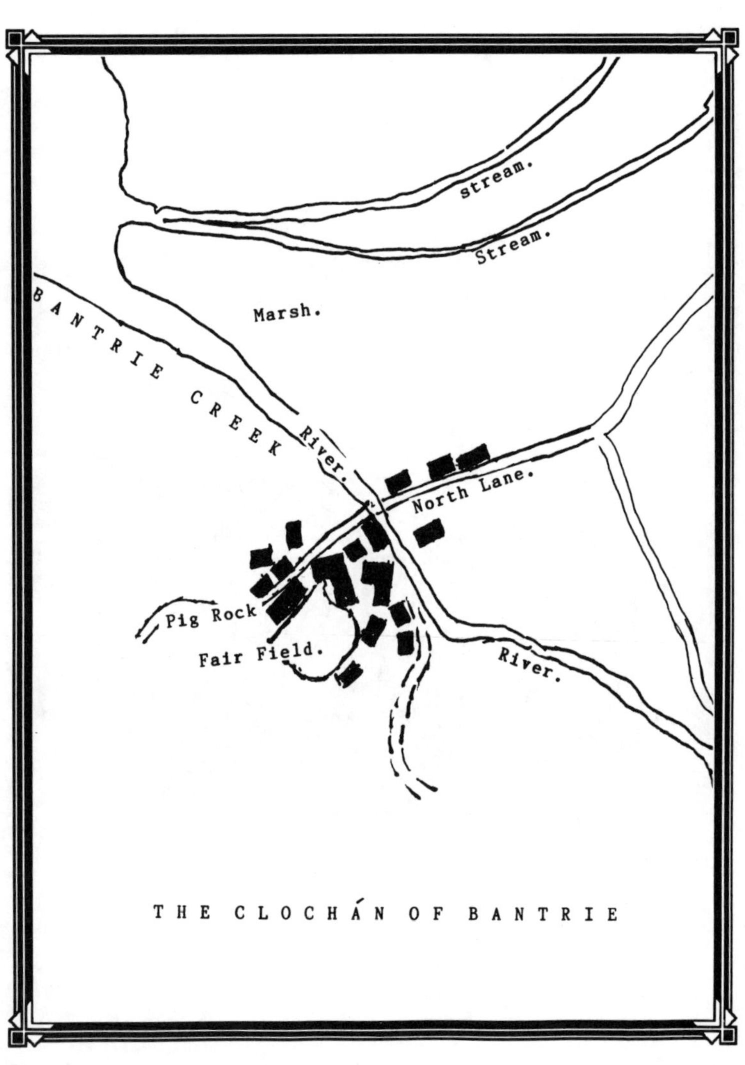
stream.
Stream.
Marsh.
BANTRIE CREEK
River.
North Lane.
Pig Rock
Fair Field.
River.
THE CLOCHÁN OF BANTRIE

— 26 —

The Despoliation of the Local Forests

In parts of West Cork and Kerry the woodlands were almost impregnable to man before the settlers arrived. Yet, in some hidden valleys near rivers or streams small settlements did exist, with sections of cleared land for the cultivation of vegetables and potatoes. As a rule, these were inhabited by the native Irish, who eked out some kind of existence from both the soil and an animal or two.

However, all this was to change from the 1560s with the arrival of some English settlers who immediately saw the vast wealth that could be gained by cutting down the trees and forests for export to Britain and other countries. Having taken possession of the land, some of these settlers started to fell the trees, hiring the Irish to carry out the work, all of which was done by saw and axe. Mules, donkeys and horses were used to move the tree trunks to a suitable place for cutting up into manageable lengths for export by ship. In this way, Bantry timber found its way to England as furniture, building material, support beams for the mines, and shipbuilding.

Ore Smelting

Seeing that a large quantity of unexportable wood remained, other settlers, in particular the Whites, decided to build ore smelters which would use charcoal made from the discarded wood. These smelters were set up at Dunboy, Adrigole, Glengarriff, Coomhola and Bantry. In time the local forests gradually disappeared, as they were denuded of oak and birch trees.

Afforestation in the Bantry area

Ore was imported from Spain and England and taken to the charcoal furnaces, where it was melted into manageable bars. What was not used on the home market was re-exported to Wales and England. There was sufficient timber in the region to keep these smelters in action until the 1750s—almost a hundred years of intense burning. The Boyles, Pettys and the Whites were said to have grown rich by the despoliation of the local forests, and such was the rape of the countryside that no wood or forest was offered for sale, in Cork or Kerry, after 1745. From the map we can see the extent of the wooded area in the south-west. Stretching from Ballingeary to Castletownbere was a section of woodland, rising to about 550 feet, and from Ballingeary to Drimoleague another broad band of woodland existed.

Yet another forest extended south-west of Bantry, while a small wood stretched from Gloun to Durrus on the Muintir mBaire peninsula. Finally, there was a fair-sized wood reaching from Parkana East to Aughaville. There were tracks, passes and pathways through these woods which had to be kept clear, to protect the traveller from the dispossessed Irish who had sought refuge in the woods. In 1612, an act was passed directing the owners of all lands to clear trees and bushes from the paths through the woods of the kingdom.

Local Industries Based on Timber

Other local industries based on timber sprang up. These included the construction of house frames, boat-building and glass-making. Of these, house-framing and glass-making were located in Bantry and Glengarriff respectively. Small timber yards grew up along the south side of Bantry Creek, while glass-making was located at Reenmeen East in Glengarriff. When the local fishing industry boomed, coopering became very important, which was dependent on timber. Coopering formed a large part of the Irish timber industry from the seventeenth century, and constituted a major source of local employment. The coopers' products consisted of staves and barrels of all sizes. Casks for wine were also made and came in three sizes: pipes, hogsheads and barrels. Oats, flour, salt and other items were also sorted and shipped in dry barrels. Meat, butter, tallow and fish were cased in small barrels. As Cork was the major export centre in the south, most of the barrelled goods were transported by sea on small luggers to that port. This is not to say that Bantry Creek did not have its own import and export trade, but this is described in another chapter.

Boat Building

It is not known whether there was a boat-building industry in the vicinity of Bantry during this period, but with plenty of native wood available, and a thriving fishing industry, some sort of local boat-building must have taken place. At one stage, there were over six hundred small fishing boats, ranging from sailing luggers to open seine boats, as well as a number of coastal vessels plying between other ports. Most of these larger ships were less than one hundred tons and about sixty feet long, with a draft of less than six feet and of round bilge construction, allowing them access to tidal river estuaries like Bantry Creek. With the rising tide they were able to get as far as the present Credit Union building on the mill stream.

Tanning Industry

Another trade which grew out of the timber industry was hide tanning, and there were four major tanneries in the town. Prior to the sixteenth century most of the hides were preserved by salting, but with the availability of large quantities of native bark from the trees to make charcoal, the transition to tanning took place.

It was the custom to strip the bark used for tanning from the living tree—especially the oak tree. In 1665 a barrel of oak bark was valued at 6s 8d. During the 1660s, the exportation of live cattle from Ireland to England was prohibited, and the number of tanned hides rose from 100,000 to 220,000 in the space of two years. With this increase in tanning, brogue-making became one of the most popular occupations in Ireland, especially here in the south-west. Sir William Petty was quoted as saying that there were 20,000 shoemakers and 10,000 tanners and curriers in Ireland. The term tanner in those days could mean a variety of allied trades, such as curriers, skinners, leather merchants, butchers and glue-boilers.

Iron Foundries

Like the mining industry in the following centuries, most of the ironworks supported considerable colonies of people, most of these being English or European immigrants brought to Ireland to provide a labour force. An example of this practice was Sir William Petty, who founded a colony of over eight hundred English in Kenmare to work his iron foundries. Here, in the Bantry–Beara region, small communities of English ironworkers sprang up near Dunboy, Adrigole, Coomhola and Bantry. The skilled workers were nearly always English, while the Irish were employed as hewers and drawers of water, the women carrying baskets of charcoal from the tips to the furnace. By the middle of the eighteenth century, the ironworks had made many inroads into the woods and forests of the south-west, which in time resulted in the clearance of all those who had sought refuge there—such as evicted tenants, 'Tories' and the native wolf population. It is of interest to note that, during the seventeenth century, there was a bounty of five guineas for a wolf's head and five shillings for the tail of a fox.

As for the wages of those engaged in wood cutting, only a few details emerge for the seventeenth century. Payment was not made per day or week but on a lot basis: £1 12s per thousand staves, fellers were paid £1 10s per ton and sawyers received 3 shillings per hundred feet. However, during the eighteenth century, workers for the estate lords were paid per week, whilst in the town the timber merchants were paid a piece rate.

The timber industry in Ireland during the eighteenth century was such that timber—mainly deal—began to be imported from Scandinavia. Shipments arrived in the harbour here to supplement the local industry. The result was the establishment of twenty-four independent timber yards in the town.

— 27 —

The Bantry Charters

If we examine the charters, which are printed in full in the Appendix, we can see how the lands of Ireland were granted to the English lords, irrespective of the claims the Irish chiefs and native people had to those tracts. They were totally disregarded—blatant colonisation at its oppressive worst.

In the first charter, Charles II granted to his 'beloved cousin and counsellor Arthur, Earl of Anglesey, Lord Keeper of the Privy Seal, the lands listed and situated lying and being in the Barony of Bere and Bantry in the County of Cork in his said Kingdom. That such lands, as listed, shall be divided into two Manors with the rights to hold markets and fairs, and that the towns and lands be divided into two Manors. That these towns and lands be henceforth known by the name of the Manor of Bantry (dated 6 February 1679) and that all the towns and lands on List Number Two shall be known as the Manor of Altham (Bere).

'And that Charles do give and grant to the said Arthur, Earl of Anglesey, full and absolute power to hold and keep markets and fairs at Ballygobban also Oldtown within the said Manor of Bantry. And he did also grant to the said Arthur full free and absolute power and authority, that he may have one or more Court or Courts of Bi-power, and all things belonging and within the said Manor of Bantry during the continuation of said Markets and Fairs, and that he shall enjoy all and singular tolls, prerequisites, customs, privileges and jurisdiction pertaining to such Markets and Fairs.' This charter was patented in the Rolls of Dublin on 15 March 1679.

From a historical point of view, there are many interesting items contained in the charter—the division of the lands into two manors, and more significantly the existence of Bantry and the baron of Bantry simultaneously as Ballygobban or Oldtown, where the markets and fairs were to be held. It is recorded that Bantry House was known in turn as Blackrock House, Seacourt House and Seafield House, prior to getting its present name. Only Seafield as a townland now exists, so Bantry, as such, must have existed in its own right. Whether this consisted of an area or section of land remains unclear.

There are early references by historians to Newtown (near Ireton's fort) and Oldtown (understood to be Ballygobban), but there is no mention of Bantry as such. Earlier references to the area mention Bantry Creek, and not Ballygobban or Oldtown Creek. So we are left with a conundrum.

The only conclusion that the author can draw at the present time is that the creek, or river, separated Ballygobban/Oldtown to the north from the hamlet of Bantry to the south, which was situated at Pig Rock Land and around Fair Field. Also, the earliest references to shipping mention that the vessels moored on the south side of the creek of Bantry—now identified as the area between the Anchor Bar and the Credit Union building.

According to the charter, markets and fairs were held in the area that was called Ballygobban, i.e. the English Market area, Upper Main Street and Pound Lane, which are on the north side of the creek. The fairs were held only on three occasions each year, while the markets were held every Saturday.

Those who traded on the appointed days had to pay a toll or duty to the local landlord of the time. This toll was collected either by his servants or agents at designated points on the roads or pathways into the town, or else at the market place. It is interesting to note that, after the battle of Kinsale, when the forces of Carew stopped in the vicinity during May 1602, a letter from one of the officers stated that they were 'Campe nere Bantrie' (see Smith's *History of Cork*). This is understood, from other references, to apply to the area around Bantry Abbey, not far from Geardha Dubh (black garden, or Blackrock Garden).

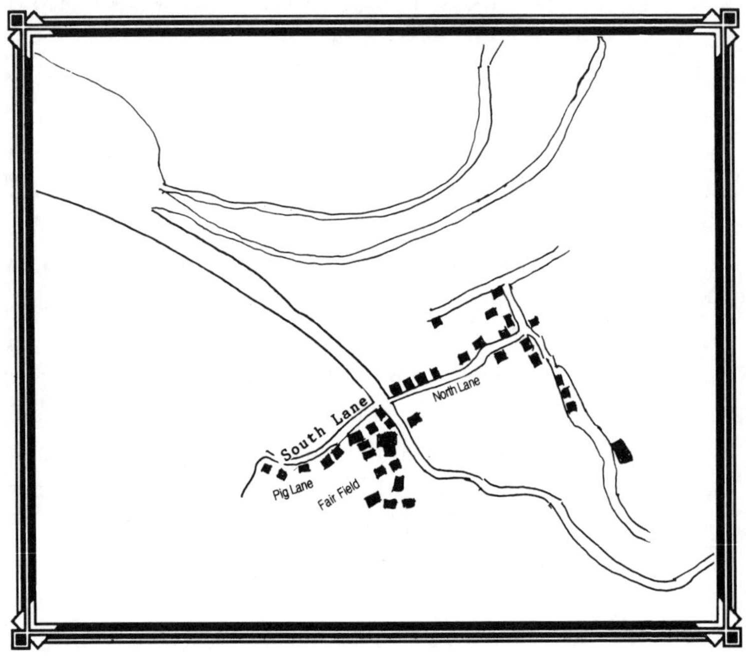

A map of early Bantry, including the Fair Field

If we consider the second charter, it states that William III (William of Orange) did grant to one, John Davys, the right to hold a fair in and within the 'town of Bantry' once yearly, on 20 November and the day following. This charter was given with the consent of Charles, Duke of Bolton, Charles, Earl of Berkeley and Henry, Duke of Galway, who were the most important landowners at that time. Davys was also given the right to hold 'a court of pie powder' in return for the sum of six shillings and eight pence per annum. This charter was granted in the year 1702, and registered in the Rolls of Dublin in the same year.

It was difficult to trace any records of the above-mentioned John Davys, but it eventually transpired that he was the pastor of Blackrock House (now Bantry House) at that time. In other words, he was acting for and on behalf of the landlord at that time. And as it so happened, it was also he who instigated the removal of the stone remains of Bantry Abbey, for the purpose of building the fish palace on the north side of Bantry and for the extension of Bantry House and its stables. This second charter only refers to Bantry town and not Ballygobban/Oldtown. It seems, therefore, that we have two charters applying to two different areas within the present town boundaries.

This second charter was transferred to the Bantry Chamber of Commerce on 28 September 1978, and the tolls were vested in the Trustees (Sean O'Luasa and Brendan Minehane at that time) in fee simple. It is believed that this particular charter was nullified by Cork County Council some years later.

In conclusion, we are left with many unanswered questions regarding the fairs and markets of Bantry:

Is the first charter still valid? Is it valid only for the days mentioned? Is it limited to the area then known as Ballygobban or Oldtown? Which charter was changed to cover the present custom of holding Fair Days on the first Friday of each month? Which charter covers the annual Pig Fair Day?

If these questions remain unanswered when this book goes to print, it will be up to somebody else to research them!

The rights of the first charter were taken over by the White family when they gained ownership of most of the domain of the Earl of Anglesey, and they acquired the rights of the second charter when they intermarried with the Davies family. So the Whites alone held the rights over all markets and fairs, as well as courts, in the barony of Bantry and could, therefore, be classified as landlords with all powers over the inhabitants.

Like Bantry, most of the other towns in County Cork received their charters *c.* 1659, yet Bantry has no record of receiving an individual Coat of Arms. The only ancient Coat of Arms in existence is that of the Whites—which happened to be adopted by the Whites of Bantry House. The present 'Coat of Arms' for Bantry was devised by Mr. Sylvester Cotter, when he was a member of the Bantry Town Commissioners.

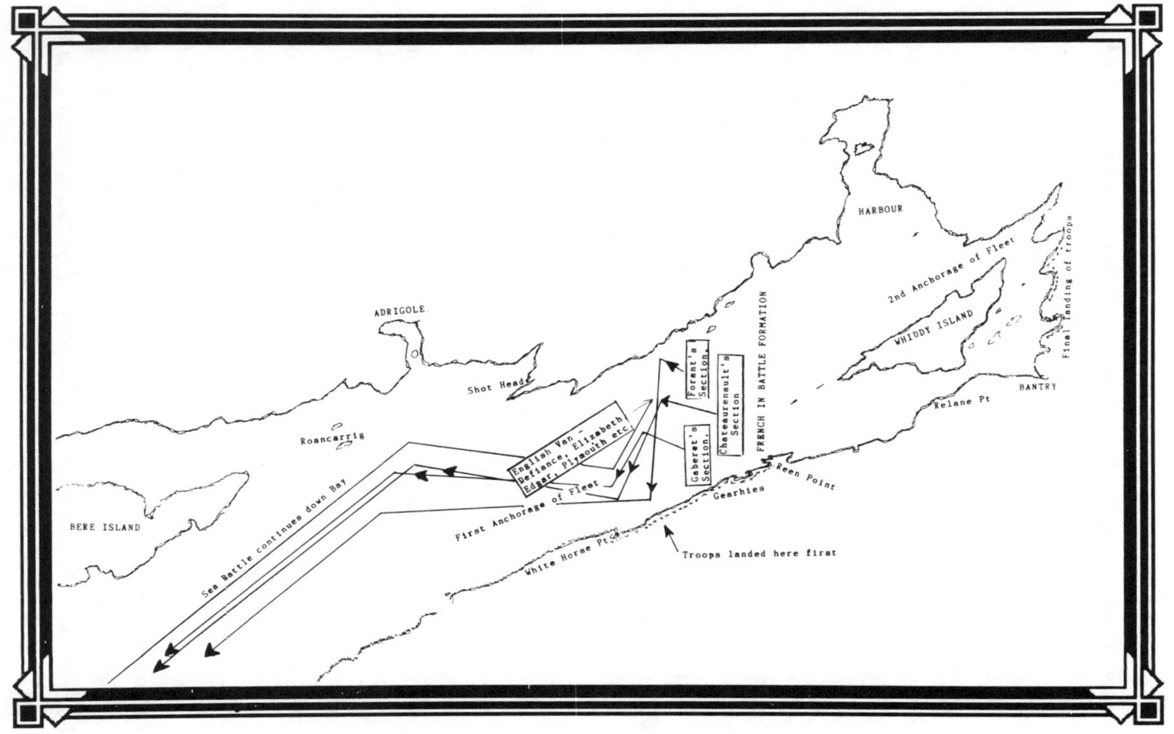
HARBOUR
2nd Anchorage of Fleet
WHIDDY ISLAND
Final landing of troops
BANTRY
Relane Pt
ADRIGOLE
Shot Head
FRENCH IN BATTLE FORMATION
Forant's Section.
Chateaurenault's Section
Gaberet's Section.
English Van - Defiance, Elizabeth Edgar, Plymouth etc.
Roancarrig
Reen Point
Gearhies
First Anchorage of Fleet
BERE ISLAND
Sea Battle continues down Bay
White Horse Pt
Troops landed here first

Part Four

From *c.* 1670–1850

— 28 —

The Battle of Bantry Bay

Considering the importance of the naval battle between the English and French fleets in Bantry Bay in May 1689, it is surprising that so little has been published on the subject. The following account makes use of French, English and independent records of the event.

In its historical context, the battle was a lost opportunity for the French to seriously impair England's domination of the seas around the British Isles. After the battle, the English naval fleet, in a depleted and barely seaworthy condition, could have been annihilated at the mouth of Bantry Bay on that May evening. All that was required of the French was the decision to make the final 'coup de grace'.

With the assistance of Louis XIV, who furnished him with ships, £112,000 cash, and arms and ammunition for 10,000 men, James II set sail from Brest with Major Gabaret and Captain Duqesne-Mosnier, and landed safely in Kinsale on 12 March 1689. In addition to the above, James was accompanied by 7,000 French troops, which were augmented with an equal number of Irish troops and some distinguished officers, including Patrick Sarsfield, Maunmont and Pusignan. The fleet that sailed into Kinsale consisted of fourteen warships, eight frigates, three fireships and eight merchantships, which carried the English, Scottish and Irish support, as well as the French officers and troops. Three days later, James and his forces marched to Cork, where he received a tumultuous reception. After a short sojourn there, the long march to Dublin began. Meanwhile, the French fleet sailed from Kinsale on the seventeenth and returned safely to Brest, while Captain Duquesne-Mosnier remained in Kinsale with three ships, in case of necessity.

On hearing of James's welcome in Kinsale and Cork, Louis decided to send additional support to Ireland, in order to create a diversion in the form of another battle front against the English. When the Louis's orders reached Brest, there were only six warships in the fortified harbour. This number was augmented during the following weeks and all the vessels were refitted and repaired, and supplies were put aboard including arms and ammunition. Despite many false notices of impending departure, it wasn't until 5 May that a suitable wind came from the south-east, and the signal was given to heave anchor. However, the fleet was becalmed as it reached the open sea and they had to drop anchor again. It was not until late on the sixth that the wind freshened out of the north-east.

Details of the exact size of the French fleet that sailed from Brest vary according to the different records of that time, but it was approximately as follows: 25 men-of-war, of 40 to 60 guns; 3 frigates of 20 to 25 guns; 6 fireships; 8 large transport ships.

The number of the military on board these vessels bound for Ireland is reported variously as from 1,500 to 6,000—most Irish historical records give the number as being 1,500. It does seem extravagant on Louis's part to send such a large escort for such a small landing force, when the large transporters could carry up to six hundred troops each.

At noon on 9 May, the van (the forward section of the fleet) arrived off the Stag Rocks outside Castlehaven, some thirty miles south of Kinsale. The whole fleet then tacked into the wind (north-east) and tried to make headway up along the coast. Two English men-of-war came within sight—to the east—and were chased for some time. Guessing that the English fleet was not far away, Admiral Chateaurenault's flagship, *L'Ardent*, changed course, and, falling off with the wind, headed west-south-west along the coast. At dawn on the morning of the tenth, the fleet rounded Sheep's Head and, tacking to windward, slowly made headway up Bantry Bay. The wind was, at this stage, more easterly and a few points to the south, so the fleet anchored off the south shore of Muintir mBaire from the 'colloch' rock east to Gearhies, leaving a number of frigates on guardwatch at the entrance to the Bay.

During the previous months, the beleagued Protestants of Ireland had sent numerous requests to William of England for assistance. William, who had not foreseen this serious development right on his doorstep, was in a serious quandary. Reports from spies in France gave details regarding Louis's satisfaction at the possible diversion on William's flank, and the distraction of manoeuvres on mainland Europe. 'The presence of James at the head of a Catholic army controlling Ireland could only add to William's difficulty and spread alarm in France' (J. C. Beckett).

William was now most anxious to send a fleet to Ireland to help his Protestant brotherhood, but, as his navy captains had all been appointed by James, he could not be certain of their loyalty to him. So, finally, on 11 March he appointed Arthur Herbert as admiral of the fleet and commander-in-chief of his invasion force. William was satisfied that he had made the right choice, as Herbert had been dismissed from office by James some two years previously. Herbert's orders were to cruise between the Irish and French coasts and prevent the French from sending troops either to Ireland or Scotland.

When he arrived in Portsmouth on 18 March, he found only six ships awaiting his command, as the remainder of the fleet were caught in the 'Downs' off Dover, due to adverse winds. News soon arrived in Portsmouth that James had already landed in Ireland and Herbert, instead of waiting for the remainder of the fleet to join him, sailed to the Downs on the twenty-fourth and met up with his fleet there two days later. Herbert transferred to the *Elizabeth* with his flag and joined John Ashby, her captain.

Despite gales from the south-west and west, the fleet finally reached the Scilly Isles on 9 April and, three days later, it was off Cork harbour. Men were sent ashore to ascertain the whereabouts of James and the French fleet. These men returned later to inform Herbert that James was already in Dublin, having landed in Kinsale a month earlier, and that the French fleet had returned to France.

Herbert remained at anchor off Kinsale for the following two days while deciding what to do next.

A severe gale sprang up and swept Herbert and the fleet as far north-east as Dungarvan, so it was not until the seventeenth that the fleet was able to regroup and return to Cork harbour. As more gales descended on his fleet, many of the warships developed leaks and became unseaworthy, giving Herbert much cause for concern. He badly needed reinforcements, but with none forthcoming he landed at Milford Haven on 23 April and immediately sent despatches to London requesting additional ships and crew. Since he had no directive to attack the French, only to harass any attempt to land troops in Ireland or Scotland, he also asked for new orders.

On 26 April, Nottingham sent a message to Herbert saying that he could now fight the French wherever he encountered them, as 'a state of war now exists between England and France'. However, the French believed otherwise—Louis did not declare war on Great Britain until 17 May.

Herbert had repairs carried out to the fleet, the vessels were victualled, and crews were 'pressed' into service. The bad weather continued, which prevented him from sailing until the twenty-seventh. He headed for Brest, but the wind changed direction, to the east, and he altered course and sailed instead for Kinsale. When he heard that the three frigates under Captain Duquesne-Mosnier had sailed southwards, followed by many other sails, he ordered his fleet southwards.

Returning to Bantry Bay and the French fleet at anchor, Admiral Chateaurenault gave orders that the troops, ammunition and arms be put ashore in the tenders, in case the English fleet appeared in the night. Anchored to the east of him were the three frigates under Captain Dequesne-Mosnier, who had been ordered to remain off the south-west coast. As night fell, the frigates on watch at the mouth of the Bay passed signals that enemy ships were in sight. This, of course, was Herbert's fleet, which was now due south off Cape Clear Island, and which, in turn, had also seen the French frigates.

The Battle

Herbert decided to lie off Cape Clear for the night, and, at dawn, he mustered his fleet and sailed south-west prepared for battle. His order of battle had been prepared and this was passed to various ships.

Meanwhile, Chateaurenault had also arranged his ships in battle formation, with Gaberet in charge of the front van, himself at the centre and Forant taking up the rear. According to the Admiral's log, the disembarkation of troops and equipment had only been completed at 10.30 a.m., while Gaberet stated that the transfer of men had almost been completed around 4.00 p.m. the previous evening.

Chateaurenault was in no hurry to attack the English fleet which was experiencing great difficulty in tacking against the east wind which blew straight down the Bay. It was 11.00 a.m. when he gave the signal to attack. The following is the list of French ships, the number of guns and their captains:

Ship (guns)	Captain
François (48)	Pannetier
Vermandois (60)	de Machault
Duc (50)	Colbert-Saint-Mars
Fendant (52)	de Réals
Saint-Michel (56)	Gaberet, Louis
Fort (56)	chevalier de Rosmadec
Léger (40)	chevalier de Forbin
Précieux (52)	de Salanpart
Capable (48)	de Bellefontaine
Arrogant (58)	de la Haterloire
Diamant (54)	chevalier de Coetlogon
L'Ardent (66)	comte de Chateaurenault
Furieux (60)	Desnos
Faucon (40)	chevalier d'Hervault
Modéré (50)	marquis de Saint-Hermaine
Entreprenant (56)	de Beaujeu
Courageux (56)	de Forant
Neptune (46)	de Palliere
L'Arc-en-Ciel (44)	de Perrinet
Excellent (60)	de Lavigerie
Sage (52)	de Vaudricourt
L'Oiseau (40)	Duquesne Guitton
Emporté (42)	Roussel
Apollon (58)	Montortier

It appears that the battle commenced about three miles west of Whiddy Island, and Chateaurenault had arranged his battle formation along the same line as the English. Firing began before the ships of the battle corps had properly established themselves in formation, resulting in the centre doubling around the van.

Gaberet's division now found itself in the centre, and the matter was further confused as Chateaurenault's section had to tack because of the closeness of land. Captain Ashby opened fire on *Le Francois*, but with a skilful manoeuvre Captain Pannetier brought his vessel around to within musket range of the *Defiance* and, when he was almost broadside, he gave the order to fire the cannons. The *Defiance* was badly damaged and her captain was killed instantly. Other English ships came to the assistance of the *Defiance*, but they in turn suffered damage from the cannons of *Le Vermandois* and *Le Duc*. Chateaurenault then entered the fray and engaged the *Defiance*, which was now under the command of Herbert himself. For some three hours they exchanged fire, until the English vessel pulled away and headed south out of the Bay with its masts and sails severely damaged. *L'Ardent* had also suffered hull damage and had up to six feet of water in the hold. The action continued in other parts of the Bay, and the French ship *Diamant*, commanded by the Marquis de Coetlogon, was seriously damaged by an explosion of ammunition which had been stored in the captain's cabin. And so the battle continued down the Bay as the English attempted to draw the French fleet out to sea. At 5.30 p.m., Chateaurenault gave the order to cease pursuit and to return to the anchorage to oversee the discharge of arms and ammunition from the fireships, which not joined the battle. Although everything was going in their favour, the French did not press home their advantage and complete the rout. This was due to the absence of the fireships, and the hostility and jealousy between the commanding officers and their younger and more ambitious admiral. These officers tacitly refused to press the advantage, and Chateaurenault had no option but to stand down.

Herbert, who had narrowly avoided a crippling disaster, made for Portsmouth with his seriously damaged fleet. Captains Ashby and Aylmer, one lieutenant and ninety-four crew had been killed adn another three hundred officers and crew were wounded.

Although both sides claimed a victory, it was obvious that the French had had the upper hand in the battle. If we examine the report of Chateaurenault to Louis after his return to France, we can see why their advantage had not been pressed home—'instead of responding to the arrival signal of his enemies, Major Gaberet had tacked in a manner which forced himself (Chateaurenault) to the head of the fleet. This manoeuvre, which was as a result of the enmity of Major Gaberet, who, not being one of my friends, did not want the deed to be too glorious for me. And as for Major de Forant—he did not hold his way in the water [he was a poor seaman]'.

When King William visited Portsmouth some days after Herbert's return, he created him Baron Herbert of Torquay and Earl of Torrington, in recognition of his 'great victory in Bantry Bay'.

Meanwhile, in Brest, Louis conferred the highest naval honour on Chateaurenault for his outstanding victory over the English fleet, which suspended their domination of the seas around the isles of Britain and Ireland for a period.

Addendum

Some French sources state that one English ship sank in Bantry Bay during the battle. There is no mention of such a loss by the English. The English did, however, mention other losses including *Edgar*, *Cambridge*, *Portland*, *Advise*, *Diamond*, *Deptford* and *St. Albans*.

Events Ashore during and after the Battle

Late on the afternoon of Tuesday 10 May, Admiral Chateaurenault decided to put all the Irish, Scottish and French militia ashore, along with the money, arms and ammunition. The five fireships, as well as two small frigates and a sloop, were brought alongside the larger men-of-war for the transfer. When this was completed, the small flotilla headed up the Bay to find a suitable landing spot. However, as darkness fell, no suitable location had been found, so the vessels moored at the rocks at the eastern side of White Horse Point. Many of the soldiers were put ashore, against their will, on the rugged terrain, and had to camp there overnight in the bitter cold and damp. Those fortunate enough to remain aboard the smaller ships had some minor comfort.

The following morning, the two small frigates and sloop tried to tack against the north-easterly wind in order to reach the head of the

Bay. Meanwhile the English fleet entered the Bay, and the French, having weighed anchor, sailed to meet them in combat. The exchange lasted some four hours in total, and was watched both by those ashore and those in the smaller vessels.

When the French fleet returned to anchor towards evening, a number of the larger vessels came to tow the frigates and sloop to the creek where the town stood. It is not known whether the ships actually entered Bantry harbour that evening.

The following morning, the remainder of the soldiers were put ashore at Bantry Creek, which was described as 'a miserably poor place, not worthy the name of a town, having above seven or eight little houses, the rest very mean cottages'. The account continues 'the least part of us could not be contained in this place, so most were sent two or three miles round to no better cottages to quarter'. The forces remained in this general locality for the next two nights, and the writer continues his description: 'I walked two miles out of town to lie upon a little dirty straw in a cot or cabin, no better than a hog-sty amongst some twenty more comrades. The houses and cabins in town were so filled that people lay all over the floors. Some gentlemen that I knew took up lodging in an old rotten boat that lay near the shore and there were others who quartered in a sawpit'. He goes on to state that 'the people are extremely poor and do not even have the change of half-a-crown'. Furthermore, good drinking water was difficult to find and he himself had to journey about half a mile outside of town to find a clear spring. 'About half a mile outside of the present town is the old town of Bantry much like the new. Upon a hill over this town and creek is a fort built by Cromwell, now gone into decay but never of any considerable strength'.

As two days were spent in landing and organising the arms and ammunition, the majority of the soldiers slept in the open fields and ditches. On Saturday morning, having located and bought some horses, the forces moved out of town and headed for Dunmanway through the high mountains and deserted countryside. Arriving in Dunmanway, which is described as having only one gentleman's house and a number of smaller cabins, the majority spent that night in the fields, without shelter, while a few were lucky enough to billet in an old straw barn.

On Sunday they reached Bandon, described as a considerable walled town inhabited by bands of brigands and lowly classes, as all the rich English settlers had fled in fear, having earlier rebelled against allowing James's forces within the walls.

From the above excerpts of a personal diary (*Journal of John Stevens* 1689–91), the reader can get a good idea of the state of the almost deserted countryside during this particular period: the abject poverty and the inhuman conditions in the cabins. All that was in every soldier's mind was to escape from the wretched place and move on to join the main army near Dublin, at a marching distance of some one hundred and eighty miles over rough terrain.

— 29 —

Wolfe Tone and the French Invasion

One point which seems to be ignored concerning the failure of Wolfe Tone's invasion is the role of the English Secret Service in France at that time. Tone himself made no reference to this in his journals, and it is not clear if he was unaware of the activities of the English at that time to frustrate any French move—either military or naval.

Many government departments in Paris, especially the Ministry of War and the Ministry of Foreign Affairs, had paid agents amongst their employees. This is now well documented.

Even Crofton Croker, an official of the English admiralty who had access to many secret papers some one hundred years later wrote that 'Hoche and De Galles, the Military and Naval Commanders-in-Chief, were very strangely on board the same vessel'. And, moreover, all the money for the expenses of the undertaking was also stored on the very same ship. Croker also wrote that he had it on the best authority that 'the Captain of that vessel had accepted a considerable bribe to sail the vessel away from the Irish coast'. He performed that task so well that 'he boldly drew on the English Government for double the amount agreed upon, which, moreover, was ultimately arranged to the perfect satisfaction of all the parties concerned'.

In 1792, the National Assembly at Paris pledged the friendship and help of the French nation to all other struggling nations. So now, in the fourth year of the Revolution, all the archives and documents regarding Ireland were brought together by the Committee of Public Safety. Hoche and Carnot, two eminent military men of that time, studied these in great detail and, when Wolfe Tone arrived in Paris, the planning of a French expedition to Ireland commenced.

But there were dark forces in the corridors of power, none more so than a French nobleman called Comte d'Antraigues (a monarchist) who acted solely for the benefit of the English in order that one day the French monarchy might be restored to power. With Pitt's money he was able to recruit men holding high positions in the most important government departments and their reports kept him minutely informed. One of his lackeys, an official in the Ministry of Finance called Vannelet, was able to manipulate the funds granted by the Directory in such a way that the expenses for the preparation of the invasion forces (both naval and military) were given out piecemeal or not at all. Ships were not repaired, equipment ordered was not paid for, food and supplies were not delivered, crew wages were not allocated and soldiers waiting (months) to embark were left without funds. This state of affairs is best described in the memoirs of La Reveillière, one of the members of the Directory:

> Success would have been certain but for the perfidious tactics of the National Treasury. The French flotillas were delayed through their waiting for the money which was indispensable to them before setting out. The Clerks of the Treasury had given us their word of honour that they would have these funds sent to Brest on a specified date. Despite our urgent solicitations, they do not do so, and thus treacherously let them go by. The English Government, too, was informed of our plans, for the officials in the National Treasury were not anxious to see the success of an expedition against the English that was undertaken in the cause of liberty.

In 1793 Hoche had considered the idea of invading England and had communicated this to the Committee of Public Safety in Paris. Later, the Directory had considered plans for the invasion of the British Isles based on the idea of disembarking groups of crack troops at various locations around the English coast. It was to be a type of guerrilla warfare, with the intention destabilising the British government. Early during Wolfe Tone's sojourn in Paris he was asked to prepare a plan for this proposed undertaking, but declined on the grounds of lack of knowledge of the English countryside.

As these plans for a major invasion of England were being considered by Hoche, Mascheret, Humbert and others, instructions arrived from the Directory that the main object now was an invasion of Ireland, in order to free it from the stranglehold of England, as 'such a detachment is to reduce the latter to be nothing more than a second-rate power; it is to take away from her the greater part of her preponderance at sea'. The undertaking was to be divided into three separate landings, and the instructions continued as follows:

1 The flotilla designed for India will bring, besides the demi-brigade necessary to assure the success of the expedition which is confided to it, 5,000 men at least of good troops, whom it

will disembark on the Irish coast, in the province of Connaught, and, if it is possible, in Galway Bay. These 5,000 men shall be taken from the Armée des Côtes de l'Océan, and you will give them the artillery necessary to maintain themselves in Ireland until the arrival of new re-inforcements. They should be able to take the whole of Connaught, with the exception of the County of Leitrim. They will occupy also the County of Clare up to the north of the river Shannon. They will carry at least 10,000 arms with them, and part of the clothing taken from the English at Quiberon will be used for the inhabitants. The flotilla for India ought to leave in six weeks, and there is not a moment to lose in disposing in advance of the 5,000 men who must be landed in Ireland. Their leaders ought to be intelligent, honest, inclined to discipline, and capable of conducting themselves with audacity and vigour.

2 A second expedition will be prepared at Brest by you, and the Minister of Marine, with whom you will collaborate. It should be ready before 1 September next. The flotilla allotted to it will take at least 6,000 men, drawn also from the Armée des Côtes de l'Océan, and composed of free corps which you will raise, and to whom you will give intrepid officers, zealous for discipline, and drawn from other corps. One part of the troops should be destined to form a cavalry troop who will provide themselves with horses at the moment of their arrival in Ireland, and you will be careful to take the same precaution for a part of the 5,000 men embarked in the flotilla for India. The Directory will send you English speaking officers, who can be employed with advantage in this second expedition which will disembark likewise in Galway Bay. As to the composition of the free corps of which we have spoken, it will be such that it can purge France of many dangerous individuals, and there will be no objection to incorporating in them former Chouans whose intentions appear to be right. The Directory should, however, bring to your notice that these free corps cannot, by reason of the Constitution, bear this title until the moment of their disembarkation.

3. The third expedition will leave from Holland at the same time as the second. The Commander-in-Chief of the army of the north is charged with their disposal. It will be of 5,000 men, the greater part foreign deserters, commanded by French officers, of whom one part is already regimented. If you can give them 5,000 red coats taken at Quiberon, send them without delay to Ostend, and warn the Commander-in-Chief, Beurnonville, who does not know the object of the armament. This third expedition is also for Galway Bay.

You will find herewith, under the numeral 1, copy of the manifesto which the French Commander in Ireland should publish at the moment of landing, and several memorials which will instruct you of the situation in Ireland.

If the resources of the French navy had permitted the Directory to carry, at the same time to Connaught the 16,000 men destined to assure the liberty of Ireland, it would not have hesitated to ask you to put yourself at the head of so glorious an enterprise which promises such happy results. To-day the Directory limits itself to recommend to you to form, with great care, the staff of the little army of Connaught. It reserves to itself the transmission of new orders on this account, but it leaves you the greatest latitude on the dispositions to be made, and will now engage itself in obtaining the funds indispensable for success.

P.S. The attempts at Chouannerie in Wales and Cornwall ought to be considered as useful diversions, capable of contributing strongly to the success of the great Irish expedition.

Signed: Carnot Rewbell Barras

Hoche was completely taken aback by this new proposal. He was summoned to Paris to examine the details of the plan and their modifications, and was assisted there by Truguet, the Minister of the Marine, a man of immense sea-faring experience who had already drawn up his own plans for the invasion of Ireland as well as England. He had reorganised the defence of France and its colonies after the Revolution and had also been behind the near destruction of the loyalist-appointed army and navy. After various sessions with Truguet, he finally came up with a plan which was presented to the Directory. It was so well received that he was immediately made Commander-in-Chief of 'the army destined to operate a revolution in Ireland'. This plan consisted of landing 15,000 troops in Ireland under Hoche which were later to be augmented by another 17,000 troops. At the same time, a proposed expedition to India with 4,000 men was being prepared for under Villaret. In fact, France under the Directory was in no state to prepare for one invasion, never mind two, as shall be seen from a detailed account of the main port of Brest.

Brest, at this time, was completely disorganised, approaching a state of utter chaos. The French currency was at an all time low in the port and promissory notes from the Directory or the various government departments were almost worthless. In fact, it was almost impossible to purchase provisions with guarantees of payment by the Office of Finance. There was also a serious scarcity of ship's equipment such as sails, rope, clothing and provisions, and even bread was a scarce commodity. Barter was the only method of doing business.

It is not surprising that the preparations for any proposed expedition got bogged down. There was unrest in the dockyards, soldiers were revolting due to lack of pay, and there was civil unrest on the streets.

The port was under the control of Admiral Villaret Joyeuse and the co-ordinator of the Marine, M. Sane. With Villaret intent on equipping an expedition for India, against the wishes of Hoche and his associates, there was a complete lack of co-ordination amongst the navy and army chiefs. Villaret believed that his proposed voyage and victory in India would make him famous and bring untold riches.

As autumn passed, the preparations for the invasion of Ireland went painfully slowly. The fact that both Hoche and Tone spent most of their time in Rennes did not help matters. It was only when news of the victories by Bonaparte in Italy reached him that Hoche realised that his position as head of the armed forces was in jeopardy, and he applied pressure to get the invasion underway. A victorious campaign in Ireland would consolidate his position, despite having to contend with Villaret. Tone sided with Hoche during any discussion concerning the conflicting expeditions, as he admired Hoche as a great general. Hoche, despite his poor background, which was often a bone of contention amongst his fellow upper-class officers, was a brilliant strategist in the battlefield, but knew almost nothing about naval matters. Hoche sought the assistance of a naval officer called Bruix, who was later to distinguish himself in the defence of the colonies. With the assistance of Bruix, the preparations speeded up and, when the proposed expedition of Villaret was cancelled by the Directory, only the lack of experienced seamen delayed departure.

With the removal of Villaret, the question of who was to be appointed Admiral-in-Chief was debated by the Directory and the Minister for the Marine, Truguet. Against the better judgement of Hoche, Tone and Bruix, the appointment went to Morard de Galles instead of Latouche Treville. The choice was far from satisfactory, as Morard de Galles was almost blind, suffered from ill-health, was of a nervous disposition and lacked confidence in himself.

Finally, during the third week of November, the embarkation of troops commenced. When further delays were announced, some of the restless troops who were confined in terrible conditions aboard the vessels mutinied, and some of the leaders of the mutiny were executed to re-establish order. As the fleet lay at anchor awaiting reinforcement by other French warships, the order was given to sail on 15 December.

As the ships lifted anchor and began to sail out of Brest harbour, the Directory in Paris came to the conclusion that the proposed invasion of Ireland should be cancelled for the time being, as Hoche was required to defend France on the home front. Truguet was dispatched in all haste to Brest with the new orders, but arrived to find that the fleet had sailed the previous day.

— 30 —

The Invasion Fleet at Sea

As it departed the port of Brest, the fleet comprised of the following ships—seventeen ships of the line, one ship of the line Rasé, thirteen frigates, six corvettes, eight transport ships, an ammunition ship and a number of brigs and small luggers (45 ships in all). There were 14,750 men on board.

The allocation of the chiefs-of-staff to the various vessels fuels the suspicion that a well-prepared plan had been laid to sabotage the undertaking. Against the express orders of Truguet, the Minister of the Marine, Admiral Morard de Galles decided who was to be in charge of the leading vessels of the fleet. The Admiral's flag was hoisted on the frigate *Fraternité* when Morard de Galles assumed command. Also on board were Hoche and Bruix, the chief-of-staff, as well as the funds for financing the invasion. Rear-Admiral Bouvet, the second-in-command, as well as the military second-in-command General de Grouchy were on another frigate, *L'Immortalité*, and Rear-Admiral Nielly was on the *Résolue*. Rear-Admiral de Richery was the only senior officer commanding a ship of the line (the *Pégase*). The largest and best-equipped vessel of the line, *L'Indomptable*, which was the flagship of the invasion, had Commodore Jacques Bedout in command. With him were Wolfe Tone—under the title Adjutant-General Smith—and his compatriots and staff. Thus, whether by chance or design, the principal officers were separated.

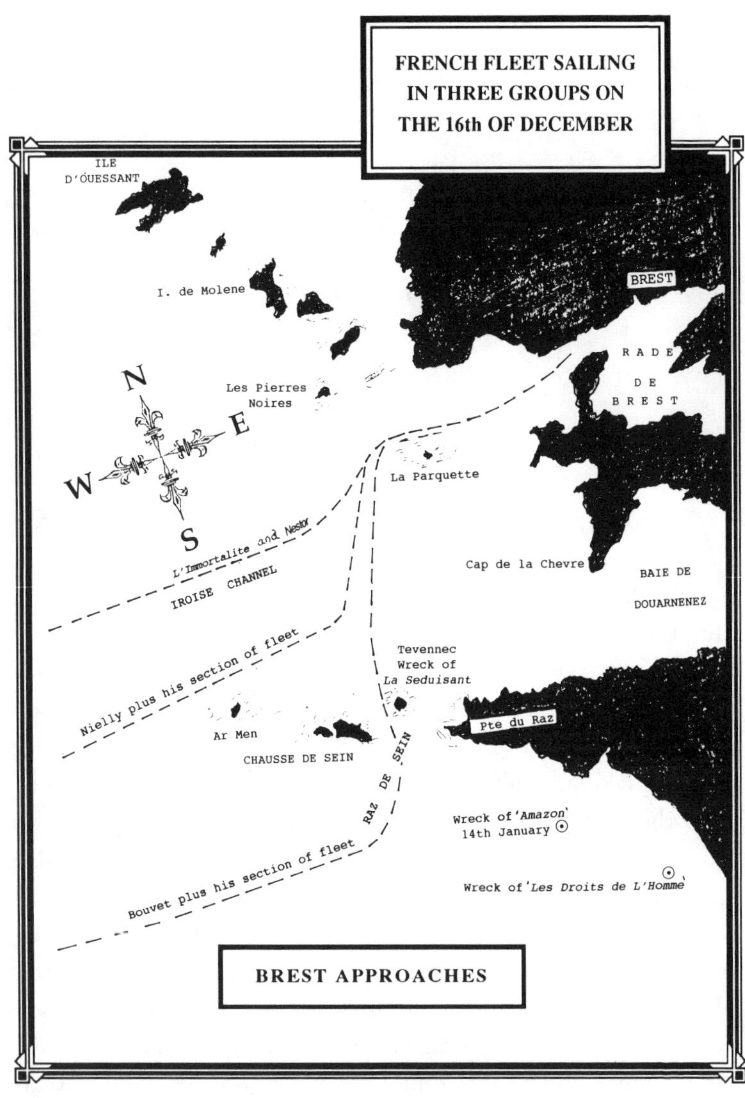

Tone was delighted to have Bedout as commander of *L'Indomptable* as he spoke perfect English. Tone was in high spirits at the time of departure, but was somewhat upset on seeing what he classified as

'French adventurers' coming on board as well as 'ladies' dressed in cabin-boys' clothes. Yet, his main worry was that the large invasion fleet would come to the attention of the English before it arrived at its destination.

This was also the principal concern of Admiral Morard de Galles as he studied the alternative routes to the open sea from Brest harbour. Due to misleading reports from merchant ships that a fleet of more than thirty British ships was sighted north of Ushant, he decided that the fleet should pass through the narrows of Raz de Sein to the south. This was a very narrow channel with many reefs and subject to strong tidal currents. In fact, no fleet had ever passed through it before. Now, Morard de Galles was directing a large fleet, recently assembled with mostly inexperienced captains and officers, to manoeuvre through the rocks, shoals and currents without mishap or danger, either an extremely foolish or a daring decision by a man whose personal knowledge of the channel was debatable.

On 16 December, at about 13.00 hours, the ships began to weigh anchor, as a strong favourable wind was blowing from the east. By 14.30 hours most of the fleet was under way, and signals were passed to steer north by south after dark when the dangerous channel had been navigated.

However, when the wind changed direction, orders were given by signals from the *Fraternité* that all following ships should proceed through the main central channel, known as the Irose, but, as night had fallen, no vessel saw the change of signals. Bouvet, in *L'Immortalité*, navigated the original channel and, on arriving at the open sea, found that he was alone. He navigated a north-easterly course for a few hours and at 23.00 hours encountered some seventeen ships which included *L'Indomptable* and nine ships of the line, plus six frigates and one transporter. There was no sign of the other thirty ships of the fleet during that night. As to the fate of these ships, the *Séduisant* was wrecked at 19.00 hours with the loss of 1,265 lives, but the others navigated safely to the open sea and were, by dawn, some thirty miles away. Hoche's ship the *Fraternité* was for some reason the last to leave her moorings in Brest harbour, accompanied by the *Nestor*.

In the foggy conditions of the following morning, the *Fraternité* and the *Nestor* were joined by the frigate *Cocarde* and later by the

Romaine. At about 11.00 hours it was estimated that Bouvet's section of the fleet was twenty miles to the south, while the remainder under Nielly was still fifteen miles astern. During the day the fog became thicker and, according to Tone, it was so dense that it was impossible to see a ship's length ahead as the three sections of the fleet sailed independently in a generally westerly direction.

When the various captains opened their sealed orders that morning they found that they contained the following directions—to sail to the Mizen Head and cruise off for five days. If no ships, arrived they were to proceed to the mouth of the Shannon and sail off for three days. If still no instructions or re-inforcements arrived, they were to return to Brest.

At noon on 18 December, Bouvet found himself some three hundred miles from the Irish coast.

At dawn on 19 December, Bouvet was joined by the ships under Nielly when a calm—described by Tone as 'this calm, this calm. It is most terrible vexatious'—descended. He was, however, to be more vexed, as he had mistaken Nielly's flagship for that of Morard de Galles with Hoche aboard. It was decided to hold a general council of war on board *L'Immortalité* which, in the absence of Hoche, was presided over by Grouchy. He formally gave orders that, as the fleet was almost intact, it was their duty to continue with the invasion and to proceed either to Bantry Bay or the Shannon to effect a landing. Even though there was a certain amount of dissent, the plan was agreed, and Rear-Admiral Bouvet took command of the fleet, which now consisted of thirty-four ships. Meanwhile, Hoche and Admiral Morard de Galles were on board the *Fraternité*, captained by Captain Fustel, over thirty miles further south. There were strong indications that Fustel was in the pay of the British at this time, especially the fact that he had succeeded in separating his ship from the rest of the fleet. As Admiral Morard de Galles was almost blind and Hoche knew nothing about navigation, only Bruix had to be outwitted regarding compass readings and distances.

French Fleet which sailed from Brest in December 1796

Avant-Garde

Ships of the Line

Nestor (74); Commodore Charles Alexandre Léon Durand-Linois
Cassard (74); Commodore Dufay
Droits de l'Homme (74); Commodore Jean Raimond La Crosse
Proper flagship of Rear Admiral François Joseph Bouvet. General Humbert embarked.
Tourville (74); Captain Jean Baptiste Henry
Éole (74); Captain Joseph Pierre André Malin

Frigates

Cocarde, *Bravoure*, *L'Immortalité* (carrying Rear-Admiral Bouvet, General de Grouchy, Captain Siméon), *Bellone*

Corvettes

Renard, *Mutiné*

Corps de Bataille

Ships of the Line

Fougueux (74); Commodore Esprit Tranquille Maistral
Mucius (74); Commodore Pierre Maurice Julien Querangal
L'Indomptable (80); Commodore Jacques Bedout
Proper flagship of Admiral Morard de Galles. General Chérin and staff embarked, including Adjutant-General Smith (Wolfe Tone)
Redoutable (74); Captain Moncousu
Patriote (74); Captain La Fargue

Frigates

Fraternité (carrying Admiral Morard de Galles, General Hoche, Captain Fustel), *Coquille*, *Romaine*, *Sirène*, *Tortue*

Corvettes

Atalante, *Voltigeur*

Arriere-Garde

Ships of the Line

Séduisant (74); Captain Dufossey
Foundered in Raz Passage on leaving.
Pluton (74); Captain Jean-Marie Lebrun
Constitution (74); Commodore Louis L'Héritier
Trajan (74); Commodore Julien Le Ray
Wattiguies (74); Commodore Henri Alexandre Thévenard

Frigates

Surveillante, L'Impatiente, Charente, Résolue (flying flag of Rear-Admiral Joseph Marie Nielly, Captain Montallent)

Corvettes

L'Affronteur (Lugger Le Vautour)

Supplementary

Ships of the Line

Pégase (74); Rear-Admiral de Richery; Captain Clément Laronier, attached to Corps de Bataille
Révolution (74); Commodore Pierre René Maurice Etienne Dumanoir-Le-Pelley, attached to Corps de Bataille

Ship of the Line Rasé

Scévola (44); Commodore Obet

Frigate armée en Flûte

Fidéle; Powder vessel

Transport Ships

Nicodème, Ville de L'Orient, Justine, *Suffren, Allègre, Expériment, Fille Unique*

All frigates were forty gun except *Impatiente* (44), *Surveillante, Charente, Siréne* (36)

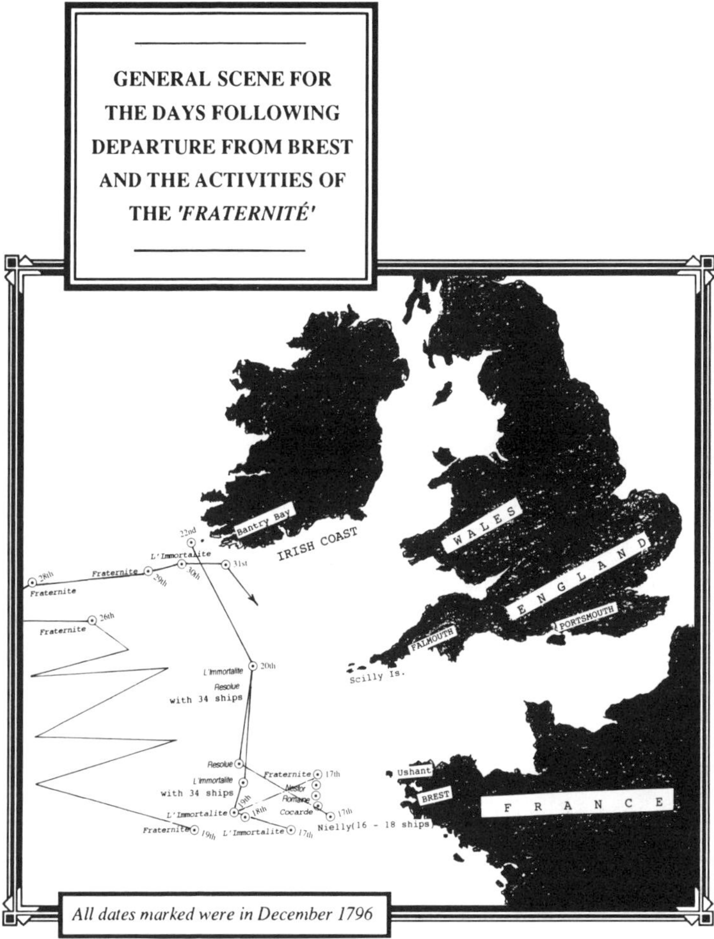

All dates marked were in December 1796

— 31 —
Tone's Arrival in Bantry Bay

Tone's diary seems to confirm that he was kept in the dark as to the exact location of the landing. It was only after the sealed orders for the fleet were opened by Captain Bedout on 19 December that Tone discovered the major change of plan.

Galway Bay was originally selected as the place of disembarkation, with the Shannon as the second alternative. The use of Bantry Bay had often been discussed between Hoche, Truguet, Clarke and others, but had been kept a complete secret, only appearing on Truguet's personal notes in pencil. No doubt, the decision about Bantry Bay was influenced by events such as the successful landing of 1689 under Chateaurenault and the detailed study of Bruix on the Bay's possibilities as an invasion point.

With the best charts available at that time, there were three locations picked out in the Bay for anchoring or disembarkation, depending on the direction of the wind. The locations were contained in the in the sealed orders which gave each ship of the fleet her precise anchoring position.

1 Berehaven Sound if wind is in an easterly direction

2 Mouth of Glengarriff harbour if wind is from the west

3 Eastern end of Whiddy Island if wind is from a northerly direction

In addition, three frigates and two corvettes were to remain at the entrance of the Bay under sail at all times, in case the English fleet were to appear. In fact, the British never appeared during the period of 21 December to 6 January.

As to the proposed landing, the following procedure was to be followed—when the fleet's boats were in the water they were to transport the troops and equipment to the beach area at the mouth of the Coomhola river, where they were to gather in formation and join the nearby road to Cork, whose capture was the primary objective.

As the reduced fleet assembled and headed towards Bantry Bay, Tone wrote in his diary—'Admiral Morard de Galles, General Hoche, General Debelle and Colonel Shee are aboard the *Fraternité* and God knows what has become of them'. At 3.00 p.m. he listed those ships, besides the *Fraternité*, which were missing—the *Séduisant* which had sunk, plus the *Nestor*, the *Cocarde*, the *Romaine* frigates, the *Mutine*, the *Voltigeur* and three other transporters. Some of these, as already mentioned, were further south with the *Fraternité*.

As the sun was setting on the calm night of 20 December (again, according to Tone's diary), seven sails were seen in the distance. Hoping that these were the missing section of the fleet, Tone stayed awake throught the night anxiously waiting for good news. Early before dawn a good breeze came up and, as daylight broke, most of the fleet were but four or five leagues from Cape Clear Island. There was no sight of the seven ships.

These ships present a bit of a mystery. According to the records of the English fleet at that time, no vessels of that nationality were in the vicinity during that period. Were they the *Fraternité*, accompanied by the *Nestor* and others? According to the log of the *Fraternité*, she was approximately one hundred miles further south.

Another important point to ponder is why didn't Captain Fustel of the *Fraternité* follow the sealed instructions of the fleet to proceed to Cape Clear and await the remainder of the fleet for a period of five days? In other words, why was the flagship *Fraternité* the only ship not to follow the orders to the fleet which were prepared by Admiral

Morard de Galles and Hoche himself? And if by some chance the *Fraternité* was amongst the seven sails spotted that late evening by the becalmed fleet, why did the lookouts not see the other ships in the calm conditions with good visibility?

Tone did not relax that evening. He was seriously worried that Grouchy and Bouvet might lack the ability to make the right decisions, and he concluded that 'if this day (twenty-first) passes without our seeing the General (Hoche) I must fear that the game is up'.

On the morning of the twenty-second, the fleet had been scattered by a gale-force easterly wind and part of the flotilla was now off Mizen Head. Tone still searched the horizon in vain for the *Fraternité*. He remarked, 'I believe it is the first instance of an Admiral in a clean frigate, with moderate weather, and moonlight nights, parting company with his fleet'. He was more than perturbed that the fleet had broken up on two occasions during the past twenty-four hours in such moderate weather conditions. To say the least, his regard for the French captains was greatly diminished.

However, it was not Mizen Head that became the landfall but Dursey Island, which was some twenty miles further west. Admiral Nielly, who was heading the starboard column of ships, found himself further west again. In fact, the whole fleet were well to the west of the Bull Rock, with a strong to gale-force wind blowing from the east-south-east. Bouvet ordered the fleet to come close to the wind and to make the entrance to the Bay. A number of Irish pilots came out from shore and joined certain ships of the line (there is a tradition that Sunday morning mass was disrupted at Cahermore Church, just north of Blackball Head, by the sighting of strange ships entering Bantry Bay. After mass, the fishermen took to their boats and rowed out to the vessels). Bouvet learned that there were no British ships in the vicinity and that Bantry was only guarded by two to three hundred militia.

On the evening and night of the twenty-second, strong easterly winds caused havoc amongst the fleet as the vessels tried in vain to beat upwind into the Bay. The sight that greeted the boats which had gained some distance was not too inviting. Tone had mentioned that he had been so near the shore the previous afternoon that he could distinctly see two castles, probably at Three Castle Head. Now, however, all that greeted him was mountain ranges covered in snow.

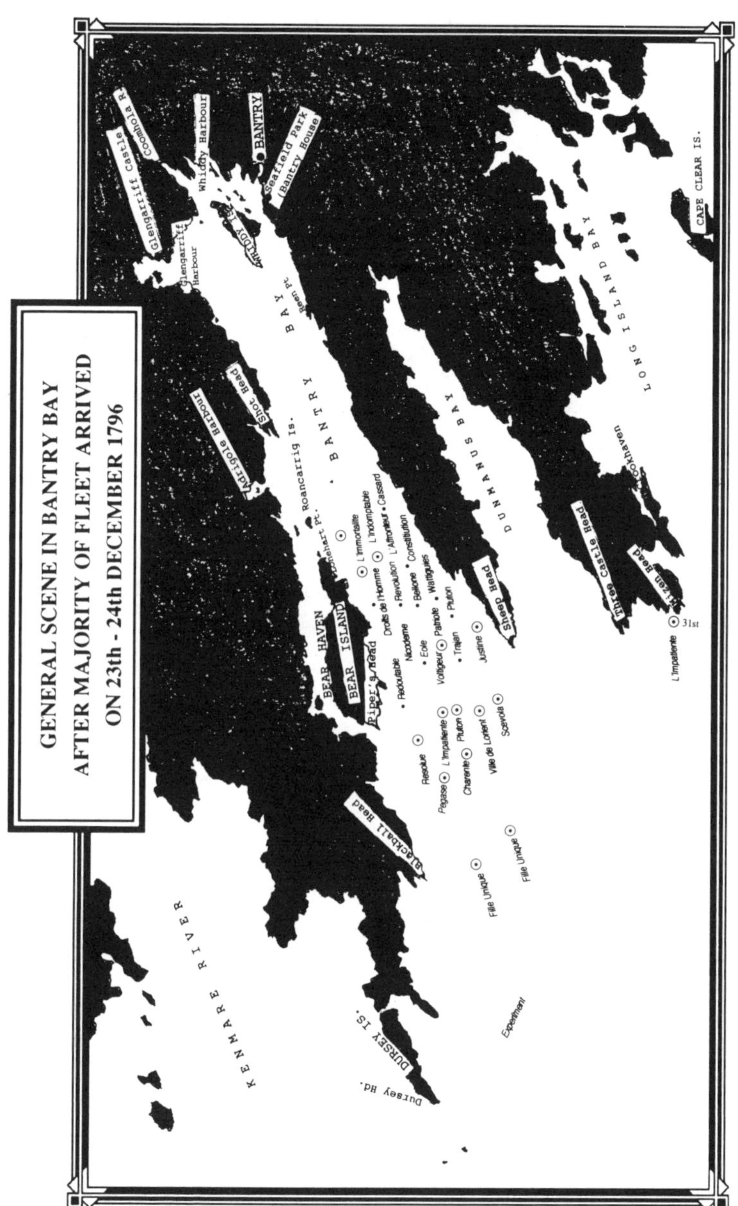
GENERAL SCENE IN BANTRY BAY
AFTER MAJORITY OF FLEET ARRIVED
ON 23th - 24th DECEMBER 1796
Glengarriff Castle
Coomhola R.
Whiddy Harbour
BANTRY
Seafield Park (Bantry House)
WHIDDY IS.
Glengarriff Harbour
Reen Pt.
BANTRY BAY
Shot Head
Adrigole Harbour
Roancarrig Is.
Lonehart Pt.
BEAR HAVEN
BEAR ISLAND
Piper's Head
Blackball Head
KENMARE RIVER
DURSEY IS.
Dursey Hd.
DUNMANUS BAY
Sheep Head
LONG ISLAND BAY
Crookhaven
Three Castle Head
Mizen Head
CAPE CLEAR IS.
L'Immortalite
L'Indomptable
Cassard
L'Affronteur
Constitution
Droits de l'Homme
Revolution
Bellone
Wattigues
Nicodeme
Patriote
Pluton
Eole
Trajan
Justine
Redoutable
Voltigeur
Resolue
L'Impatiente
Pegase
Charente
Ville de Lorient
Scevola
Fille Unique
Experiment
L'Impatiente
31st

Around noon, *L'Immortalité* was making some headway and finally, by about 4.00 p.m., dropped her anchor between Lonehart harbour and the south shore. Slightly later, *L'Indomptable* also dropped anchor, as well as fourteen other ships which included the *Wattiguies, Éole, Cassard, Constitution, Patriote, Trajan, Pluton, Révolution, Droits de l'Homme, Bellone, Voltigeur, L'Affronteur, Vantour* and the *Nicodème*.

During the early night, the *Résolue*, under Nielly, was off the Piper Sound (the western entrance to Berehaven harbour) in poor visibility, falling snow, and severe squalls when the *Redoutable* collided with her and broke her bowsprit, foremast, maintop mast and mizen mast. With such severe damage, Nielly fell away south-west and finally managed to drop anchor off Blackball Head while he shot off cannons and flares for assistance.

As the remainder of the present fleet—some twenty vessels in all—had been blown out to sea and 'were nowhere to be seen', Tone was completely disheartened—'I find our means so reduced by the absence of the missing, that I think it hardly possible to make an attempt here with any prospect of success'. Consequently, he proposed to Chérin that the landing at Bantry Bay be abandoned and that they sail to Sligo Bay, where Tone himself would land with the volunteers and what arms remained aboard the various ships.

On the afternoon of the twenty-third there was a slight improvement in the weather. It was an opportune time for Bouvet to organise what ships were in the Bay and take them to Berehaven Sound as the original plan had stipulated. Yet nothing happened, except that the *Droits de l'Homme* moved her anchorage southwards as she had been too close to the rocks off Bere Island.

The further improvement of the weather on the morning of the twenty-fourth meant that the landing of troops by boat was a distinct possibility. Signals were passed from ship to ship, and all the main officers were rowed over to *L'Immortalité* to discuss the situation and have a council of war with General Grouchy. Despite the circumstances, it was a good-humoured conference, resulting in a decision to land what troops and equipment they had the following morning. On reboarding their own vessels, orders were given to set sail and attempt to make the designated 'anchorage' to the north of Whiddy Island. Here the accounts differ as to what anchorage was the destination—Berehaven Sound near Waterfall and Bank harbour, or that 'at the head of the Bay'. Tone's journal indicates that they were trying to head for the latter, while Grouchy's account mentions the former. Yet Grouchy was also aware of possible landing places on the south side of the Bay—Gortnakilla, Loughane Creek (Gearhies) and the two beaches inside Reen Point which were all sheltered from the easterly wind.

In the event, it mattered very little, because as night fell the ships dropped anchor not far from their original positions. Bouvet, before dropping anchor at 4.00 p.m., signalled that he was proposing to make a landing at Bank Place, and two ships were sent in to protect the landing place, but before this could happen the weather deteriorated rapidly and by 6.00 p.m. another severe gale had blown up from the east.

During the night—Christmas Eve—the weather deteriorated further into a full-blown easterly storm. Tone was disheartened, but did not lose hope. He proposed to Captain Bedout and the other officers on board that the present fleet should up anchor and head for the Shannon and try to make a landing there, but, as it was impossible to inform the remainder of the fleet of this proposal due to the atrocious conditions, this plan could not be followed.

The morning broke on Christmas Day with conditions worse than the night before—not only was it out of the question to attempt any disembarkation but some of the ships were finding it increasingly difficult to hold their anchors and were dragging, despite the fact that they had two or three anchors down. As the ships buried their forecastles in the angry swell, sheets of spray driven by the cold howling wind drenched everybody to the skin. With soaking wet clothes and lacking food, the crews and troops huddled in whatever shelter they could find. Bouvet, for his part, thought that the best course of action would be to weigh anchor, but conditions were so bad that this was impossible. However, as daylight faded at around 4.30 p.m., his starboard anchor cable parted and his port anchor was dragging. Fearing that his ship would be driven onto the rocks of Bere Island, he cut the port cable and headed out of the Bay, while signalling to the other ships to do likewise. At 19.30 hours a vessel passed *L'Indomptable* with shouts of 'coupez vos cables', but Captain Bedout decided to hold on until morning light.

L'Immortalité, with General Grouchy and his officers, headed for the open sea. Running before the storm-force gale her top-gallant sails were shredded, resulting in the vessel lying broadside to the terrible seas. Driven in the south-westerly direction for the following three days, she found herself about 285 miles south of the Mizen with winds moderated. Grouchy wanted to return to Bantry Bay or else head for the Shannon estuary, but Admiral Bouvet pointed out that he had only one anchor, no good anchor cable and barely enough food aboard. The crew and troops were at the point of mutiny and there was no other vessel in sight. After a violent argument with General Grouchy, he decided to sail for Brest and arrived there on 1 January.

Meanwhile, on the morning of the twenty-sixth, Tone took a long look at the reality of the situation and summed it up thus—'we have lost two Commanders-in-Chief, the four Admirals, and have but fourteen ships remaining at anchor. Well, let me think no more about it; it is lost and let it go'. As the gale continued, everyone aboard the different vessels became more despondent.

The wind abated and the sea moderated on the morning of the twenty-seventh and the conditions allowed another council of war to be held aboard *L'Indomptable*. This was presided over by the Irish General Harty, as all other more senior officers had either left the Bay or could not come aboard.

Bedout reported that all ships were running short of provisions and that they had only two guns and about four thousand troops if a landing was made. Tone realised that the province of Munster would be least disposed to assist a French invasion, and pushed those present to attempt a landing at the mouth of the Shannon as a last resort.

At 4.00 p.m. what remained of the fleet—seven of the line and five frigates or smaller ships—weighed anchor. *L'Indomptable* had to cut her cable to save herself from going aground on the rocks. As the ships departed Bantry Bay during the darkness of late evening, the gale turned into a full-blown hurricane from the east-south-east. As *L'Indomptable* ran before the wind on a single jib she was opposed by a rogue sea, and water poured into the aft quarters. Tone was awakened and, seeing the trunks and gear floating around in over three feet of water, thought that the ship was sinking. Resigned to his fate, he returned to his hammock and calmly awaited death.

However, *L'Indomptable* survived the night and on the morning of the twenty-eighth arrived at the mouth of the Shannon. After waiting in vain for more than twenty-four hours for the other ships of the line, they set course for Brest at dawn on the twenty-ninth, and arrived on 1 January.

If Captain Bedout and Tone had decided to remain in Bantry Bay throughout the gale until 29 December, the whole story might have been different, as there was a complete reversal of fortune—but it came too late.

On the morning of the twenty-ninth, with her sails in tatters, the French corvette *Renard* slowly made her way up the Bay and anchored to the north of Whiddy Island (the primary anchorage). She was followed later by a number of her companion ships who had stayed at sea riding out the storms. These were followed by two foreign merchantmen—an American ship called the *Beaver* and a Guinea trader called *Sisters*. The *Beaver* anchored to the north-east of Whiddy Point, while firing her cannon and indicating she needed a pilot or assistance. Meanwhile, *Sisters* anchored near the *Renard*.

As the afternoon progressed, more French ships began to arrive—the *Redoutable*, *Tourville*, and frigates *Cocarde* and *Romaine*. All vessels anchored to the north of Whiddy Island. On the following day, 31 December, the *Surveillante* limped up the Bay with canvases torn, masts broken, all guns thrown overboard to lighten the vessel, and leaking like a basket. On board was the cavalry Commander General Mermet, the ruined saddles, some troops but no horses. As the ship was unfit to make the return trip to France, it was decided to take off everything of value. Two days later, on 2 January, she was scuppered and sank about a mile off the western point of Glengarriff harbour.

Meanwhile, with the arrival of more French vessels, including the *Fougueux* and the *Nestor*, there was again a sizeable French presence in the Bay, amounting to some four thousand troops.

After a council of war attended by Lemoine, Mermet and Watrin—all generals—plus the naval representatives, it was decided to cruise outside the Bay for the next two days, as they did not wish to be trapped by the south-westerly gales, or by the English.

Before the French departed from their anchorage north of Whiddy, they boarded the *Beaver* and *Sisters*, forced the crews to leave their ships and, having removed everything of value and what food and wine they could find, they torched the two ships. Both ships sank where they had lain at anchor—the *Beaver* off Ardnagashel and *Sisters* about half a mile north of Whiddy Island.

Due to changes in the weather, from gales to calm, the French vessels did not clear the Bay until 6 January and, after cruising off the Bull Rock for a period of three days without being reinforced, they set course for Brest and arrived there on 13 January.

Besides the *Surveillante*, the only other casualty was the frigate *L'Impatiente*, which was driven onto the rocks west of Crookhaven on 13 December with a loss of five hundred and ninety-four souls. Both ships were of the French frigate class.

As to the fate of the *Fraternité*, which had on board Admiral Morard de Galles and General Hoche, from Christmas night she ran before the south-easterly gale without sails. On the morning of the twenty-sixth, another large ship, *L'Immortalité*, was seen also running before the weather. Thinking that this was a British ship, the *Fraternité* put on all available sail and ran before the storm for thirty-six hours to evade her supposed pursuer and during this evasive action sighted three other sails (no doubt part of the fleet).

After the storm on the twenty-eighth, the *Fraternité*, now about three hundred miles to the south-west, steered a course for Bantry Bay. It seems that on that night *L'Immortalité* crossed her bows once again without being identified. By the morning of the twenty-ninth she had covered a distance of over one hundred and twenty miles and had already sighted a number of other sails in the distance. However, on that afternoon, the *Révolution* and the *Tortue* were encountered and messages exchanged, which brought Hoche and Admiral Morard de Galles up to date regarding the events in Bantry Bay.

Despite the bad news, the Admiral gave orders to head for Bantry Bay, with the *Révolution* and the *Tortue* following. During the night, in good to moderate conditions, the three vessels lost each other. At midday on the 30th the *Fraternité* was thirty miles south-west of the Bull Rock and, as the wind increased from the same direction, she ran before it on her starboard quarter. In these conditions she should have made landfall within four hours at least, but this did not happen. The morning of the 31st found her sailing a few points off her previous course but further away from the coast, and without sighting land. At nightfall Admiral de Galles ordered a change of course, and the *Fraternité* headed home to Brest.

There is no satisfactory answer as to why the *Fraternité* did not arrive in Bantry Bay or follow the sealed instructions prepared by Hoche and others. Perhaps she was not intended to reach her destination.

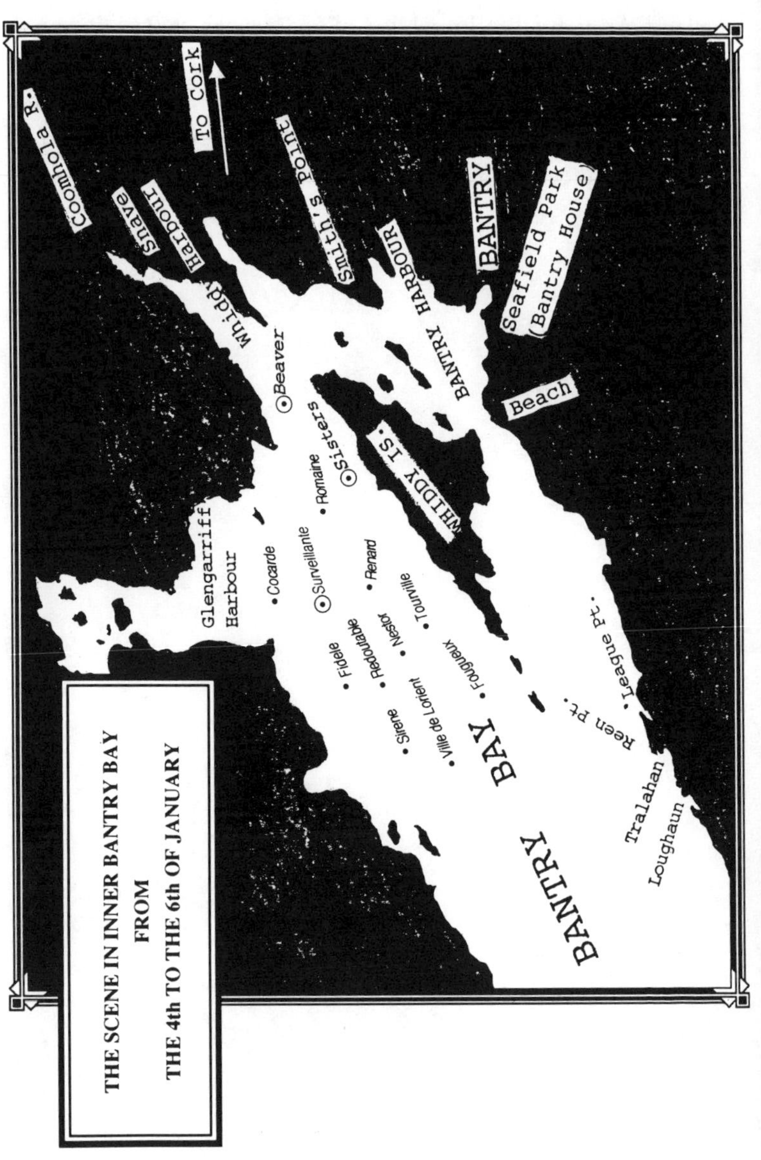

THE SCENE IN INNER BANTRY BAY
FROM
THE 4th TO THE 6th OF JANUARY

— 32 —

Too Soon and Too Late

Before moving on from the ill-fated invasion it is necessary to examine briefly the overall situation in Ireland just prior to the invasion and the main events around Bantry Bay from the first sightings of the French ships.

As Frank McDermot states in his biography of Wolfe Tone, 'the French arrived both too soon and too late'. A number of the leaders of the United Irishmen, including Keogh, Neilson, Russell and Teeling, were in jail at that time. In addition, the two principal leaders, FitzGerald and O'Connor, were not in the country. The only rebellious part of the country was Ulster, where the effects of the Indemnity and the Insurrection Acts had caused many to join the outlawed United Irishmen. In fact, the French were misled into believing that the whole of Ireland was at the point of insurrection, with a widespread reliable rebel force in waiting. Munster, as a whole, was satisfied with the status quo, and there was, in fact, considerable anti-French feeling after the humiliation of the Pope. The leaders of the United Irishmen who were at large did not believe the news of the French fleet's arrival in Bantry Bay, and even the personal assurances of Hoche and Tone, through their emissaries O'Shee and MacSheehy, were doubted.

When the French fleet was first sighted, it was mistakenly believed to be British, or else a convoy of traders from the colonies. The Irish pilots who made their way to the ships at the mouth of the Bay were convinced that they were returning merchant ships from the west. Even the English thought that the French fleet had gone south to Portugal.

The first news to arrive in England that a French fleet had been sighted near Bantry Bay came from the British sloop *Kangaroo*, which put into Crookhaven to get an officer to Cork with the important news. He arrived there on the night of 22 December. Almost simultaneously, a dispatch rider sent by Mr. White, an English landlord in Bantry, arrived with the news that some local fishermen had gone out to the ships thinking that they were British and had been detained and later released. When these men had come ashore at Berehaven, they were obliged to make an affidavit before O'Sullivan of Cooliagh who sent it to Bantry to Mr White. This O'Sullivan, a descendant of the family of O'Sullivan Beare, was a prosperous Catholic landowner in that area. He also sent a message by boat across Kenmare Bay to his uncle Maurice O'Connell (uncle of Daniel O'Connell), informing him of the French fleet's arrival. This message was sent to Lord Kenmare by O'Connell, and he, in turn, sent it to Cork.

As to the attitude of the local people, there was a general fear that the French were coming as invaders and not allies. As a French force of some 80,000 troops was mentioned to the Irish fishermen, it is little wonder that the local Irish feared a foreign invasion, as is evident from the following letter.

'Bearhaven 22 December 1796

To Richard White.

My Dr Friend,

The French fleet consisting of twenty-eight ships of the Line and some small vessels are this moment off this harbour all beating up for Bantry. What we are to do or what is to become of us God only knows.

I am as Ever, yr

SAML BAYLEY

Later, a second dispatch rider arrived in Cork with further news from Mr. White—reporting the capture of some French officers and men after their longboat went ashore on Bere Island. For this service to the Crown, as well as for organising his militia and tenants and posting lookouts on the hills surrounding the Bay, Mr. White was later rewarded by being raised to the peerage as Lord Bantry.

When the news of the French arrival in the Bay was received in Cork, Kingsmill, who was in charge of the naval forces, sent Lieutenant Pulling in the cutter *Fox* to Mizen Head, while General Dalrymple sent Lieutenant Gerard Gibbons, a military officer, to Seafield House, Bantry, to monitor developments. Gibbons was selected because he had a very good knowledge of the coastline and had relations in the town of Bantry. He also spoke perfect Irish. It was through him that all dispatches were sent to Kingsmill concerning the movements of the French fleet. It is worth noting that in their dispatches of 31 December Gibbons states—'The French cruiser *L'Impatiente* carrying twenty-five pounders, three hundred and twenty men and two hundred and fifty troops was wrecked this morning [thirtieth] near this place Bantry Bay. Five men were only saved, one being the Irish pilot.' The location of this loss was in the first gully north of Mizen Head which has an almost sheer cliff face.

When Admiral Nielly sent his longboat to assist *L'Immortalité*, it was blown ashore on Bere Island during the late evening of 24 December. Lieutenant Proteau and his crew were apprehended by a detachment of yeomanry under the command of Daniel O'Sullivan of Cooliagh. Later, on the twenty-sixth, Proteau was taken to Bantry under escort to be interrogated by General Dalrymple from Cork. Dalrymple was billeted at Seafield House (Bantry House), which had been put at the disposal of himself and Eyre Coote of Bandon. It seems that Richard White had sent his family to Bandon for safety. Later, Dalrymple sent Lieutenant Proteau to Dublin Castle for further interrogation.

The longboat from the *Résolue* was brought to Bantry House, where it was stored until 1944 when Mrs. Shelswell-White presented it to the National Museum of Ireland. The present Bantry longboat is built to the same design.

Daniel O'Sullivan of Cooliagh was rewarded by being given the freedom of the City of Cork, a beautiful sword and twenty guineas for each member of his yeomanry. He was also designated Commander of the Berehaven Royal Infantry by the English government in Dublin.

There was also an expedition ashore for fresh meat on Bere Island or the mainland by the crews of one of the French vessels at anchor. This was met by local opposition and the French returned empty-handed.

When Richard White received further details as to the strength of the French forces, he ordered his Protestant yeomanry forces (about fifty men) to protect Seafield House, and to stand on guard at Beach strand and at Smith's Point ready to engage the enemy should a landing be attempted.

— 33 —

The Sequel to the Attempted Invasion

The arrival of the French fleet caused great anxiety in Ireland, especially in the south. Those charged with maintaining the fabric of government, such as the military and political appointees of the Crown, had cause to worry. The threat of an invasion alone was enough to paralyse the meagre finances of the nation. As soon as the news of the arrival of the French had reached Dublin there was a general run on the money-market, as many people withdrew their deposits and called in debts. Camden, the then Lord Lieutenant of Ireland, wrote to Pitt requesting financial assistance to cover the costs of increasing the armed forces and the building of defences against a further invasion.

General Dalrymple, who was in charge of the Cork garrison, wrote in his many dispatches that 'at Bantry Bay, in particular, something must be done [proper fortifications], its vicinity to Cork, its ease of approach will ever make it an alluring feature'. One of the results of this statement was the building of the fortifications (batteries) on Bere, Garnish and Whiddy Islands some years later.

An interesting letter written by the Lord Lieutenant of Ireland to the Duke of Portland, dated 10 January, Dublin Castle, and printed in the *London Gazette*, contains the following excerpt:

> Many prominent examples of individual loyalty and spirit have appeared. A useful impression was made upon the minds of the lower Catholics by a judicious address from Dr. Moylan, Titular Bishop of Cork. I cannot but notice the exertions of Lord Kenmare who spared no expense in giving assistance to the Commanding Officer in his neighbourhood and who had taken into his demesne a great quantity of cattle which had been driven from the whole coast.

All cattle from the Bantry Bay region had been driven to the interior, so as to deprive the French of meat supplies.

As for Richard White, who had put his house at the disposal of the Generals Dalrymple and Eyre Coote and had extended every hospitality, a letter of gratitude from Eyre Coote gives us some interesting details:

> My dear White,
>
> Colonel Blake will deliver to you the forty guineas you were so obliging to lend us (during our stay). I cannot inform you how much obliged I am to you for all your kindness—venison, hares, woodcocks, scallops, oysters, and what not.
>
> God bless you, most affectionately yours,
>
> *Eyre Coote*

It is surprising that there is no mention of the wine cellar, which, being well-stocked and very valuable, was a cause of deep concern to Richard White. In fact, he stationed a section of his yeomanry to protect it at all costs if the French landed.

The failure of the French in Bantry Bay did not put an end to Hoche and Tone's obsession with freeing the country from English rule. 'It was a business that the Republic would never give up' Hoche stated to Tone. However, another expedition to Ireland was postponed for the time being. Hoche was appointed commander-in-chief of the army and Tone joined him as his foreign correspondent.

Meanwhile, in Ireland, the awakening of the revolutionary spirit spread southward from Ulster to Munster where a state of anarchy prevailed. Tithes were not paid and notices appeared everywhere exhorting tenants not to pay rents. Those who conformed to the law had their cattle killed and their crops and barns burned. Conspiracies abounded to murder the landlords. Even in Bandon there was a plot formed amongst the inhabitants to rise against the armed forces. The soldiers were to be seduced and General Eyre Coote was to be murdered.

Two year later, O'Connor, one of the leaders of the United Irishmen, was arrested at Margate in Kent on his way to France. He was sent to Dublin as a state prisoner. The other principal leaders, betrayed by Tone's brother-in-law Reynolds, were arrested in Dublin. Lord Edward Fitzgerald, on the run with a price of one thousand guineas on his head, was betrayed by the Catholic barrister Francis Magan, captured after a skirmish and later died of his wounds.

Notwithstanding these events, the rebellion of 1798 went ahead. Without its leaders it completely lacked cohesion and was soon brought under control, but not without atrocities taking place on both sides, fuelled by religious and social animosities. Cruelty reached a degree scarcely paralleled in later history. Murder, house-burning and floggings were widespread. The militia were completely out of control and scoured the countryside with the hangman's rope and the cat-of-nine-tails. The people of the countryside feared for their lives. The slaughter of 350 insurgents at Vinegar Hill still serves as a reminder for those who abhor man's inhumanity to man.

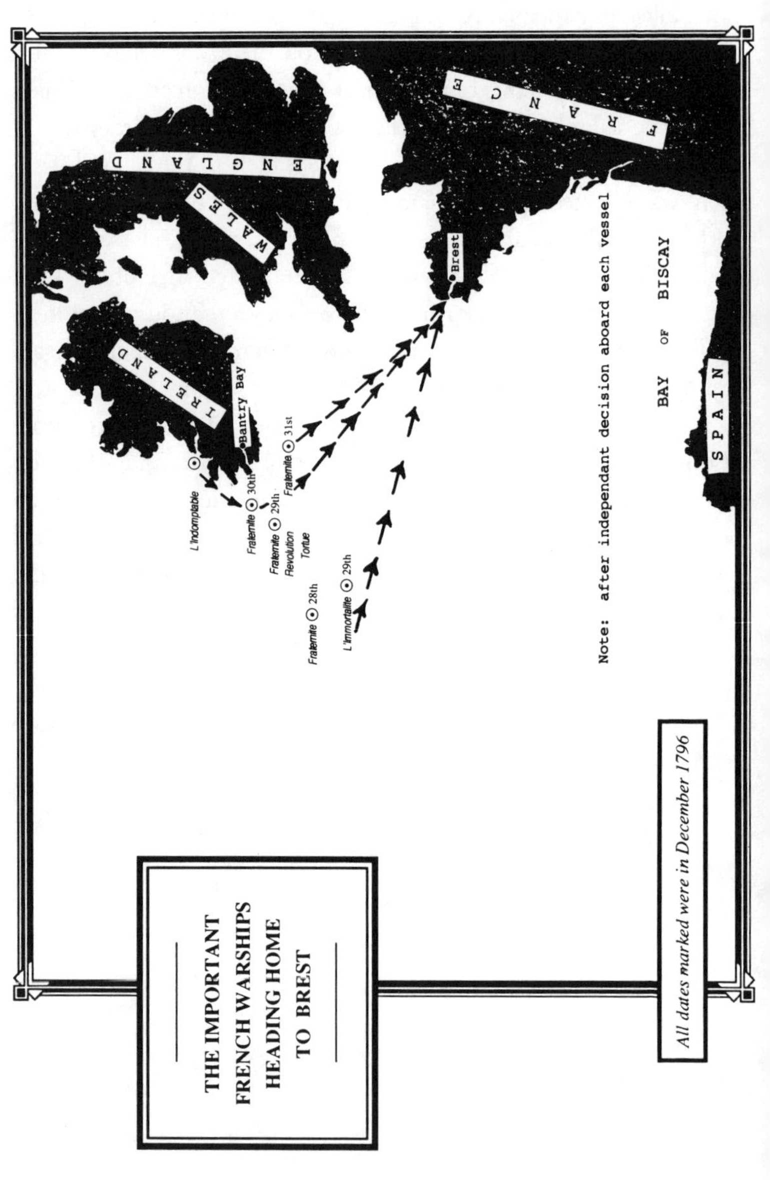
THE IMPORTANT FRENCH WARSHIPS HEADING HOME TO BREST
All dates marked were in December 1796
Note: after independant decision aboard each vessel
IRELAND
Bantry Bay
WALES
ENGLAND
FRANCE
Brest
BAY OF BISCAY
SPAIN
L'Indomptable
Fraternite 30th
Fraternite 29th
Revolution
Tortue
Fraternite 31st
Fraternite 28th
L'Immortalite 29th

— 34 —

The English Fortification of Bantry Bay

Fearing further invasions by the French after the Wolfe Tone episode, the Admiralty in London decided that proper fortifications should be built on Bere and Whiddy Islands to safeguard the English position in Bantry Bay.

It is believed that work commenced first on the fortifications on Bere Island around 1798. The defensive Martello towers in Corsica served as a blueprint for the construction of four similar towers on the island, at Lonehart, Rerrin, Clochlann Hill and Ardagh Hill. Besides these round towers, an additional square fortification was built at Rinndubh. Situated near each tower was a gun battery. Building stone was shipped from the south of England and Cork and any additional material required was quarried locally.

The fortifications built on Whiddy Island were somewhat different and referred to as 'redoubts'. The western redoubt was built at a suitable location to protect the southern entrance to the harbour, while the eastern one commanded a vantage point to defend the main north channel entrance. The central redoubt was built on the highest point of the island and had a commanding position over the inner harbour itself. Nowadays these redoubts are referred to as the 'gun batteries' of Whiddy Island.

Work commenced on the construction of the batteries on 16 December 1803, under the supervision of English ordnance engineers. The main contractor was a local named O'Mahony and, at the height of the construction, over five hundred men were employed. Carts, horses, mules and all equipment were transferred to the island by either boat or timber raft from the mainland.

The western battery was built on rock, while the sites for the eastern and central batteries had to be excavated manually using hammer and chisel, crowbar and shovel. The rock encountered was mostly shale and slate. On 18 October 1804 the western battery was completed and was described at that time as 'a Martello tower of unusual magnitude constructed at the north-west point of Whiddy Island with an interior diameter of two hundred and forty feet'.

The location of the central battery is most interesting, as it was previously the site of one of the largest forts in the region. Early charts of the inner Bay indicate that this fort had occupied an area larger than the perimeter of the present battery and was surrounded by two large circular mounds on the hillside.

The excavation of the sites was carried out by the descending spiral method. Most of the materials were dumped on the northern slopes. While the excavation continued, large timber rafts were built ashore and these, in addition to a number of small luggers, were used to transport the cut stone from a shoreline stone quarry at Ardnamanagh to the stone slipway at Croangle. The large stones were then transported by carts pulled by teams of six to eight mules or horses to the construction sites. When the outer and inner walls of the moats were completed, the centre was then filled in, with the exception of a stone-walled well which was built off-centre to catch and store rainwater for the occupants. On the inner walls, raised platforms suitable for gun mountings were incorporated at strategic locations.

The central battery was the main base, so officers' quarters, soldiers' barracks, warehouses, a cannon and shot armoury and a gunpowder store were built. These were mostly constructed of imported red brick in archway style and can be seen to this day. Eighteen cannons, ball and gunpowder were first shipped from Plymouth to Cork and then to Bantry on a ship of the line.

With the completion of the central battery and the installation of six large guns, a force of seven artillery officers and 188 soldiers were transferred from the Queenstown (Cork) barracks. An additional timber structure had to be built adjacent to the battery on the south-east slope to alleviate the cramped quarters of the soldiers. This building also housed some of the company's horses. On 29 December 1804 it burnt down, resulting in the loss of twenty-four horses which were trapped inside.

Some months later, a decision was made in London to withdraw the defence force on the island, and the batteries were left in the hands of a local English merchant called Iremonger who in turn employed three local brothers called Murphy to look after the batteries. About a year later, as the batteries were no longer regarded as strategic, only one man was employed as a caretaker for all three, and his job continued until 1807. Shortly after Napoleon's escape from Elba in 1814, the English decided to build a Martello tower on Garnish Island. It was more for show than for actual defence of the Glengarriff harbour, as it was only manned by one officer and ten soldiers, plus a single small cannon. It was eventually closed in 1825.

Accepting that Bere Island and Berehaven harbour provided the most strategic location on the Irish coast for their continuous domination of the western approaches, the British naval authorities began to move in their forces early in 1890. However, it was not until the arrival of the 'dreadnoughts' on the scene of sea warfare that the British War Department examined the defences of Bantry Bay and came to the conclusion that Berehaven harbour had to be properly protected while its fleet lay at anchor. As the dreadnoughts required more than thirty hours for their boilers to raise enough steam for any engine movement, they were defenceless against sea attack while at anchor.

The year 1898 saw the creation of a fortified naval base in Berehaven harbour, after the compulsory purchase order of 17 March 1898 and the eviction of tenants from the sites marked out for the defensive artillery bases. During the period 1898 to 1911, the six main gun batteries were built and the large guns were brought by ship from Spike Island (Queenstown) and off-loaded at Laurence's Cove at the eastern end of Bere Island. Five hundred men were employed during certain periods of the construction.

— 35 —

Famine in the Bantry Region

Before we recount the events of the famine in this area, we will first have to examine the overall background in Ireland leading up to this period.

In 1829 'high farming' was introduced into Ireland by the English. This was a system which changed the Irish landscape from smallholdings of a few acres, which sustained the majority of those who lived in the countryside, to large farms of wide open spaces for the cultivation of grain and substantial herds of cattle. Nearly all landowners, both large and small, endeavoured to take advantage of this change in land use. In order to rid themselves of small tenants, cottiers and so forth, they contracted with shipping agents and companies for passage to the Americas for these unfortunates, on a 'lump sum' basis (passage only).

During 1844, the Poor Laws were in operation, whereby all those, rich or poor, who had a roof over their heads, had to pay a tax for the relief of those less well-off. The Devon Commission decided that the only way to get rid of the Irish peasantry was by emigration, 'peculiarly applicable as a remedial measure'. To accomplish this, the Commission decided on the consolidation of all farms over eight acres. This proposal aimed to 'rid' the country of over one million Irish.

Even though the Irish harvest of 1845 was one of the best on record, it was nearly all exported to Britain, and no notice was taken by the authorities of the reappearance of the dreaded potato blight. A few 'experts' came over from England to examine the situation and reported back that it was 'nothing to worry about'. When questions were asked in Parliament some two months later about the seriousness of the situation and the plight of the starving masses in the countryside, the government of the day pretended to be surprised at the arrival of the famine. It is interesting to note that, even at this stage, the official numbers recorded of those who had died of starvation and famine had been 'doctored', and only represented less than one tenth of actual numbers.

In June 1846, Peel introduced the Coercion Bill for Ireland. This involved an imposition of a curfew, from sunset to sunrise, on the population, and anybody found outdoors during this period was considered to have broken the law, and was therefore liable to transportation for a period of fifteen years, or else three years in prison. In this context, we must remember that up to forty per cent of those living in the countryside were now living on the sides of the road.

Then came the repeal of the Corn Laws, which allowed grain to be imported to Britain from all other countries. This automatically lowered prices, and the Irish farmers felt the brunt of derisory prices for their products. As the bottom fell out of the market, the English buyers and shippers made 'a killing on the market' by shipping out the cheap grain to an English port, transferring it to another vessel and bringing it back again to Ireland, and with the assistance of a subsidy, selling it at the highest price possible to the starving thousands. It is estimated that over £8 million worth of grain was exported to Britain at this time.

To relieve the poor in Ireland, Parliament granted the sum of £50,000, an amount equal to that given to the British Museum in London at the same time. The money was to be used for 'public works' (any work which was unproductive, like building a road to nowhere) and had to be paid back by a levy on all landowners, including the lowliest tenant. To supervise the distribution of this grant, up to 10,000 civil servants, taken from the ranks of the English classes in Ireland, were recruited. Very little money, therefore, found its way to alleviating the poor by providing employment which would provide cash to purchase the basic, and overpriced, foodstuff for survival. With a change of government in England, the Coercion Bill was defeated on 25 May 1846. However, the gross disinformation on the exact numbers of deaths continued, so as not to alarm the English public at the horror on their doorstep.

What followed is almost unbelievable to us in this day and age. Parliament introduced a Relief Act, then a Labour Rate Act for public works, both of which were to be funded by the very people they was supposed to assist, i.e. the starving masses. In the countryside there were additional public works commissions and more salaried civil servants—in fact there were more people administering the various relief schemes than workers who benefited. Extermination or emigration was the motto of the day.

The poor starving farmer had few options, with the bailiff and his henchmen knocking at the door of his little cabin even before the harvest was brought in. Then there were public works, the Relief and Labour Rate Acts, the 'county cess' collectors, and, finally, the Preserver with Decrees, all to be paid out of his meagre income. If he sold his land, he would be considered homeless, and liable to transportation with his family. So he, like many others, had little option but to slave on, and finally perish from starvation in his bothan.

Matters got worse still during 1847. Those who managed to become employed on public works and had any possessions (i.e. land) were immediately dismissed, so many of these had to sell their farms to get work and money to buy essential food. Yet, when these works were purposely terminated, at short notice or otherwise, the labourer was then considered homeless and liable for transportation. In other words, there was no solution to his problem—either starve or be transported.

Finally, as the charity food began to trickle into the Irish ports, it was automatically stored or distributed by the agents of the English government, and very little of it reached the hungry, as it was sold on the open market at exorbitant prices.

Having explained the general situation in Ireland up to and during the early part of the famine, let us return to the Bantry region. At this time, Bantry was a very prosperous town enjoying a lucrative sea trade, fisheries, grain production, livestock production and commerce. The population of the town, despite the dire housing problems, was increasing drastically, with people sleeping in the streets, hovels, yards, sheds and barns.

The failure of the potato crop was devastating for the small farmer, who either held his small plot of ground by short lease, or by no lease at all. He existed either on potato, milk or crushed oats. He could not avail of his crops, which were grown to cover his rent, and he could not slaughter his cows, as he would then have no milk. As the farmer became weaker due to lack of food, he was unable to provide the landlord with his labour, and was therefore thrown off the holding and left by the side of the road with his family.

With nothing to eat, the only alternatives were to seek food and shelter in the nearest town, Bantry, or else die on the roadside. As a last resort there was the new workhouse, but one had to be destitute and penniless to be admitted. No matter how sick and hungry the people were, they were loathe to seek refuge there, both from a sense of personal pride and also a hatred of being called destitute. Instead, the people wandered around the town begging for food and refuge, with many of them dying on the streets and byways, and in old vacated hovels.

The workhouse itself was built in 1845, and could accommodate about six hundred people. It was funded by the Poor Law rates which were levied on all buildings and lands within the Bantry Union. This covered the area from Dursey Island to Sheep's Head in the south, and had a population of approximately 50,000. The next nearest workhouse was in Skibbereen. A Board of Guardians for the workhouse was elected from the landowners and prominent, mostly English, businessmen. This board consisted of: J. W. Payne (Lord Bantry's agent), Arthur Hutchinson (Ardnagashel Manor), William Pierson (civil engineer), George Bird (lawyer and part agent for Lords Bantry, Castletownbere and Bandon), Richard White (Coomhola Lodge), Richard O'Donovan (fish exporter), Timothy Murphy (brewery owner), Arthur Hutchins (landlord of Ardnagashel), William Vickery (innowner), Robert Warner (merchant), Michael Murphy (mill-owner), Samuel Hutchins (landowner), Patrick O'Sullivan (landowner at Ballylickey) and James Downey (merchant). The clerk was Henry Spencer and the medical officer Thomas Tisdall of Donemark. The official in charge of the workhouse was Mr. Roberts, whose wife acted as matron. During this time the Catholic chaplain was the Revd. T. Barry, whilst the Protestant minister was a Revd. B. Halliwell.

Admissions to the workhouse were slow up until August 1846, but, with the potato crop failing for the second consecutive season, matters took a sudden turn for the worse. In August there were about two hundred people in the workhouse, but the numbers grew rapidly as more and more people came in from the countryside, reaching nine hundred by the end of that November. As trade and commerce within the town and surrounding area began to decline, the money collected to run the workhouse diminished. The Board of Guardians found themselves in a serious quandary when the bank in Skibbereen would not honour their cheques, and it was only the generosity of some of the Guardians and other charitable people that enabled the workhouse to stay open.

As the steady stream of starving families filled the approach roads to Bantry from every direction, the town authorities decided that in order to prevent a mass influx of destitute people bringing fever and typhus into the town, various 'soup kitchens' would be introduced, both as a means of feeding the needy and also of keeping the afflicted out of the town. Even these meagre sources of food were brought under English law with the 'Rules for the Establishment of Soup Kitchens', dated 31 September 1846, whereby those who subscribed the sum of 1s 9d (8p) per month were issued with tickets entitling the holder to two pints of soup per day. These soup kitchens were located at vantage points on the main access routes into the town:

1. Near the present West Lodge Hotel, for those coming from Muintir mBaire, Durrus, Colomane, Caheragh and the Skibbereen direction.
2. At Newtown, near the present Wagner factory, for those coming from the north, which would include Kealkil, Coomhola, Glengarriff, Adrigole, Castletownbere and even Kenmare.
3. Near the present schools at the Black Bridge for those making their approach from Drimoleague, Castledonovan and lands to the east.

Other minor soup kitchens were also set up by the Board of Works near Dunmanus Castle, Caheragh, Durrus, Drimoleague and Ballydehob, but these were unable to cope with the vast numbers seeking relief, and the people soon had no option but to journey further to the now overflowing workhouse at Skibbereen, or else head for Bantry.

Lord Berehaven, heir to the Earl of Bantry, gave £20 in October 1846 towards the soup kitchens in his domain, while the Hutchins families of Ardnagashel set up and financed their own soup kitchen. To alleviate the hardship in the countryside, and to give the poor and starving paid employment by which food could be purchased (albeit at a price), the Labour Relief Act, through session in Bantry, granted the sum of £3,540 to the barony of Bantry in November 1846. This sum was spent on drainage on the estate of the Earl of Bantry—the filling-in of the Square, from the courthouse to opposite the Church of Ireland gates—roadworks at Kilnavanig, Cappanaloha, Kilmacomoge, Borlin, Keimaneagh, and a section of the road from the present West Lodge Hotel to Rooska.

Towards the end of that month the Poor Law Rates were not bringing in enough money to purchase food for the workhouse, and traders refused to give credit. The population within the gates had by this time risen to nine hundred people—one can only imagine the terrible sight within its walls. Disease also began to spread at this time, with serious outbreaks of fever, typhus, dysentery, diarrhoea and cholera. These diseases broke out even within the walls of the workhouse, which had three deep spring wells within its boundaries. It seems that all the main freshwater wells of the town were contaminated, either by decaying human or animal bodies within, or else by design. Many aspects of the famine in Bantry have been well documented, but I can find no reference to the clearing of water supplies and wells, as cholera was caused by drinking contaminated water.

This was not the first failed potato crop to be experienced in Ireland. One other such period was between 1740 and 1741, when it is estimated that over 400,000 people died. Also, in 1822, the crop failed due to very bad weather, and the potatoes rotted in the ground. It is not known how many died during that year, but death was recorded as being due to typhus and dysentery rather than hunger. The records for 1846 also show that the exportation of corn, beef, butter, pork, hides and so forth was valued at £8 million. There were 127,000 acres under oats, 114,000 under wheat and 44,000 under barley. Over 95% of all wheat and oats were exported to Britain. At this stage, in early 1846, there were an average of twenty deaths per week at the workhouse alone—this figure does not include those who died in the town or vicinity. As starvation increased weekly, a limited amount of food, sent by charitable organisations, began to filter into the various towns, including Bantry, by late February 1846. To protect their market, the local businessmen arranged for the food to be stored in the mill at Donemark, the warehouse on the quay, and the English Market owned by the Earl of Bantry. It was decided that the food was not to be released until all supplies in the area which could be sold commercially had gone, and then, if the need arose, the food would be 'sold' at the market price prevailing at the time. Eventually, a local relief organisation was established, and the food was released and distributed 'at cost' in the early spring.

During the summer of 1846, conditions continued to deteriorate, due mainly to fever and cholera. However, when it became obvious that the potato crop was again going to fail, everyone realised that things were going to become much worse. Those who had returned to sow the land, or who had managed to survive up to now, saw no option but to seek help elsewhere in the towns. The great influx had now begun in earnest. By August, various organisations were set up to meet the situation. The workhouse numbers increased. Streams of destitute people were continuously at the gates, crying out to be admitted.

With conditions deteriorating drastically in the workhouse, and with fever now rampant amongst the inmates, it became impossible for those running the workhouse to do their job, to the extent that some of the female paupers had to be called on to assist the sick and fever-ridden patients. By this time it was almost impossible to locate uncontaminated water, so many patients suffering from fever died of thirst.

To cope with the vast numbers now seeking assistance, a number of annexes to the workhouse were opened by voluntary helpers. These were situated at Main Street and Donemark mills, and there were two on the quayside.

In order to escape the utter destitution in the area, those who were fit enough to make the sea journey to the West Indies or the United States signed on for the outward passage, to make a new beginning with their families on those distant shores. Those who had money paid the going rate—about £3 per person, or £10 per family—which covered the passage only, so those embarking had to bring enough food for the journey.

Those without money who sought passage negotiated with local agents acting on behalf of the ship and plantation owners. Contracts were signed with free passage exchanged for a period of plantation work, which amounted to fifteen years hard labour. This was little less than slavery. It must be remembered that the vast majority of those people seeking passage spoke only Irish. In all probability, they did not understand that when they marked their 'X', they were in fact signing their lives away.

The 'black winter' was now upon the starving people. The workhouse was overflowing, the staff unable to cope. The mortality rate rose to about fifty per week, with dysentery and fever the main causes of death. In January 1847, a fever hospital adjoining the workhouse was opened. It was designed to hold twenty-six patients, but within weeks there were one hundred and twenty people within its cramped confines.

In February 1847, an English representative of the British Relief Association arrived in Bantry and visited the workhouse. He also visited the soup kitchens in the area and arranged a grant of £50 towards the voluntary work of the Hutchins at Ardnagashel.

At this time the workhouse at Skibbereen was overflowing, and the deaths in that town and area were reaching exceptionally high figures. Skibbereen was rapidly becoming the worst affected town in Ireland. With no hope of assistance, the people there began to head for Bantry, which was already the only centre of relief for the population stretching from Dursey Island through to Keimaneagh, Castledonovan and the Durrus and Muintir mBaire area.

As the death toll mounted, the 'hinged coffin' began to be used at the Abbey graveyard. We do not know how many of the Bantry population were buried there, as there is no exact record of how many died during the famine period of 1845 to 1847. It is estimated that the population of Bantry in 1844 was between 5,500 and 7,000, and that the number buried in the famine pits was around 1,500 to 2,000. As nobody knows how many wretched people came in from an area that stretched from Glandore to Dursey Island, it is impossible to give any idea what percentage were Bantry people who perished during the period. As cholera, dysentery and fever were rampant, we cannot estimate how many died from starvation alone. From the available records, it seems that about five per cent to seven and a half per cent of Bantry's population perished.

Souperism

In a present-day re-examination of the Famine, the emotive words 'souper' or 'souperism' bear looking at. Most historians shy away from this particular subject, and say that it was just famine myth, with no basis in actual fact. Yet, although they may be exaggerated through time and retelling, the facts that have been handed down contain some indication of past reality. It is undeniable that there were those ultra-Protestant proselytisers who tried to take advantage of the terrible circumstances of the poor by offering them soup on the condition that they would renounce their Catholic faith and convert to Protestantism—in the hope of initiating a 'Second Reformation' in Ireland.

There are many references to souperism in Connaught—especially Galway, Mayo and Sligo—and closer to hand on the Dingle peninsula, but little is recorded concerning West Cork and the Bantry region. There are a number of minor references, giving a limited view of what actually occurred, and, with limited documented evidence, I shall try to give a brief description of what happened.

Seeing that the poor were in terrible distress, there was an influx of Bible societies into Ireland. Having mastered the Irish language, they went into the countryside preaching. The main theme of their teaching was piety and resignation to the will of God. Since they used food and soup as an enticement to attend their meetings, many of the destitute attended. Because of the guarantee of receiving something to eat, some people then joined these Biblical societies. When there were a substantial number of converts, small religious ghettos, which fell under the protection of Evangelical churchmen, were established in the countryside. It was not until the arrival of the fanatical Scripture Readers of the English Ladies' Auxiliary Society that the clerics of the Catholic and the Established Church took notice, as civil unrest began to manifest itself amongst their respective congregations. The clergy had little time to contend with this wave of proselytism in their midst, trying as they were to cope with the distress of their flocks in the time of famine. They also did not have the time to admonish those who took it upon themselves to carry out vendettas against the 'jumpers', as they were called.

We do not know if the Irish Society of Evangelists had a person in charge in Bantry itself, but they did have a superintendent in Castletownbere in 1849. While the local clergy, both Catholic and Protestant, did all they could for the starving masses at their doors, even by going short of food themselves, the superintendent had a more than adequate supply to keep his soup kitchen going. We have no record of those who changed religion in the region, but, up to recent times, certain families were still referred to as 'turncoats'—a local equivalent of 'jumpers'.

It was not only the enticement of the soup kitchens which made some individuals and families change religion at this time. The role of the various Bible societies in places of authority—like the English and Irish parliaments—in obtaining independent funding and influence over who could get work, under the Poor Law Act, in the areas where they had colonies, was also a great inducement to change religion.

To relieve the starving, and to give the menfolk the opportunity to work, whereby they could earn some money to purchase food, certain works were designated for each area. Here in Bantry, the works commissioned were the filling in of the Square, rebuilding the Glebe walls of Bantry House, and the construction of the road from the docks to the Abbey. However, they were strictly under the control of the English nominated civil servants, and work was not given on a first come first served basis, but only to those who had influence, such as being of the 'correct' denomination, or who had converted to one of the societies. With no sign of improvement in the situation in the country, and the 'black spring' approaching, the English government passed a temporary Bill (10 Victoria c7), better known as the Soup

Kitchen Act, which became law in February 1847, under which food was to be provided directly to the starving people by government-sponsored soup kitchens. However, local authorities were slow to implement this new legislation, as they found it difficult to find willing helpers to man these kitchens, which attracted the starving, the fever-stricken cholera carriers and dying people. With the Catholic clergy fully occupied with bringing the 'last rites' to the dying all over the countryside, it was left to the local rector, or parson, as well as to members of the societies, to organise the soup kitchens with any help they could get from their own congregations. Finally, it must be said that the Protestant rector, Alex Hallowell, and his parishioners did give what monetary assistance they could to purchase food, also helping the starving and assisting at the official soup kitchens. Father Barry, who more often than not went to bed hungry, and his dedicated band of followers also did everything they possibly could under circumstances of great hardship.

The Voice of the Poor

Was sorrow ever like to our sorrow?
Oh, God above!
Will our night never change into a morrow
Of joy and love?
A deadly gloom is on us waking, sleeping,
Like the darkness at noontide
That fell upon the pallid mother weeping
By the Crucified.

Before us die our brothers of starvation;
Around are cries of famine and despair;
Where is hope for us, or comfort, or salvation—
Where—oh! where?
If the angels ever hearken, downward bending,
They are weeping, we are sure,
At the litanies of human groans ascending
From the crush'd hearts of the poor.

We never knew a childhood's mirth and gladness,
Nor the proud heart of youth, free and brave;
Oh a deathlike dream of wretchedness and sadness,
Is life's weary journey to the grave.
Day by day we lower sink and lower,
Till the Godlike soul within,
Falls crushed, beneath the fearful demon power
Of poverty and sin.

So we toil on, on with fever burning
In heart and brain;
So we toil on, on through bitter scorning,
Want, woe and pain;
We dare not raise our eyes to the blue Heaven,
Or the toil must cease—
We dare not breathe the fresh air God has given
One hour in peace.

We must toil, though the light of life is burning,
Oh, how dim!
We must toil on in sickenss, feebly turning
Our eyes to Him,
Who alone can hear the pale lip faintly saying,
With scarce moved breath,
While the paler hands, uplifted, aid the praying;
'Lord, grant us Death!'

(Speranza—Lady Wilde)

Part Five

From *c.* 1850 to the Present Day

Chapel and Woollen Mills, Bantry.

– 36 –

The Bantry Fairs

It is interesting to note that the Irish word for fair—*aonach*—also means fury or rage. This, quite possibly, derives from the ancient fairs or 'gatherings' being an occasion not only of commerce, but also of personal, family and tribal rivalry. These ancient fairs were usually held on hill tops or high ground, like the southern area under Curran, Coomhola, where there is a gentle slope and some flat land. The ancient year was divided into two seasons which commenced on 1 May and 1 November, and these were the main dates on which the gatherings were held for the division of land (commonages) and tithes. These dates, on which land tenure is based right up to the present day, were referred to as the Gale Days. Small hamlets or *clochans* grew up at certain vantage points, such as river crossings or crossroads, and trade gradually became concentrated in these locations. So it was that the hamlet of Bantry Creek came to be situated on the south side of what is now Bridge Street. Here, on the high ground behind the clochan was the area known as the Fair Field, where the early trading of sheep, goats, pigs and other animals took place.

It was not until the emergence of Bantry as a real town, and also with the influence of the English settlers, that the location of the fairs was changed to the English Market and the Pound at Market Street. Freeman, on his tour of Ireland, stated that 'the Irish kept to their own fairs', and, in doing so, 'took great custom and profits to the depression of the boroughs and the trading towns' which had been set up by the English. Following many deputations to the English Parliament, an Act was passed in 1431 whereby control of all fairs was passed to local English landlords.

As the town enlarged gradually in its south-eastern corner—the area between the present Chapel Street and Market Street down to Vickery's Inn—the fairs took to the streets, lanes and pathways, until the mill river was covered in as far as the courthouse. Then, when the present Square was covered in, that area became the location for one of the major fairs of West Cork, from the latter half of the nineteenth century right up until the late 1950s. Then the introduction of the cattle marts at Skibbereen and Bandon, and the withdrawal of the railway service to Bantry in 1961, sounded the death knell of the famous Bantry Fairs.

Fair day in The Square c. *1892*

Some fairs were of more importance than others during the course of the year. October and November was a critical time for the farmer, with the approach of the long winter months. It was a time to sell his good cattle in order to raise enough money to maintain his family and his remaining livestock through the winter months. May and November were the months of the great cattle fairs in Bantry and the February, March, July and August fairs were mainly dedicated to the sale of horses, sheep, wool and general farm produce.

With the transfer of the fair from the limited space of the English Market to the wide expanse of the Square and surrounding area, the toll and tariff collectors of Bantry House positioned themselves at the main entrances to the town—the West Lodge of Bantry House, Custom's Gap (now the Boston Bar), the Brewery Cross (near the Hospital Cross) and at the Pigeon Loft (across from Whooley's shop on the Glengarriff Road).

Besides all the activity of trading livestock and country produce, the fair was also the occasion for the monthly excursion into town of the country folk, a time for them to renew old acquaintances, meet distant relations and pass on news of important events. Money and coinage was extremely scarce in those early days, so all negotiations were carried out either by barter or by the weight of butter, the main item of trade in those days.

For those living as far afield as Adrigole, Lauragh, Kenmare, Keimaneagh, Drimoleague, Ballydehob and the Mizen peninsula, it was a journey of twenty to thirty miles, so people would start the trek to Bantry on the morning prior to the Fair Day. In fact, most of the cattle drives arrived in town from early afternoon on the preceding day. The sight of a herd of cattle being driven by a farmer and his children in bare feet, while his wife handled the horse or donkey pulling the cart with the younger children covered by rough blankets, was a common one on the approach roads. Loaded on the cart would be the small churn of country butter, baskets of eggs, and wicker creels of chickens, ducks and possibly rabbits. Others arrived with just a young calf, a few sheep, a large sow or boar, or a ram in the creels. From midnight onwards large numbers of the country people began to arrive in town. The noise on the approach roads would gradually increase, until the air was filled with the lowing of cattle, the bleating of sheep and the grind and rattle of carts. The shouting of farmers to their children, or whistling to their dogs could be heard echoing through the narrow streets, as the scrabble for the most advantageous bartering locations in the Square commenced. On finding a suitable spot, the animals were gathered together into a small space while the cart was unloaded and the goods for sale were displayed. Small fires were lit with a bit of dry kindling, and cans of water were boiled to make tea for those that could afford it. Others just drank buttermilk and ate some brown cake brought with them for the journey.

By 5.30 a.m. the hotels and eating houses were already opened and serving food. The pubs normally opened at 7.30 a.m. but the back doors were always left ajar from much earlier. The blacksmiths and saddlers would already be at work, to take advantage of the early morning trade. It might be worth recalling that at the turn of the century there were seven hotels, about twenty eating houses, fifty-two pubs, eight blacksmiths and three large tanneries in the locality.

At dawn, the Square and adjoining streets would be full and the town alive with people. Buyers and farmers haggled over prices until the deal was confirmed with a slap of hands. No deal was completed without the question of 'luck-money', which was usually agreed by a slap on the back or a tap on a child's head. The townspeople descended on the Square in droves to purchase butter, fowl, fresh eggs, vegetables and 'bastible' cakes, which were cakes baked in an iron pot (known as a bastible) over a fire. A long line of meat stalls extended down Main Street, the fish hawkers would be in their usual places on New Street, between Vickery's Hotel and the Bridewell Lane. Sides of bacon, pig's legs (crubeens) and heads were displayed outside Crowley's, Seano's and Warner's shops.

Bantry Fair always seemed to be damned by rain and bad weather. This was sometimes ascribed to the time when these gatherings or patterns were banned by the local Catholic clergy, sometime around 1855, as occasions of 'profanities, fights and lewd pagan customs'.

There were those who came to town and spent their mornings in the pubs drinking spirits and pints of stout on an empty stomach, and by 11.00 a.m. they would emerge onto the streets arguing and fighting. This was an extension of the old 'faction fighting' where, on occasions, whole families fought with stones and blackthorn sticks over some old inter-family dispute.

With the introduction of the railway, most of the livestock was shipped out by cattle wagons, with train loads departing nearly every hour from noon onwards. It has been estimated, though not officially recorded, that up to one thousand cattle were dispatched in this way on the main Fair Days of August and September. The agents of Bantry House stood on the roadside outside the Terminus Hotel and all levies were paid in cash before the cattle were allowed through to the Station yard. By early afternoon, most of the trading had been completed and it was time to make smaller purchases at the stalls or local shops. Amusements began on the streets, while occasionally a circus visit coincided with the Fair Day. By 4.00 p.m. the Square and streets began to empty as the country folk left for home. As the last train departed around 7.00 p.m. the town was deserted, except for some stray animals, lost dogs and a few drunks lying in a stupor on the pavements or streets.

Those days are now gone and almost forgotten, and have been temporarily replaced by the spectacle of hawkers of all nationalities selling their wares on the first Friday of every month.

Fair Day in Bantry

— 37 —

Recent Festivals and Customs

Many of the old customs and festivals are disappearing nowadays. Unless they are written down for the enlightenment of future generations they will be lost.

In a preceding chapter, I explained the old druid customs and traditions. In the following pages I will record some of the local customs and festivals which existed up until the late 1950s. These contain a mixture of old druidic and early Christian practices.

There were two methods of dividing the year into four seasons, one which consisted of the 'true quarters of the year', and the other which was called the 'crooked quarters of the year'.

The True Quarters

A quarter from Lunasa to Samhain
A quarter from Samhain to St. Bridget's Day
A quarter from St. Bridget's Day to Bealthaine
A quarter from Bealthaine to Lunasa

The Crooked Quarters

A quarter from St. John's Day to St. Michael's Day
A quarter from St. Michael's Day to Christmas
A quarter from Christmas to St. Patrick's Day
A quarter from St. Patrick's Day to St. John's Day

The true quarters are derived from the ancient druidic calendar year, while the crooked quarters represent the Christian calendar of the feasts of the important saints in these islands.

The following examples are a few of those which come to mind.

Lá Coille'—1 January

Children would be up and about early in the morning so that they could ask the first person they saw, other than family, for a New Year's gift, such as a brass coin—a halfpenny or maybe even a penny.

The Brideóg—1 February

On St. Bridget's eve, children were accustomed to go from house to house with their faces blackened with soot. One of the young girls would hold a straw doll in her arms. In olden times this straw doll had a dress of oat-straw with a binding string around the waist, a similarly made jacket and a peak cap made of straw on its head. When the group entered a house, the woman of the house would approach the straw doll and stick a pin in Brideog's chest. Then the children would start singing and dancing, and if the woman was satisfied she would give them a present of some kind. As St. Bridget's Day replaced an ancient druid feast-day, it is quite possible that it came from deepest Africa, where the ancient Voodoo religion was first practised. The custom of young girls going from house to house around the town with a doll in their arms and asking for 'a penny for the Biddy' was still in practice right up to 1954 in Bantry town.

St. Bridget's Cross

On the days and nights leading up to St. Bridget's Day, many hours were spent in each household making St. Bridget's (or St. Brigid's) crosses for the neighbours. They were given by one family to another as a good luck charm, and were usually kept tied up to the rafters, over the fire, or under the thatch. They were supposed to protect the house from fire, accident or sickness. This type of cross had its origins in ancient pre-druid culture (originating in Hindustan), and belief in its good luck could not be obliterated from the minds of the early Christians.

St. Patrick's Day—17 March

Before the introduction of the custom of wearing a sprig of shamrock on a dress or lapel and a green badge in honour of St. Patrick's Day, the custom in the not too distant past was that little girls wore a multi-coloured cloth cross on their right arm. The boys, men and older women wore fire-blackened sally (willow) twigs in the shape of the cross on their right arm. Doubtless this custom was to remind people that, even though St. Patrick's Day was a day of celebration, Lent was still in force. This practice was more likely to be found in the countryside.

Good Friday

The practice of visiting the graveyards to pray for the departed was, and still is, widespread throughout the country—including visiting the old Cillineach (children's unconsecrated graveyards). As for the custom of eating fish, there were many variants, especially of not eating freshly caught fish, but using the salted ling, cod or haddock which had been preserved in the shed or outhouse. If salt fish was not available, people would go to the beaches and rocks to collect periwinkles, clams and limpets to make a shellfish soup.

May Day—1 May

On the eve of May Day, children went out to collect green leaves. When the sun had set, these sprigs of green were tied to the doorknob or handle of every house to signal the arrival of summer. In the countryside, the same custom of collecting the green sprigs before dawn was followed. It did not really matter what kind of sprig was collected—often it was bog myrtle, hazel, ash or holly, but 'ash and hazel' were considered more lucky. These sprigs were left under the eaves or thatch until the following year.

St. John's Eve—23 June

This was a reminder ofone of the old pagan customs. On this night bonfires were lit in every clochan, village or town. It was a night of celebration, with music, dancing and merriment. In olden times the old women said the Rosary at the bonfire and took a dead ember home for luck before the festivities commenced.

St. Stephen's Day—26 December

This was the day when the Wrenboys called to the local houses with a dead wren hanging from a long stick with a green branch on top. The bird had coloured ribbons around its neck. As these groups made their way through the countryside, they played music and sang the Wren's Song, of which there are as many versions as there are parishes in the country. The basis of such a practice is not really known, except for an account where a wren tapped a drum with its beak and alerted the Cromwellian forces of an ambush. After the resulting massacre of the Irish forces by the English, the wren was considered to be a bird of ill omen.

Shrove Tuesday—Skelligs Night

Marriage was prohibited on the mainland during Lent, so many young couples took the opportunity to avail of the ceremony on Skellig Island. The old calendar was still followed on the island—the time difference was about ten days.

As Shrove Tuesday approached, one of two methods of conveying the message that it was time to make a decision was followed.

One was the 'listing', a type of comical matchmaking, whereby some of the local wits would draw up a list of the most incompatible bachelors and spinsters in the area, and post it on the doors of local grocery stores and pubs in the morning.

The second was when groups of young boys would pull a collection of old pots, pans, buckets and an old bath around the town with fires burning, on Shrove Tuesday night, to alert any young couples who had considered going to the Skelligs to get married.

Faction Fighting

Faction fighting attained a degree of notoriety in certain parts of West Cork, especially around Drimoleague, Enniskeane, Ballygurteen, Ballinhassig, Cahermeen, Gougane Barra and Ballydehob. These bloody events frequently ended in death for the participants. Faction fighting was well documented in both the English and local press of the day, as well as by historians and travellers.

I have been unable to locate any serious reference to faction fighting in the Bantry region, but no doubt it did take place, as the conditions for these occasions did in fact exist during this turbulent period of Irish history, between 1775 and 1840. Even as late as the early 1940s, I can recollect minor skirmishes between groups of men brandishing blackthorn sticks, on the Square on Fair Days.

Faction fighting was, in a sense, a way of life. Sometimes it was 'just for the hell of it', but more often than not it had more serious root causes. The most likely of these would be long-standing grievances between families and their kin. This 'bad blood' between families could usually be traced to the purchase, sale or letting of land, where the opposing family had in the past held some tithe on the property concerned and had been dispossessed. Regardless of this fact, they were still of the opinion that they should have a say or some participation in any deal.

Another cause of the fighting could be when an arranged marriage fell through due to the withdrawal of either party over the agreed allotment of livestock, money and rights of residence. It was usually on the male side that a decision against the size of the dowry was made, leading to the marriage being called off. In these circumstances, the family of the prospective bride were normally incensed, as it was likely that the girl's marriage prospects would be damaged irrevocably and she would end up as a spinster.

The people of the time regarded the exercise of the law as futile, especially regarding disputes over lands or marriage, so they preferred to settle their differences in their own fashion—usually with sticks and stones. This system of settling local disputes and family grievances owes its origins to events of earlier times, such as the tradition of cattle raids and the emergence of secret organisations. The 'Whiteboys', so called because they wore white tunics over their clothes, first evolved in Country Tipperary as a type of Robin Hood band whose main object was to ease the economic difficulties of the peasants and to protect them from the whims and brutality of the landlords. From 1760 this type of protectionism spread southwards to Cork and Kerry. One of the main strongholds of the Whiteboys in this region was the area between Kealkil, Borlin and Kilgarvan. However, as the main objective of the Whiteboys changed to self-gratification by robbing and terrorising the poor as well as the rich, local support waned and eventually disappeared.

We must also remember that during this period, from 1760 to the 1830s, the state of the country was such that it was continuously preparing for invasion or uprisings. The countryside was alive with young men marching and preparing for battle. Due to the lack of arms, they used staffs, long branches and smaller blackthorn sticks with knobs on the end, in place of 'real' weapons. In some localities they were even trained in the proper and most effective use of these temporary weapons. Hence, when local rival families engaged in battle, there were many young men well versed in the most deadly use of the ordinary stick.

The main occasions on which the rival families came into direct contact and conflict were the summer fairs, the religious celebrations at holy wells, or at the patterns (open-air dances).

The June fair was the time when inter-family hostility was most likely to come to a head. The day was usually fine, and by late afternoon when business had been completed the farmers, their families and helpers retired to the local pubs to 'wet their whistles'. Having fasted since dawn, a few drinks took immediate effect and in no time tempers became frayed and insults began to fly. Soon, the rival families were on the streets, with the men flaying one another with blackthorn sticks and the women and children throwing stones. Sometimes the local police intervened, but more often than not they let the fighting continue until the bloody combatants called a victory or truce.

The increasing frequency of civil unrest, drunkenness and debauchery at these events eventually forced Dr. Murphy, titular Bishop of Cork, to forbid any festivities at these events. This ban appears to have been a result of riots which took place at Gougane Barra in September 1818 preventing religious celebrations from being completed.

It was chiefly the work of Daniel O'Connell and the clergy preaching from the altar that brought an end to faction fighting. The temperance movement, the Great Famine, and finally the Land League movement in the 1880s were other factors which led to its demise.

The expression that there is 'black blood' between certain families can still be heard in local conversation. Memories die hard in rural areas, especially those of unfair land deals or evictions, or when some poor girl was sadly 'done by'. During my researches I have often been amazed to discover that local or family animosity owes its origins to events which took place decades or even centuries ago.

Many writers, Anglo-Irish as well as Irish, made reference to faction fighting, including our own T. D. O'Sullivan in his famous lines:

> We've seen the wedding and the wake,
> The pattern and the fair;
> The stuff they take
> And the heads they break,
> And the fun they make down there.

(from the ballad: 'Ireland, Boys Hurrah')

Patrick O'Donnell, in his book *The Irish Faction Fighters*, suggests that the fighting derived from the influence of 'long-tailed families' (those with many relations) rather than any specific motive. Notable among these local families were those with old clan names, such as the O'Sullivans, Walshes, Neills, O'Donovans, Crowleys and Sweeneys.

– 38 –
Emigration

Little is known about the emigration of the Irish to the colonies of the West Indies and the United States during the early 1600s. However, as ships departing from Liverpool, Bristol and London called into the Irish seaports of Youghal, Cork, Kinsale, Baltimore, Castletownbere and Dingle for fresh supplies of provisions, it is quite likely that some Irish did join the vessels, either as crew or as working passengers on the outward journey.

Looking back over the available records, we find a Sir Walter Harcourt obtaining a charter from James I to sail to Guyana in 1609. It is not documented whether he actually called at an Irish port on his outward journey, but on his homeward journey he did encounter some problems in locating Crookhaven for shelter. In 1612, Sir Thomas Roe commenced his expedition to the 'Indian Gates' (West Indies), having on board a number of Irish families who wished to be settlers. There is no record of their surnames, but we do know that he put in at a port on the south-west coast of Cork.

With an increase in shipping to the west during the early part of the seventeenth century, it is certain that many Irish did, in fact, decide to make a new start in the colonies to escape the troubles in Ireland at that time.

From 1615 to 1653 there is little documentation on English vessels calling into Irish ports on the south-west coast. Captain John Vernon, acting for the British merchants Sellick and Leader, offered his services to the Crown to transport Irish children to New England in early 1653. In June, a Colonel Phaire advertised in Irish ports for men to work in the colonies. A sum of fifteen shillings was offered to those who wished to avail of the opportunity. The small print added that each man would be 'free' after four years, having worked off the cost of his passage, clothes and food. Also in that month, a Colonel Stubbers, who was the governor of Galway, tried to organise the transportation of over one thousand Irish from Connaught. There is no evidence as to whether or not he was successful. Meanwhile, Joseph Lawrence, who was a wealthy merchant, obtained a licence from the king to transport the Irish to the 'Canadian Isles'.

In July we find Colonel Phaire trying to organise transportation of some four hundred Irish through the ports of Cork and Kinsale.

Most of the vessels sailed westward from London, with Barbados as their ultimate destination. The English who sailed were those who wished to make a new beginning and included adventurers, sons of wealthy gentlemen, farmers, general craftsmen, potential settlers, and servants. Between 1612 and 1642 these early English emigrants had established the most perfect colonial aristocracy in the Americas. They had brought with them the English common law, and institutions, the system of English parishes and the English Church.

They adopted the cultivation of tobacco, and as this required many workers on the land the demand for labour intensified. The years from 1627 to 1640 are called the 'tobacco age' in Barbados.

In 1627, a Sir William Courteen organised the first real settlement in Barbados. He sent two shiploads of colonists to Barbados under the command of John and Henry Powell. Until this time, various wealthy individuals had organised privately funded expeditions to the West Indies with great financial success. No semblance of law and order was introduced until Courteen's associate, the Duke of Carlisle, had a governor, Henry Hawley, nominated in 1639. He introduced a policy of distribution of land to the settlers. Almost forty thousand acres were granted to about 240 settlers during the period 1628 to 1630. The smallest parcels of land were thirty acres, while the large tracts were distributed in minimum lots of five hundred acres. It is worth noting that 1,000-acre lots were sold for £1,000. Even though the land was cheap, and therefore an incentive to those who wished to journey to the colony, there were major hidden obstacles. The land itself was covered in rainforest, which was extremely difficult to clear. In addition, there was the extreme heat and tropical diseases such as malaria and fever. It appears that only very young people were engaged in clearing the land, as over sixty-five per cent of the inhabitants were under twenty-four years of age—those who had bound themselves to four years' work in the hope of getting about ten acres of land in return. During the 1630s, there were an average of sixteen vessels a year sailing out of London for Barbados and calling into the south-west Irish ports on their outward journey.

From the Barbadian records, we can see that Ireland was a prime source for the supply of servants during this period. In 1636 there is a ship listed as having brought fifty-six Irish men and women from Kinsale. A Thomas Anthony also organised two other trips from Kinsale in the same year. Unable to recruit enough young Irishmen, he signed up more women than he required, assuring the ship-owners that all of these women were 'between seventeen and thirty-five years with very lusty and strong bodies'. Those who survived the voyage were sold as slaves for five hundred pounds of tobacco each.

In 1638 a Thomas Rous lost eighty of his 350 'passengers' during the voyage to Barbados. There were seven more 'convict' ships sailing for Barbados around this period. Because of its poor quality and the importation of the 'Virginia' type taking over the market, the Barbadian tobacco prices dropped on the English market. The planters in Barbados switched, around 1642, to the production of sugar cane, which in just ten years became the boom export. This, in turn, created a greater demand for labourers. The island planters found that their indentured white servants could not cope with the amount of work, and so they negotiated with the privateers to bring in African slaves. Soon the white servants found themselves toiling in field gangs with black slaves.

In the 1640s and '50s, most of the young Irish and English shipped to Barbados were those who had been imprisoned for some misdemeanour—or else were 'Barbadosed' (Shanghaied). There were also many who were shipped out as servants or workmen, such as carpenters, coopers, smiths and masons.

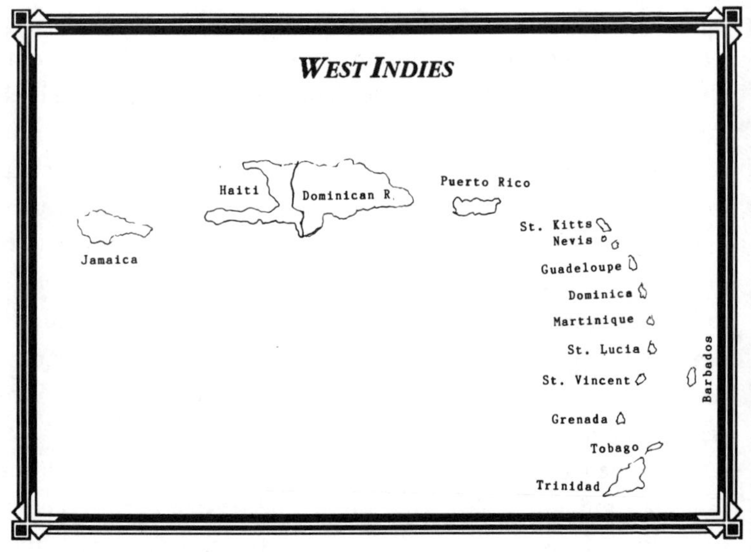

Map of the West Indies

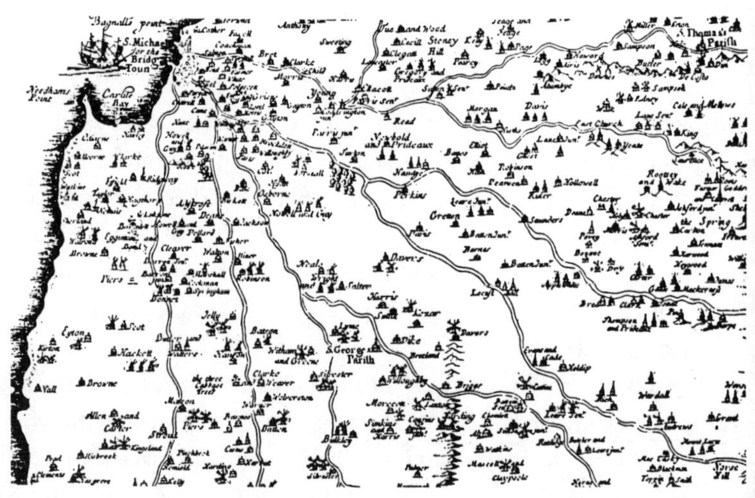

Detail from Richard Ford's New Map of the Islands of Barbadoes *c. 1674*

It was not until the early 1650s that the port of Bristol entered into the sea trade with Barbados and the other islands. Bristol merchants and shipowners kept records of those who joined ships destined for the West Indies and the colonies, but did not record those who joined ship in the southern ports of Ireland.

Meanwhile, Barbados was gaining the reputation among white people as a slave colony, so the numbers leaving from Britain dropped dramatically. Richard Ligon, the historian, puts the population of Barbados at 50,000 whites and 100,000 slaves in 1652. With the influx of black slaves, many of the settlers in Barbados moved to the Leeward Islands of Montserrat and St. Kitts. Included in these numbers were many of the Irish emigrants. In Montserrat alone they constituted over two-thirds of the population.

To Hell or Barbados

The question of the transportation of the Irish to the West Indies and colonies after the Cromwellian conquest of the country is very poorly documented. Initially, it was mostly a clandestine practice operated by London and Bristol slavetraders in collusion with a number of English families who had established themselves in the south-west of Ireland.

Oral tradition here in the south-west of Cork is very strong on the subject, and the phrase 'to Hell or Barbados' supersedes the expression 'to Hell or Connaught'.

While marching south in the early spring of 1650, Cromwell sacked Irish strongholds in east Munster and south Cork. Part of his army marched into West Cork and plundered the area. Those captured were collected at the ports and imprisoned. The prison overflow was shipped off to Barbados on the first available vessel. The going rate for prisoners was equivalent to 1,500 pounds of sugar per man.

During 1654 the transportation of the Irish continued unabated. Not even young people escaped this fate. Orphaned children were rounded up by the soldiers, while children with no father were taken from their mothers. The English government contracted with the Bristol slave merchants for the removal of these Irish to the West Indies and the Americas.

Children were hunted down like animals, forcibly put aboard ships and sold to the shipowners, captains or agents at 21 shillings each for the healthy ones. The young males ended up as slaves in the sugar cane fields, while the females worked in the planters' houses as maids or mistresses. The indentured servants who had gone to the islands voluntarily were paid 10d per day, plus a free house and a plot of land, usually less than half an acre. The house and land were given on condition that the occupier worked for the planter five days a week, nine hours per day. If the servant wanted more land, he had to work extra hours for it, or else deductions would be made from his meagre wages. If these servants did not work the hours demanded, they were thrown off the land.

When many of the Irish found themselves in this position they joined forces, set up little villages on abandoned land and went from one estate to the other in 'jobbing gangs'. In Barbados, law and order was extremely weak, and most plantation houses were like fortified citadels. This breakdown in law and order during these early years was in fact due to the stupidity of the planters, who supplemented wages by a gill (half pint) of rum. Many of the quick-thinking Irish took advantage of this custom and opened 'shebeens' or small shops, where they sold black-market food and liquor. Governor Warner of St. Kitts ordered all Irish Catholics to the island of Montserrat in 1632. An early census of this island contains the following Irish names: O'Sullivan, O'Donovan, Lynch, Gibbons, O'Shea, O'Mahony, O'Callaghan, Murphy, Scully, Shannahan, Sugrue, Croghan, Leahy. There were twenty-two O'Sullivan families, sixteen McCarthys and twelve O'Donovans on the island.

As the demand for black slaves from Africa increased, more and more ships were prepared in England for the trade. These were mostly ex-merchant ships which had their open cargo holds converted into three decks. The bottom section was called the slave deck, and running around the inside of the hull were two further platforms. The average space for an adult slave was 5.5 feet by 1 foot two inches by 2 feet, which meant that the slave could not lie down or change position during his or her incarceration for the long voyage from Africa to the West Indies. The minimum allowance of fresh water was one teacupful every three days, while food was distributed by a specially chosen half-wit in the stinking cesspit of the ship's hold.

The Bristol merchants were the most active in this horrendous trade. Their vessels destined for the West Indies headed to the coast of Cork, where they picked up meat, fish, wheat, flour, water, fresh vegetables, housing timber and transportees. The voyage to the West Indies and back took about two months. Irish transportees were paid for in kind or, more often than not, by instalments, or Bills of Exchange, which were negotiable in Bristol or London for cash.

From 1655 to 1657, it appears that there was mass transportation to the West Indies, and amongst these were numerous priests. Many sources mention that the Bristol, London and Liverpool merchants and slave traders had agents in the Irish ports. Many of the original Loyalist settlers in Ireland, having been dispossessed by the Cromwellian forces, left Ireland voluntarily for the colonies—the choice was either to live under Cromwell's slavery, or to be treated as Barbadian merchandise.

Detail from Richard Ligon's Map of Barbados c. *1650*

Amongst the early Cromwellian officers to occupy the Loyalist and Irish properties in south-west Cork at this time were the following: Arundel, Benchley, Blair, Blake, Boyd, Carey (Carew), Clarke, Evans, Hardstaff, Hutchins, Hutchinson, Ironmonger, Levis, Nagle,

Osborne, Power, Roycroft, Summers, Pain, Tobin, Vickery, Walters, Ward, Waters, White, Wolfe and Young.

According to the Revd. J. Grace, who visited Barbados in 1669, he found that the white slaves had been arriving on the island at an average annual rate of eight thousand during the previous ten years. These statistics are just a sample of transportation from the British Isles during the reign of Charles II. What happened before this time is open to conjecture, as the merchants or slave traders were continuously petitioning Cromwell to grant them permission to transport the Irish to the 'Indian Gates'.

After 1650, over 45,000 men were banished from Ireland, and several shiploads went to Barbados. Up to, and including this period, most of the Irish who ended up in the West Indies only spoke Irish, so it was not surprising to note that Irish was spoken in Barbados, Montserrat, St. Kitts and parts of Jamaica. Going through the shipping records of vessels engaged in trade (including the transportation of Irish) from the south-west ports of Cork, we continually encounter the ships *Providence*, the *Two Brothers* and *Good Fellow*. It has been handed down by tradition that *Two Brothers* was a regular caller to Bantry, where she collected supplies of food for the West Indies. Barbados at this time was seventy per cent dependent on the import of goods, including salted and cured fish for its slaves. In Bristol we find the names of Robert Cann, Robert Yate and Thomas Speed amongst the main merchants and slave traders, while here in Bantry we find that Walters of Whiddy Island was an agent for Yate and Speed.

In the records of Barbados from 1654, there were many reports—most of them unfavourable—regarding the Irish as the following records show:

6 December 1654—Garrett Plunkett, Martin McCarthy and Daniel O'Mahony 'jump ship' from the vessel *Two Brothers* under Captain Barron.

15 January 1665—Cornelius Bryan was brought before the courts for insulting an Englishman.

1 September 1657—Peg Donoghue and Walter Walsh were accused of breaking up their master's home—they got thirty-one lashes each.

An Act was passed in 1657 forbidding the 'free' Irish from wandering around the island and threatening the plantation owners.

Cardinal Moran wrote that 'a Government Order published on 20 March 1655 states that in the four proceeding years some 6,400 Irish had been disposed of to the English slave dealers'. The Rinuccini manuscript states that 'to the island of St. Christopher (better known as St. Kitts) several thousand Irish and whole colonies were transported as slaves'. A Father Hartigan from Paris wrote on 30 March 1643 that, during the reigns of James I and Charles I, 'I received a petition of 25,000 Irish who had been forced into exile and had settled at St. Kitts and the neighbouring islands'. Archdeacon Lynch, at the time of the Clonmacnoise Gathering on 4 December 1649, wrote, 'In one year, since the last war, 40,000 men were transported from Ireland into foreign countries'. Petty himself puts the number of boys and women 'sold from Ireland to the planters of the American islands' at 6,000, while Lingard gives the figure as 60,000.

As the deaths of Irish slaves or servants were not recorded in those early days, it is impossible to enumerate the number of transportees. But availing of the various censuses for the different islands, we estimate a figure of about 25,000 Irish transportees for the years up to 1656.

The Immigrant Ships

This phrase was first coined in 1787, which was eleven years after the Declaration of Independence in the United States. It is not known how many people emigrated in the period between 1600 and 1795. The so-called Puritan Migration between 1628 and 1640 totalled only some 20,000, with an average in the following years of 10,000 per annum. The total emigration during the eighteenth century is put at 450,000. Prior to the Great Famine, Ireland had the highest population density in western Europe.

The emigrants to North America fell into two categories: those pioneers who settled in the wilderness and helped establish a new society, and those who arrived later when the country's laws and customs had been established.

The first mass movement to America began after the Napoleonic Wars, reaching its peak in the 1850s. The second was in the 1880s and the last in the decade prior to the outbreak of the First World War. It is estimated that some 35 million people emigrated to America up to this time.

In the hundred years from 1820 to 1920, numbers emigrating to America break down as follows:

Germany, 6 million; Ireland, 4.5 million; Italy, 4.2 million; UK, 4 million; eastern Europe, 4 million; Russia, 3 million Jews fled Tsarist persecution; Scandinavia, 2 million.

The root cause of mass emigration was hardship at home, due to a massive increase in the population, the collapse of agricultural order, the industrial revolution, famine and changes in the social order. Of all those who emigrated, almost one-third eventually returned to their homeland.

Up until 1880, the majority of the migrants came from Ireland, the UK, Germany and Scandinavia. Towards the end of the century, the majority were Slavs, Greeks, Hungarians and eastern European Jews.

The following is a breakdown of the influx of Irish into America:

1846 to 1855	1.3 million
1856 to 1865	0.5 million
1866 to 1875	0.54 million
1876 to 1885	0.49 million
1886 to 1895	0.55 million
1896 to 1905	0.35 million
1906 to 1915	0.28 million
1916 to 1925	0.15 million

Some of the main destinations for Irish emigrants were Baltimore northwards to Boston, Detroit eastwards to Rochester, Chicago, Cincinnati, St. Louis, New Orleans and San Francisco.

Those Irish who left their country were made up of the enterprising, the restless, the ambitious, the unfortunate and the discontented. There were starving peasants, unskilled labourers, artisans, businessmen and wealthy farmers and all these were mainly concentrated in the 15 to 35 age bracket.

Adieu to Innisfail

Adieu! The snowy sail
Swells her bosom to the gale
And our bark from Innisfail
Bounds away.
While we gaze upon thy shore
That we never shall see more,
As the blinding tears flow o'er
We pray.

Ma vourneen be thou long
In peace the queen of song,
In battle proud and strong
As the sea.
Be saints thine offspring still,
True heroes guard each hill,
And harps by every rill
Sound free.

In the dreary hours of eve,
O though round her Indian bowers
The hand of Nature showers
The brightest, glowing flowers
Of her sphere;
Yet not the richest rose
In an alien clime that blows
Like the briar at home that grows
Is dear.

Though glowing breasts may be
In soft vales beyond the sea,
Yet ever, *grá mo chroí*
Shall I wail
For the hearts of love I leave,
In thy stormy shores to grieve,
Innisfail!

But memr'y o'er the deep
On her dewy wing shall sweep,
When at midnight hour I weep
O'er thy wrongs;

And bring to me, steep'd in tears,
The dead flow'rs of other years,
And waft unto mine ears
Home's songs.

When I slumber in the gloom
Of a nameless foreign tomb,
By a distant ocean's boom,
Innisfail!
Around thine em'rald shore
May the clashing seas adore,
And each wave in thunder roar
'All hail!'

And when the final sigh
Shall bear my soul on high
And on chainless wing I fly
Through the blue,
Earth's latest thought shall be,
As I soar above the sea,
'Green Erin, dear, to thee
Adieu!'

Richard Dalton Williams

— 39 —
Mining in the Bantry Area

The copper mines at Mount Gabriel were worked during the Bronze Age, *c.* 1500–1300 BC. It is estimated that over 4,000 tons of rock from thirty-two Bronze Age mines was extracted from Mount Gabriel over a period of time. Very primitive means were used to extract the copper—lighting fires against the rock face and waiting for cracks to appear and then prizing the pieces out. The main use of copper at that time was to make bronze implements and arms such as swords, daggers, axe-heads and arrow tips. This was achieved by mixing the copper with tin in extreme heat.

Around this period the largest worked tin deposits were found in Cornwall, so there must have been a certain amount of sea trade with the south-west corner of England in those days. An interesting point to note is that the early Phoenicians are said to have journeyed to the British Isles in this period of time to acquire copper and tin, as the sources of these minerals in the Mediterranean had been exhausted.

It is not known who worked these early mines—whether it was the native population or 'foreigners'—or who had introduced the primitive methods of extracting the copper from the rock. There is no evidence of extraction taking place near Mount Gabriel, but there are indications of some smelting sites to be found on the Muintir mBaire peninsula. Whether the presence of these smelting sites in this location indicates some other simultaneous mining activities in that area can only be surmised.

From the 1830s there was a considerable amount of mining activity in the Muintir mBaire peninsula. On the invitation of the English settlers in the area, a number of mining entrepreneurs descended on the region, with a get-rich-quick mentality, to exploit the mineral wealth. This was probably due to the growing success of the copper mines at Allihies across at the north side of the Bay, which reached the peak of its production in the 1830s. A number of companies were incorporated by Act of Parliament to work Irish mines throughout Ireland, and their objective was to make trials and reopen old copper mines. Many new companies were formed, some of them fraudulent and merely designed to profit the promoters and directors who had purchased old leases cheaply and then sold them to a company in which they were shareholders.

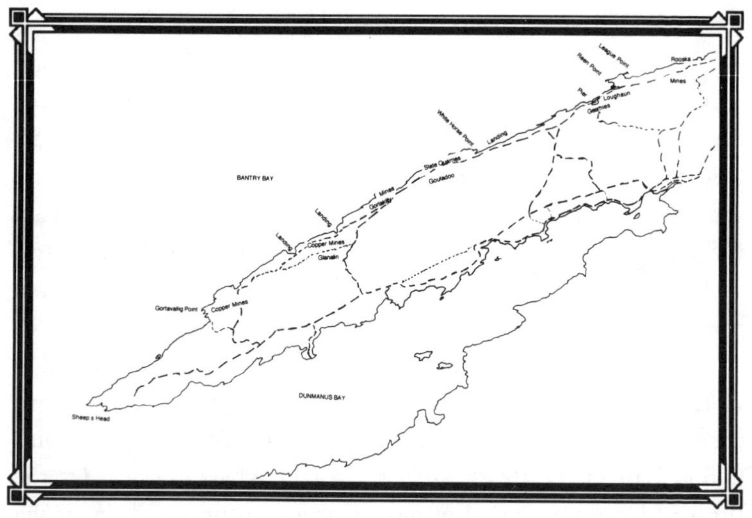

Map of the Sheep's Head peninsula and associated mines

It is not known how many of these 'shady operations' occurred in the Bantry region, and especially on the Muintir mBaire peninsula. However, the amount of local subscriptions to the various undertakings indicate that those involved were considered trustworthy.

In 1845, a Captain William Thomas is said to have 'discovered' the

Gortavallig copper seams. It is not known whether he was a geologist or had mining experience. It is not known either whether the site had been worked in the distant past. Captain Thomas was joined by a Colonel Beamish, who became chairman of the mining company. Work commenced with a small capital investment, but, as the location was inaccessible by sea, a road ten miles long was built in eleven weeks from the mine site eastwards to the sheltered inlet south of White Horse Head, where a strong pier was built.

It is believed that over ninety tons of copper ore was mined during the first year of operation and shipped to Swansea. If this is true, then the Gortavallig mine was more productive than the Allihies mines across the bay.

Despite its apparent success, the mine was closed down and abandoned in 1847. This may have been due to a lack of workmen (these were the famine years), to seawater entering the shaft works, or that the mine's 'life' was shorter than expected.

Despite this setback, various other mines were opened on the peninsula—Killeen North on the water's edge, Glanruin (Cuas), Lissaremig and Rooska, as well as a number on the Kilcrohane side of the peninsula. A Mr. Walter Woods and a Colonel Swart were involved in opening the Lisaremig, Cuas and Rooska mines. The assayist's report is rather interesting, as it estimates the following figures.

1. Lissaremig and Cuas yielded thirty-two per cent copper and two grams of silver per ton
2. Rooska yielded twelve per cent copper and seventy-three per cent ounces of silver per ton

Bearing in mind that the mines at Allihies were producing ten per cent of copper per ton, these were exceptional figures and were verified by Messrs. Bath & Sons Limited, the well-known and respected copper smelters of Swansea who had received the first shipments. Despite the great potential of the mines—now operated by the Bantry Silvermining Company—no government funding or financial assistance was forthcoming, so the mines closed when funds ran out and the Cornish miners who had been engaged in the mines departed and their newly constructed stone houses were abandoned (ruins can still be seen in the vicinity of the old mines).

When a Mr. Rathbone, Managing Director of South Berehaven Mines, wrote to the Geological Survey Office to request up-to-date geological survey maps for the Muintir mBaire peninsula, they were not forthcoming. Despite the favourable assayists' reports, this office did little to promote these ventures with government offices. All of this leads one to believe that there were forces in high places doing their utmost to prevent the possible growth of the Muintir mBaire mines.

Further accounts of the mines can be found in an article by F. O'Mahony in the *Bantry Journal* and in *History of the Berehaven Copper Mines* by R. A. Williams.

Other types of mining commenced in the area around 1880, including the mining of very good quality slate.

The earliest slate quarries were at Gouladoo, about one and a half miles west of White Horse Head on the Muintir mBaire peninsula. These were operated by a Captain O'Flaherty of the Bantry Slate and Slab Quarries and were subject to a lease of some ninety-two years at a rent of £11 per annum. Employing about fifty men and producing 40,000 slates per week, it appeared to be a prosperous business. Slates were exported to Cork and were also used locally for the many houses under construction.

There were a number of other slate quarries in the area, and the principal one of these was at Dromkeal near Snave bridge. This was operated by a Mr. Lissabe and had direct access to the sea for shipment. The quarry was taken over by the Belfast Slate Company, with a Mr. W. B. Ritchie as director. The lessee of the property was the Earl of Bantry (White). Under this new arrangement the operators of the quarry were obliged to pay a down payment of £300 and one-twentieth of the royalties to Bantry House. In 1866 there were fifty men employed at the quarries. Even though there was a great demand for the slate quarried, the company suddenly ceased production early in 1868 and all the plant, machinery and ready slate were auctioned off. Another slate quarry was located at the top of Vaughan's Pass, where slates were extracted mainly for use in Bantry town.

The barytes mine of Derriganocht was located outside Bantry, on the road to Lough Bofinne—these first of its kind in Ireland. It was opened and operated by the Liverpool Barytes Company Ltd. and later became known as Storer's Mines and Mills—from the name of the company representative, a Mr. Storer.

The exact date that the mine was opened is not known, but appears to have been prior to 1900, as a special railway siding was constructed to facilitate the crushing mill when the railway extended around the town in 1892. From the mill, the barytes was loaded onto railway wagons and taken to Cork for shipment to the UK.

During the height of production there was a twenty-four-hour shift system in operation—thirty men in each eight-hour period. The rate of pay for these shift workers, working six shifts a week, was 30 shillings (£1.50) per week, while those engaged in the separation of the barytes from impure rock was 12 shillings (60p) per week.

The barytes was removed mainly by crowbar and sledge. The holes for the dynamite were made by a miner and driller. When the holes were cleaned out by a 'buchee', dynamite was put in place, the siren was sounded, and the mine was cleared before the explosion occurred.

A boilerhouse and large steam winch were situated over the main mine shaft. These were used both to transport the men up and down and to bring the barytes rock to the surface in large steel buckets. On the surface it was loaded into large carts by hand and then these carts were pulled by teams of horses to the crushing mills near to town. According to the records, a Mr. J. J. Crowley (grandfather of Mr. Jimmy Crowley, of the Square) was the haulage contractor.

When the main shaft began to run out of suitable barytes, a number of deep cuttings were made nearby. These cuttings were up to eighty feet deep in places, but they did not prove very productive.

As the Troubles started, Mr. Storer, fearing for his life, moved out and a Captain Daly took over the operation of the mine and, together with a Mr. Henry Downey, continued the workings until 1922, when the mine closed down.

A point worth mentioning is that the late Ned Cotter TD and Ted (Reagh) O'Sullivan TD worked in the mines in their early days.

In the early 1950s an attempt was made to reopen the mines. New machinery, winches and pumps were installed and, as soon as the mine shaft was emptied of water, barytes was once again extracted. When sufficient amounts were accumulated, the barytes was then transported to Bantry pier and loaded onto cargo ships of about six hundred tons. The mining continued for a few years and then closed down again. The reasons given for the closure at that time was lack of further investment and the on-going problem of water seepage into the shaft.

As to the other mining ventures in the Bantry region, there are various ambiguous references principally to the mining of iron ore by the Whites for their smelters in the area—at Castletownbere, Adrigole, Glengarriff, Coomhola and Bantry. It appears that the main source of iron ore was located near the smelter at Coomhola, at Glengarriff, and at another location on the coastline of Roaringwater Bay. These sources were soon exhausted and the iron ore had to be imported by ship from England.

A reference to a glass-smelting furnace at Reenmeen East near Glengarriff is worth mentioning. Little is known about this operation except that it was probably worked by the Whites who found suitable mineral deposits near that location.

Many surveys have been carried out in the Bantry region during the recent past by various companies. The results were encouraging and it only remains to be seen whether there are sufficient deposits to make any undertaking a viable proposition.

Remains of the dam at the Coomhola mines

—40—

Road, Rail and Sea Routes to Bantry

From the late 1850s until about 1905, a steamship service ran between Cork and Dingle, calling at various ports, including Castletownbere, on its round trip. The first vessel on this route was a steamship called the *South Western*. In 1876 the route was taken over by the *Rio Formosa*, a vessel owned by the Clyde Shipping Company. This ship was later joined by the *Rockabill*, *Skelligs* and the *Valentia*.

There was no fixed schedule until the 1890s when the weekly round trip from Cork to Dingle was introduced. When there was cargo, the ports visited included Schull, Castletownbere, Bantry, Kenmare, Sneem and Cahirciveen.

The SS *Fastnet* sailed from Cork on a Tuesday and arrived back the following Sunday. Some passengers were catered for and the cost of the round trip was 22s 6d, which excluded food.

To maintain this valuable service, the Congested Districts Board paid an annual subsidy of £500 to Clyde Shipping Company, but in 1940 when this subsidy was discontinued the service was withdrawn. According to the records, the Cork and Bandon Railway Company was formed in 1844. Amongst the members of the Board were the Earl of Bandon, Lord Carbery and the Earl of Bantry. On his journey to

Bantry and Glengarriff in 1858, the Price of Wales availed of the train service as far as Bandon. The West Cork Railway Company was incorporated in 1860 and in the following twenty years the towns of Ballineen, Dunmanway, Drimoleague, Skibbereen, Clonakilty (1886), and Kinsale were all connected by rail to Cork.

In November 1879, work commenced on the railway line between Drimoleague and Bantry, and this link was officially opened on 4 July 1881. The terminus at Bantry was situated in front of the present hospital. The cost of this extension was £105,000. The extension from the hospital site to the vicinity of the Square was built during the period 1891 to 1892 by William Martin Murphy.

With the completion of this railway link between Cork and Bantry, trade in the south-west increased. With a further extension to the north pier, a thrice-weekly cargo service from Bantry to Castletownbere was introduced by the Bantry Steamship Company with the newly chartered *Countess of Beara*. The CBSCR held 3,375 ten-pound shares in the Bantry Steamship Company.

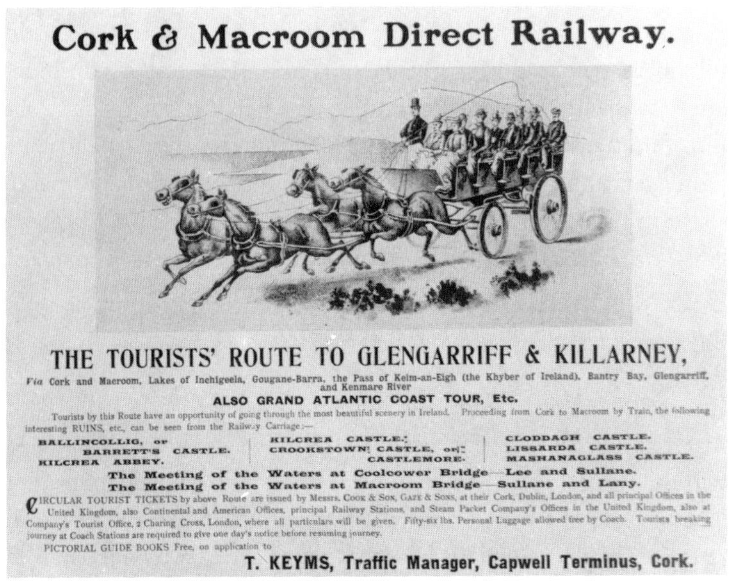

Advertisement for Cork to Macroom railway

With the building of pier facilities at Glengarriff and Adrigole, again with the assistance of the Congested Districts Board in 1906, the service grew to include Bere Island and Castletownbere. To cope with the additional services, the *Lady Elsie* was purchased by the Bantry Steamship Company, financially assisted by the CBSCR who invested £2,000 in paid-up shares.

During the famous Cork Exhibition of 1902, many visitors enjoyed the daily round trips to Bantry and Glengarriff. The following years were the boom years of the railway line and excursions, and to help to ease the load the Lady Betty Balfour was brought from the Shannon for the summer season of 1905, and introduced on the Bantry to Glengarriff route.

The Sunday Excursion Special from Cork to Bantry became extremely popular from 1902 to 1913, with loaded trains arriving at the pier-head platform around 12.30 p.m. to catch the boat. The round trip to Glengarriff was 1s 6d (7.5p) with the added pleasure of a ship's band on board. This new service also provided an attractive way to get from Cork to Killarney, as after a forty-minute boat trip the journey could be continued by coach from the pier at Glengarriff.

Sailing on weekdays connected with the train's arrival and departure at Bantry. There was a period of interruption to the Castletownbere service during the First World War, but it continued afterwards with the *Lady Elsie* until 1936, when the *Princess Beara* was introduced on the route. This vessel continued with cargo and a few passengers until 1946, when the service was discontinued, due mainly to the improvement of road links to Glengarriff and Castletownbere. The *Princess Beara* was laid up in the harbour, sold to some Spaniards in 1949 and spent her last days in the port of Vigo, before being abandoned and cut up on the beach at Bouzas.

In 1946, CIE proposed a new hotel for Glengarriff, but this never materialised. During 1947 and 1948 the railway pier was dismantled, without opposition, thus depriving Bantry of a valuable port asset. The first diesel-engined train was introduced on the line to Bantry in 1954. This shortened the train journey to about two hours. In 1961, CIE management came to the conclusion that the line was not viable and it was closed on 31 March 1961.

West Cork Railways

Opening of New Lines and Services

Early schemes	1836–43
Bandon–Ballinhassig	1849
Cork–Ballinhassig	1851
Kinsale branch	1863
Cork & Macroom	1866
Bandon–Dunmanway	1866
Dunmanway–Skibbereen	1877
Allman's Tramway	1876
Drimoleague–Bantry	1881
Clonakilty branch	1886
Shannonvale Siding	early 1890s
Courtmacsherry Line	1890–1
Bantry Bay extension	1892
Baltimore extension	1893
All-out Strike	1898
Trips from Cork–Bantry	1899

Vessels of the Bantry Bay Steamship Company

SS *Countess of Bantry*
Built in Belfast in 1884. An iron vessel with a Compound Steam Engine, it was 92 feet long and 17 feet wide. It was withdrawn from service in 1935.

SS *Lady Elise*
Built in Greenock in 1906. A steel-plated vessel with a Compound Steam Engine, it was 87 feet long and 19 feet wide. It was withdrawn from service in 1936.

SS *Princess Beara*
Built in Greenock in 1901. A steel-plated vessel with a Compound Steam Engine, it was 115 feet long and 21 feet wide. It was withdrawn from service in 1948.

SS *Lady Betty Balfour*
Built in Paisley in 1884. A steel-plated vessel with a Compound Steam Engine, it was 70 feet long and 14 feet wide. It was withdrawn from service and scrapped in 1922.

First Train to Bantry

Skibbereen Eagle (4 July 1881)

Special train from Cork (Albert Quay) on Sunday 3 July for Directors' party. Opened to public following day (Monday 4th).

The Bantry terminus is an exceedingly neat and handsome structure. The contractor, Mr. Dowling, exceeded what he had to do in erecting such an edifice, and on coming under its friendly shelter [it was a two-storey building, with a roof over the platform and tracks—see layout plan]. Mr. McBirney, Dublin (CBSC Chairman), was first to step out on the covered platform, followed by the Directors, lawyers and commercial men. A wagonette from Vickery's waited for the train.

Serious Accident, Bantry Train Wrecked, Four Injured

Cork Constitution (8 July 1887)

The Mail train, which left Cork at 3 o'clock yesterday morning, on approaching the Bantry terminus, moved rather faster than usual, running over the turning table to the end of the line and in doing so knocked away the buffer stop. This portion of the line is built on an embankment, some half a dozen feet high, over which the engine fell, pulling with it the carriages, a van and a wagon. So great was the speed that the engine and neighbouring carriage were partly embedded in the ground.

The driver, Kiely, was thrown off and seriously injured, as well as fireman Twomey. The guard of the train, who was at his brake, was thrown against it, his chest coming in contact with the said brake, and being thrown down he received a severe shock. There was only one passenger, Captain Shea, late of the *Augusta*. He was thrown down, and complained of having received a great shock and some slight injury to his back.

Information of the accident was telegraphed to Cork, and the services of Dr. Cotter, the Company's consulting physician, and Dr. Guiseni, resident physician of the South Infirmary, being secured, a special train immediately proceeded from Cork to Bantry.

Chapter 40

Royal Traveller

On Monday 16 July 1888, Prince Edward of Saxe-Weimar travelled the Prince of Wales route, joining the 8.35 a.m. morning train from Bantry (Old Station) to Cork (Albert Quay).

Opening of New Station at Bantry

CBSC Advertisement in Skibbereen Eagle

On and from Saturday 22 October 1892, the new station at Bantry, near the pier, will be open for public traffic, and the present station at Bantry will be closed.

All trains starting from Bantry New Station will leave *ten minutes earlier* than at present, and all down trains will arrive at Bantry ten minutes later than at present.

For particulars, see timetables.

Alex Gordon, General Manager

Albert Quay Terminus, Cork

7 October 1892

Lady Betty Balfour, *the* Countess of Beara *and a two-masted schooner at Bantry pier*

The Countess of Beara *and the* Lady Elise *at Bantry pier*

The Countess of Beara *loading at Bantry pier with a cargo ship anchored in the bay*

Back o' Whiddy

Off from Bantry pier we start
Sailing—or it may be rowing—
Lads and lasses, light of heart,
On to fair Glengarriff going.
Oh, the harbour's smooth enough,
But some heads get queerly giddy,
Once we dip in waters rough
Round the point and back o' Whiddy.
Then there's chaffing, back o' Whiddy;
Fearful tales
Of sharks and whales
And huge sea-serpents, back o' Whiddy.

Soon we've cause for tender cares
(Thanks, oh, thanks, sweet rolling ocean!)
And we hear delightful pray'rs
Uttered with intense emotion;
Sometimes, too, when waves and wind
Would try the temper of a 'middy',
Language of another kind
Is freely spoken back o' Whiddy.
But that's no harm—when back o' Whiddy;
It has a charm—when back o' Whiddy—
At least I know
I judged it so,
Long, long ago—when back o' Whiddy.

Sing the beauties of Glandore—
They deserve such celebration;
Say good things of Baltimore—
A safe retreat, a pleasant station;
Praise what bays and creeks there by
From Mizen Head to Ringaskiddy.
But after all, the trip for me
Is that which takes me back o' Whiddy!
Oh, the long waves back o' Whiddy!
Oh, the strong waves back o' Whiddy!
Oh, the joys
That—girls and boys—
We knew when boating back o' Whiddy.

Anon

— 41 —

From the Rising to the Truce

As nationalist momentum grew, a branch of the Ancient Order of Hibernians (AOH) was founded in Bantry during 1909. The Irish Volunteers were formed in December 1913 and the AOH supplied it with its first officers and most of its fifty recruits.

During the remaining winter months and early spring, training exercises were held in the Town Hall and, as numbers increased, training took place on the adjoining road, now known as Parade Field. However, as a result of the controversial speech of Redmond on 20 September 1914, there was a major split in the Volunteer movement and the Bantry numbers fell to about twenty men.

On the Saturday before Easter 1916, people from all over West Cork made the journey to Drimoleague to hear Terence MacSwiney speak. A group of fifteen volunteers travelled from Bantry in a horse-drawn cart which carried a rowing boat with a flag flying from its mast. This effort, no doubt, was to remind all those present of Bantry's link with revolutionary forces, whether they came by sea or land. These fifteen men were a section of the original group recruited in December 1913.

The following Saturday, orders were received that they were to march to Kealkil by noon on Easter Sunday. After parading at first mass, they made an uneventful march to Kealkil. They waited, as instructed, to join up with the Ballingeary troop for further action. However, a Sean O'Hegarty arrived with instructions to return home. Somewhat despondent at not having taken part in any action, the men all returned to their respective homes, without being arrested by the RIC or British army patrols. Afterwards the group became inactive and the majority of the Volunteers ceased to be members.

Following the Easter Rising, the Irish people saw things in a different light. The Irish Parliamentary Party was finally identified in its true role—as a puppet of the English Government. During the following years, those elected to represent the people were those who had the welfare of Ireland at heart—Count Plunkett, Joseph McGuinness, Eamon de Valera, William Cosgrave, Arthur Griffith and many others.

In the early months of 1917, the Irish Volunteers in Bantry were reorganised. Under a Battalion Commander, the following were elected: Captain—Ralph Keyes; 1st Lieutenant—Robert Lynch; 2nd Lieutenant—Michael Crowley; Adjutant—Michael Harrington; Quartermaster—Jack O'Mahony. The company became known as the 'A' company of the 14th Battalion, Cork Brigade. Other companies were formed in Glengarriff, Coomhola and Kealkil.

The British still occupied the country with a large army and a network of outposts held by the Royal Irish Constabulary. Every post in the civil administration was occupied by those who were loyal to the Crown. The main objective of the army of the Irish Republic was to break the power of the Royal Irish Constabulary in the countryside. The RIC—or 'Peelers'—was not a police force but a well-armed military force whose duty it was to keep the country under British rule. Every town, village and outpost had an RIC barracks, and these were manned by Irishmen who had sworn allegiance to Britain and who spied on the local population.

In April 1917, a US transport ship en route to England was torpedoed off the Mizen Head. Large quantities of petrol in metal containers came floating up the Bay. The fishermen of Whiddy Island salvaged what they could and hid the drums on the island. About two months later a request went out for petrol—which was severely rationed at that time—to assist Eamon de Valera in his effort to visit every part of County Clare before the pending election. Realising de Valera's campaign would be seriously damaged without the use of a vehicle, the local Volunteers called a hurried meeting. Word was passed to Whiddy Island an during the early hours of the following mornin one of the seine boats left the slipway on the island, crossed the harbour and landed at the corner of the Black Strand beach. Aboard were twenty full 'jerrycans' of petrol, bound in rags in full potato bags. Under the eyes of the British army patrols, these were carried by horse and cart through the town to the railway station and put on a train to Cork, under the protection of the RIC officer and men. A few days later the 'bags of potatoes' arrived in Limerick, where they were collected and transported to a destination in County Clare. With this mixture of American petrol and Whiddy potatoes, de Valera won the seat.

On 7 October 1917, a meeting was held in a large field at Newtown to hear Michael Collins, the Countess Markievicz and Geroid O'Sullivan speak on the Republican efforts to rid the country of English domination. After Collins' speech, the Countess appealed for recruits to form a branch of Fianna Éireann, and nine were selected. This became the only branch in West Cork, outside of Bandon. When Michael Collins and Count Plunkett had visited Skibbereen two months previously on 25 August, a large battalion of Volunteers had attended the parade.

Being in dire need of arms and explosives, the Bantry Volunteers attacked the powder house of Derryganaugh barytes mines, early in January 1918. They removed a quantity of gelignite with fuse and a box of detonators. Meanwhile, men worked by night at Jack O'Donoghue's in Gourteenroe making hand grenades and bombs out of cans stuffed with nails, bits of iron, a stick of gelignite and a fuse sticking out of one end.

A few weeks later, two members of the RIC returning from patrol in Glengarriff were attacked at Donemark, on the corner opposite the present golf course. Dan O'Mahony, together with eight Volunteers, carried out this attack. One of the men, making use of a heavy blackthorn stick, captured a rifle and two hand guns. Those involved in this action were Ralph Keyes, John Begley, Michael Walsh, Willie Brennan, Thomas Breen, Richard McCarthy, Cecil Keyes and John O'Sullivan who kept watch. Later on in that year, 1918, when the

British government tried to impose conscription, the Irish desire for freedom from the British yoke became stronger. There was a great influx of young men into the Volunteer movement, and in Bantry alone 175 applied for membership.

Shortly after the end of the First World War, plans were made for a general election, in both England and Ireland, to be held in December. In nearly every constituency, with the exception of Ulster, those elected pledged refusal to attend the British Parliament or to recognise Britain's right to govern Ireland. Those deputies who were not in jail at the time met in Dublin in January 1919. They established the first Dáil Éireann, and declared Ireland, *de jure*, an independent republic. Following this meeting, the Volunteers came under the authority of General Mulcahy and Dáil Éireann—they had become the Army of the Irish Republic. The title 'IRA' was never officially adopted, but was a popular name which came into general usage during the following years of conflict. On 5 January, a meeting of all the staff officers of the Volunteers was held at Kilnadur, near Dunmanway. Those attending were Michael Collins of GHQ, Thomas McCurtain—his Adjutant, Florence O'Donoghue and representatives from each of the West Cork battalions. After this meeting, the Volunteer movement in West Cork became known as the West Cork Brigade. It was also decided that Frank Hurley's house on the outskirts of Bandon would become the Brigade's headquarters. Communication between the battalions was by means of young men riding bicycles between town and villages, either by main roads or by-roads, depending on British surveillance and army traffic. All notices between Bantry and Castletownbere were passed on by using one of the crew of the SS *Lady Elsie* or the *Princess Beara*, namely Danny McCarthy.

Early in 1919, the British army moved into the Bantry workhouse, which they used as their local headquarters. These were the King's Liverpool Regiment of some two hundred men under the command of Colonel Jones, who was a fair and respectable man who would not tolerate any excesses by his men. The sick and infirm who were in the workhouse at that time were thrown out, and on hearing of their plight Lady Shelswell-White of Bantry House took them in. This act of charity no doubt saved Bantry House from the torchers' flame the following year.

In addition to the above army presence, there was an RIC garrison of sixty men stationed between the army barracks at the top of Barrack Street, the barracks/jail on the Square (now the left section of the Bantry Bay Hotel), Glengarriff Road (next to Murphy's monument works) and the officers' quarters on the north side of the Square (O'Sullivan's house).

Late in 1919, authorisation was granted in Dublin to carry out attacks on enemy barracks in West Cork from the beginning of the following year. The formation of permanent 'columns' in Brigade areas of the countryside became known as 'flying columns', and were noted for their guerrilla-type warfare in carrying out swift and sudden attacks, raids and ambushes.

At this time, the Bantry town battalion consisted of 107 active members out of a total force of 154, but they were ill-equipped, with a few rifles and hand guns at this time.

Apart from the above-mentioned locations of the British army and RIC barracks, there were eight RIC members stationed in Kilcrohane, six at the Eccles in Glengarriff, and four on Whiddy Island, plus reinforcements of twelve military. Only Bandon and Kilbrittain had forces of a similar strength.

The most daring exploit of the Bantry battalion was the raid on the British naval sloop *ML 171* at the railway pier on 16 November 1919. At 7.00 a.m. that Sunday morning, word was passed on to the Volunteer command that the sloop had berthed at the pier. The Volunteers met and drew up their plan of action with the aid of information—including the layout of the sloop and the crew's activities—passed to the group by Danny McCarthy of the *Princess Beara*. Amongst those present were Maurice Donegan, Sean Cotter, Michael O'Callaghan and Ralph Keyes.

Watchmen were placed at strategic locations to keep an eye on the activities of the RIC and the military. Eight men then proceeded to the railway pier in small groups. When the first pair, Donegan and Keyes, arrived at the lower platform of the pier they saw the man on watch descend the forward hatchway, and they immediately jumped on board. Shouting that they had a bomb, they closed the hatchway and were then joined by the other Volunteers. The crew, fearing for their lives, offered no resistance, merely watching as the armoury was broken open with a sledge-hammer. Six rifles and two heavy black boxes were quickly removed and passed along to the others on the pier.

Avoiding the town, the Volunteers made their way along the strand to the north, to Cove, with their booty. They headed to the Boys' School by a circuitous route which took them across Barrack Street, Glengarriff Road and the railway line to their destination. There they found the ladder was too short to reach the loft opening as planned. In their anxiety they decided to call on the local sacristan for help and he agreed to hide the boxes and rifles in the church attic.

Keeping a watchful eye on the nearby army barracks, they crossed into the small wood and down into the church grounds. Within minutes they had scaled the long ladder at the back of the church, passing up the boxes from one to another until everything was stashed away in a dark corner, where it remained hidden for some time.

The men made their way home, amidst the commotion of the general alert which had sounded minutes earlier. The houses of all suspected Volunteers were searched, roadblocks were mounted at every exit of the town, but nothing was found.

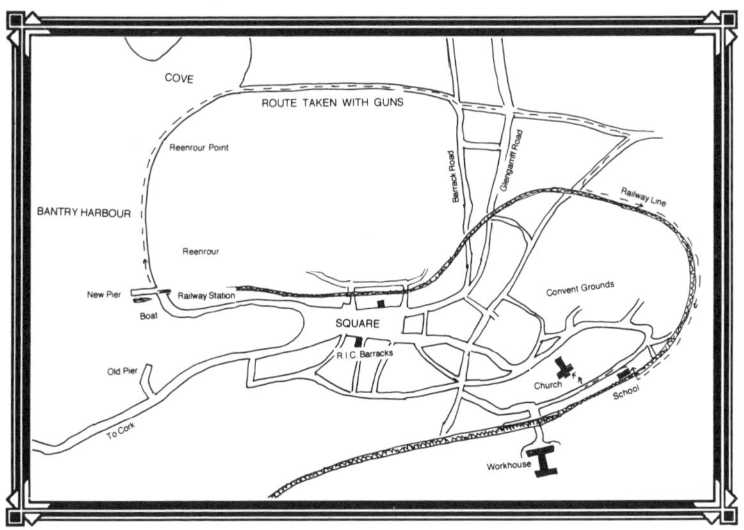

The route taken by the attackers of the ML 171

After this event, the Volunteers stepped up their activities against the RIC and British army. An ambush was prepared for a returning army column from Glengarriff at Snave bridge.

For some reason as the vehicles made their way to the ambush site they stopped, and the soldiers jumped out with their rifles cocked. On seeing this, the proposed action was immediately called off and the men hurriedly escaped through the fields to Coomhola. Nobody knew whether the army had been 'tipped off' or whether one of the soldiers had seen some movement or the sun's reflection from a rifle.

An attack on the RIC barracks in Durrus was mounted by a selection of Volunteers from all the local columns. This took place late one night, after trees had been felled across all the incoming roads, and sentries posted.

Despite their superior numbers and adequate fire-power, the Volunteers were unable to take the building due to the strong resistance of the twelve RIC men inside. As a last resort they fired the building, but, with dawn approaching, the smoke and fire from the building and the necessity of returning home to go to work without attracting attention, the commander in charge called off the attack.

The following period was one of instability, as the RIC took their revenge on the town of Bantry. Systematic searches of all known possible Volunteers' houses began. However, due to prior knowledge of the raids, all the Volunteers had left their homes and sought refuge in safe houses in the Mealagh and Coomhola valleys. When the RIC failed to find Michael Crowley at his home, they shot and killed his invalid brother Con, in his bed in front of his sister. They fired David O'Mahony's house while his wife and children were inside. However, they escaped the fire with the assistance of their neighbours. Many other houses of suspected Volunteers were ransacked and set on fire that particular night. Seeing that things were getting out of hand, the Bantry Company Column openly paraded in full arm dress on protective duty, while the British army looked on.

Sean Cotter was later arrested and sent to Wormwood Scrubs prison, where he joined other locals who had been arrested earlier, such as Flor Begley (Bandon), Ralph Keyes (Bantry) and Frank Hurley. Both Keyes and Cotter were released after a hunger-strike of twenty-three days.

Chapter 41

Newspaper Reports of Extreme Unrest in Bantry

Crime Denounced

Cork County Eagle & Munster Advertiser (3 July 1920)

A night marked by the utmost composure formed a strong contrast to the many sleepless and weary hours which the sorely-tried people of Bantry town have had to endure for some weeks. In agreement with the request made, and the undertaking given by the leading business men, neither a soldier nor a policeman was to be seen in the streets from the early hours of last night. A large body of Volunteers became the custodians of the peace, and from ten o'clock to daybreak they maintained an interrupted watch and guard over life and property. Up to eleven o'clock groups were assembled discussing the latest chapter of horrors, while others, manifestly suffering under extreme nervous tension, were rather reluctant to enter their dwellings, fearing a renewal of the burnings, or perhaps worse. The assurance that 'All's well' coming from the Volunteers, who, with the clergy and principal business men of the town, patrolled the streets, had its comforting effect, the people soon retiring, and when the midnight hour rang out not a sound was heard, save that of the steady, measured tread of the Volunteer patrols. With the Volunteers were Very Revd. Canon Murphy and Fathers M. O'Leary, J. V. Hurley and M. J. Lynch, Drs. J. O'Mahony and P. Cullinan, J. P.s together with Mr. J. Travers Wolfe, Crown Solicitor, also contribute to the preservation of the peace. Further particulars gathered today at the scene of the murder of Cornelius Crowley, accentuate still more the atrocious nature of the crime. The shots poured into the body of the poor cripple were discharged at such a close range that the bullets passed clean through his attenuated frame while he lay in bed appealing for mercy. Two bullets were found in the bed, and one, beneath the wound which is in one of the victims hands, appears to have been received in his vain endeavour to protect his body. The bullets, which are of a large pattern, are in the possession of Dr. J. O'Mahony, the local surgeon. It is stated that the house of the Sinn Féin Mahony family had been subjected to visits from the police.

Questioned again today at her humble dwelling, the mother of the victim stated that there were four men in the attacking party, all of whom had blackened faces. One was tall and acted as leader. Having entered the house, the lighted candle which she had placed on a table, was at once extinguished, and the party, who carried flashlights, immediately proceeded upstairs to the bedroom, three of them remained on the landing, while the fourth member of the party did the deadly and revolting work.

An ugly incident occurred after midnight on Wolfe Tone Square. When one of the Volunteer pickets, of which Very Revd. Canon Murphy was in charge, was passing the police barracks a number of police came out in a threatening manner and said they would not have any Sinn Féin Volunteers policing the town. Very Revd. Canon Murphy prevailed on the police to return to their station and eventually this was done. Whether the constables were armed is not quite clear, but it is asserted some of them had revolvers. There has been no incident, so far, in the town, but there prevails a distinct atmosphere of unrest.

Funeral of the Victim

It is gratifying to be in a position to record the fact that no untoward event has disturbed the apparent calm which has set in in the town of Bantry, unfortunately the scene of recent harrowing occurrences. The situation, however, calls for very careful handling, having regard to the very glaring instances of provocation with which the people are being daily confronted. The Very Revd. Canon Murphy is being ably assisted by his curates, the leading men of the town and the people generally, in his rather arduous ask to protect life and property. The streets are being patrolled nightly by local magistrates, acting in co-operation with voluntary civilians, and it must be said that the personal sacrifices displayed in the preservation of peace are beyond all praise.

The body of young Crowley, who was murdered at Barrack Road, was removed to the Parish Church on Saturday evening, the remains being received by the Very Revd. Canon Murphy P.P. and the priests of the parish. Business in the town was suspended and the blinds drawn. Nearly all creeds and classes joined in the sad function. The prayers having been said and the Rosary recited, the people, acting on the counsel of the respected and popular pastor, quietly dispersed.

The funeral on Sunday was most impressive and of exceptional large dimensions. It was over two miles in length. On all sides the deepest sorrow was manifested towards the poor victim of so foul a murder. Immense contingents of Volunteers participated in the funeral, and when the Abbey graveyard, which is situate about three miles from the town, was reached, the scene presented was most touching. The officiating were Very Revd. Canon Murphy, Revd. Fathers Lynch, O'Leary and O'Mahony.

The body having been placed in the grave, Very Revd. Canon Murphy recited the Rosary in Irish, when the prayers for the dead had been said. The people very fervently joined in the responses. Three volleys were fired over the grave by the Bantry Volunteers.

At the close of the sad ceremonial, Very Revd. Canon Murphy advised the people, especially those from outlying districts, to proceed home peacefully.

The coffin was enveloped in the Republican colours, and in addition to the relatives the following marched in the procession, which was led by the clergy, namely Sean Hayes, TD MCC; Donal Oge O'Callaghan, Chairman Cork County Council; Con Crowley, Cork City Sinn Féin Executive; Sean Jennings, Chairman Cork Board of Guardians; Alderman P. Higgins, HC, Cork Corporation; Patk. Barrett, Cork RDC; T. Coughlan, G. Grace, P. Crowley, etc., Skibbereen; Stephen O'Neill, J. Nyhan, etc., Clonakilty; P. S. Brady, RM; Dr. J. J. O'Mahony, JP; Dr. P. Cullinane, JP; G. W. Biggs, JP; C. O'Donovan, JP; W. H. O'Sullivan, JP; J. Travers Wolfe, CS; members of Cumann na mBan, each carrying beautiful wreaths. Next came contingents of Volunteers from Bantry, Coomhola, Caheragh, Glengarriffe, Kealkil, Drimoleague, Castletownbere, Bunawn, Skibbereen, Schull, Ballydehob, Dunmanway, Drinagh and Clonakilty; members of the Bantry branches Transport Union, the Staff of the G.P.O., Bantry; the National Teachers, Bantry; and representatives of the local railway officials.

At the Masses on Sunday references were made to recent occurrences in the town. Speaking at the eight o'clock mass Very Revd. Canon Murphy, PP, said the events of the past week beginning with the shooting of Constable Brett, which occurred outside the parish on Monday, and the shooting of the young man Crowley in the town, in the early hours of Friday morning, were so appalling that he hoped through the infinite goodness and mercy of God they would not witness a repetition of them. The murder of the poor cripple boy was a crime for which it would be hard to find a parallel. Now that he was called away he (Canon Murphy) asked for the earnest prayers of the congregation. He had gone to his home in Heaven. In this present time when passions were strong and feeling ran very high the people should endeavour, notwithstanding every provocation, to keep themselves calm and cool under the very trying situation that existed in the town. By the destruction of the premises of a local merchant the lives of a number of children were endangered. During the past few evenings he was glad to say they enjoyed perfect calm, and this reflected the highest credit on the magistrates and other residents, whose arrangements were carried out to the letter, the people leaving the streets and going to their homes. All this showed that if the military and police had been withdrawn from the town the existing turmoil would soon disappear. He exhorted the congregation to pray earnestly that God may help the people in the crisis through which the country was passing.

Addressing the congregation at ten o'clock Mass, Revd. J. V. Hurley, CC, said the gospel and epistle he had read were especially appropriate to the events to which he was about to refer. The gospel contained the teaching of Our Divine Lord with regard to the fifth commandment, to which he had drawn their attention the previous Sunday in connection with the shooting of an unarmed policeman. Unfortunately, the law of God was grievously violated last Thursday night—a night of terror in the town—when a poor innocent boy was shot in bed, notwithstanding his piteous cries for mercy in the presence of his aged and terrified parents. This boy had never injured anyone, and though he was suddenly before his Maker he (the reverend preacher) was sure he was well prepared. Apparently the same criminal gang went then to burn down a house in the middle of the town, giving the family barely time to escape with their lives. It would be impossible to enumerate the other crimes against life and property committed and attempted the same night. His object in denouncing these crimes against the law of God was not to inflame the minds of the people. As a Christian Minister, his duty was to urge them to remain calm and patient in submitting to the provocation to which they were daily being subjected. It was the duty of every right-minded person to denounce these outrages, and at the same time it would be wrong for any person to seek revenge by unlawful means. The virtue of patriotism obliged them to subordinate their private interest to those of the nation. He appealed to them when paying their tribute to young Crowley at his funeral that day not to be guilty of any act of aggression that might cause the armed forces of the Government to turn their guns on them and cause the loss of many innocent lives.

At the last Mass, Revd. M. O'Leary, CC, said last Sunday he referred to the shooting of Constable King and condemned it. Unfortunately, today he had to return to the subject, for during the week there were two further shooting tragedies, one in the town of Bantry, and the other just outside the parish, but both victims were parishioners of Bantry. He now condemned as strongly as possible both these shootings, as they were against the law of God. Of course, the families of the victims had the sincere sympathy of the people of Bantry. Besides the shootings, he also referred to the setting on fire of a shop and dwellinghouse in the town, which he said was practically equally as bad, as the consequences might have been terrible—that house in which there were a father and mother and several young children. No matter what people's political views were, they should observe God's laws in all things.

Incidents in the Town

On Saturday, a young man named Sullivan, a Gaelic League organiser from Glengarriffe, received very rough treatment at the hands of two plain-clothes policemen, for no apparent reason, and an eye-witness states that a loaded revolver was placed to the young man's face.

A woman who had been employed in the police barracks left on Saturday through some cause, the nature of which has not been definitely disclosed. The police complained to County Inspector Greer who informed the magistrates, who have been doing patrol duty, that if the woman did not return to the duties he would put a picket of military and police on the streets that night. It was later intimated to the justices by two plain-clothes constables that in the event of the woman failing to resume the police would not stay in the barrack during the night.

It was a critical problem, the solution of which was supplied by the Very Revd. Canon Murphy, who on representations being made to him secured the woman's return, and the incident, which threatened to develop to an unlooked-for degree, closed, much to the relief of the magistrates concerned with the maintenance of peace.

Another incident occurred on Saturday not calculated to advance the welfare of the town. A lorry, in which a mixed party of police and military were seated, displayed a Union Jack in a manner likely to inflame the feelings of the populace. Mr. Walter Biggs, son of a local Unionist JP, who is an extensive employer in the town, came in for rather harsh treatment from a party of police, who in turning their motor lorry, entered his avenue at Ardnagrena. His remonstrance led to a mauling, which was, however, not serious.

There were many rumours abroad during the past couple of days, one of which was that the dwelling of Mr. J. Downey, Glengarriffe, who is believed to be identified with Sinn Féin, had been attacked and burned to the ground. This and reports of a similar kind had no foundation in fact.

The burned down shop and premises of Mr. David Mahony, Sinn Féiner, Barrack Street, who conducted a large general business, represents a loss of some thousands of pounds. His escaping with his wife and children was nothing short of providential. The premises are situated in a most congested part of town. The rear of Vickery's Hotel abutted on the narrow street. There were stored large quantities of petrol, and but for the speedy and successful efforts of the townspeople in coping with the alarming situation the entire block of houses would have fallen prey to the conflagration.

Inquest Falls Through

Mr. Coroner Neville, in the Courthouse on Saturday, proceeded with the inquest on the young man, Cornelius Crowley. District Inspector Oates and Head Constable Gleeson represented the authorities. A party of military with fixed bayonets were posted outside the Courthouse.

The names of the following jurors were handed in by Sergeant Sullivan who stated they had been duly summoned—Messrs. Geo. W. Biggs, JP, Peter Cronin, Edward Brookes, David O'Mahony, John J. Murphy, John Kennedy, Mark Sullivan, Christopher Sullivan, Denis Cotter, John Wiseman, Timothy McCarthy and Patrick Moriarty.

On the names being called out it was found that six jurors were absent, and by order of the Coroner a policeman called the names outside the Court, but there was no response.

A juror said the notice was short, and if he were given half an hour he would secure the absentees.

District Inspector Oates—That would be a most illegal course to adopt. They were summoned in the ordinary way and fourteen others were called upon. If they don't choose to come in we can't help them.

Coroner—I don't see how we can proceed.

Sergeant Sullivan said he had personally served the six men who did not attend Court and had called on thirteen others.

Replying to a juror (Mr. Biggs), District Inspector Oates said he was not going to depart from the ordinary procedure. The police had done their best to get jurors. It was not the first time the police had failed.

There were now three adjournments within ten days.

Coroner—It is very awkward that people summoned have not attended.

Sergeant Sullivan—I have been insulted in houses I went into.

Head Constable Gleeson said every house the police went into they were insulted, and the police said they would not undertake the same duty again. District Inspector Oates pressed for the imposition of fines.

The Coroner was understood to make no order with regard to fines, and remarked that he was sick of fining.

Under the circumstances the inquest fell through.

Attempt to Burn a Policeman's House

An unsuccessful attempt was made to set fire to the residence of Constable Cleary and his family on Friday night at Bantry. The military and police were confined to barracks and civilians and Irish Volunteers patrolled the streets and kept order.

Situation at Bantry—Magistrates Meet—Armed Trawler Arrives—Guns Trained on Town

A meeting of local justices was held this evening when further measures were discussed in connection with the keeping of the peace by the civilian patrols. The outstanding incidents of the day were the holding up of the Bantry Bay Steamship Company's vessel, *Lady Elsie*: the presence of an armed trawler lyng off the pier, and an upset in the train arrangements. Some half-dozen policemen bearing arms, who had been on duty in the town during the Quarter Sessions, proceeded to return to Castletownbere, but the crew of the *Lady Elsie* refused to work the steamer, which lies tied up at the pier with the police on board. The armed trawler arrived in the inner harbour on Saturday. She has her guns trained on the town, and is in wireless communication with her military barracks. Some commercial travellers who had been doing business here were much disappointed this evening, when they found that booking by the 4.50 train from Bantry did not extend beyond Drimoleague.

Steamship Hold-up

The armed constables returning from Bantry to Castletownbere, who were on board, and by reason of which the steamer was held up, were taken off on Tuesday night and returned to barracks. In the morning they were taken down by the armed trawler which was in the harbour since Saturday and landed in Castletown. About an hour after, the held-up steamer took her departure with her cargo and passengers for Castletown. A rumour got abroad that another party of armed policemen or military may go on board the *SS Princess Beara* on her journey from Bantry to Castletown at 1 o'clock. When the hour arrived none of these forces were on board or around, and the steamer proceeded on her way. There were a number of returned Irish-Americans aboard. It being a Roman Catholic holiday, there were large crowds in the town, but everything passed off quietly, and there were no disturbances of any kind. The tension and excitement of the past week appear to be easing a little, and it is to be earnestly hoped that there will be an immediate return to the normal, and that it will then be maintained. The police and military kept to thir respective quarters. The civilian guard had charge of the patrolling of the streets and maintaining order. This they did in a very satisfactory and creditable manner. A spirit of forbearance and commonsense on all sides would very soon smooth away all trouble and difficulties here.

Daring Raid at Bantry—ML Boat Attacked (18 *November* 1919)
On Sunday night, about 10.15 p.m., a daring raid was made on a Government boat by the New Pier, and 6 rifles and 3 revolvers taken. The men in charge were surprised and fastened down, while the raiders made good their escape.

Immediately armed military and police searched the town and raided several houses. Armoured cars scoured the roads. Some went after the Dunmanway footballers who had left about 9 o'clock.

The police are very reticent. No arrests have been made. The whole affair is shrouded in mystery, and great excitement prevails.

The ML boat from which the arms were taken has left this morning. It is not clear if any ammunition was taken.

No one is allowed on this pier lately by the railway watchman.

The number constituting the raiding party is not known. Some of the ML crew were on shore.

Monday evening—The mysterious disappearance last night of six rifles and three revolvers from the Govenment ML boat is the sole topic of conversation here all day. Bantry is their headquarters. There were two of these boats lying off the pier on Sunday. Each has a small gun, being submarine chasers. They were just close to the SS Lady Elsie, which plies between here and Castletown with Glengarriffe. To reach the ML boat therefore the raiders must have crossed over the Lady Elsie from the pier, or come by boat up to her.

The watchman on the Lady Elsie has lately been taken off. The two men staying on board her were asleep in their bunks, when at 10.30 p.m. or so they were roused by the military and police inquiring after the raiders. These being in their quarters long before, neither saw nor heard anything, and were able to throw no light on the matter. These members of the crew of the ML boat were battened down by the raiders, and a voice shouted to them that if they attempted to come up they would be shot. The missing rifles and revolvers were in a box or enclosure, which was forced open. A small hatchet found on deck was the only clue left. Any ammunition is believed to be down in the magazine.

Those in the adjoining ML boat, too, neither heard nor saw anything, it is said. In fact no one appears to have seen the operations, or can tell of the number, the affair was so quietly and quickly done. The occurrence must have taken place about the hour of ten o'clock p.m. About 11 o'clock all the local available police and military were making diligent and exhaustive searches in all suspected quarters. Rooms and beds were examined, persons questioned, armed cars and lorriers were going all night. To-day the search is being continued. Both the ML boats left here. At 12 o'clock the Lady Elsie was taking in her cargo as usual. The whereabouts of the missing arms is still unknown. That no one was hurt everyone is thankful.

Our Bantry correspondent, wiring last night, said—the three men on board the Government boat when raided were having tea in the forecastle at 8.50 p.m. on Sunday, when suddenly the hatchway closed down and one, who attempted to put up his head, was promptly directed to withdraw, or it would be blown off. The arms were in the chart-room—six rifles, six bayonets, three revolvers, three rounds of ammunition. These disappeared. On the table was £5 10s in cash, some cigarettes and tobacco. These were left untouched, implying that arms was the objective. At 9.20 all had vanished.

Detailed Account of Bantry Tragedy

Cork County Eagle & Munster Advertiser (29 August 1920*)*

A night and day of tragedies have closed here, leaving the citizens stunned and dazed at it all. In the excitement and consternation that prevailed in the town yesterday afternoon when Constable Haugh was shot dead and three other constables who were with him at the tragic time had such a narrow and providential escape, it was impossible to get reliable information from which to pen a coherent and correct account of the shocking occurrence. This, following so closely on the tragic deed which was enacted at Glengarriff the previous night, and which almost all of the people only learned that morning from the papers, and they being busily engaged in discussing that awful deed, they were doubly alarmed and stunned. Now, however, it is possible to give in some detail the circumstances leading up to and surrounding the tragedy. Owing to the excitement caused amongst the police force here on account of the Glengarriff shooting on Tuesday night, when Constable McNamara was shot dead, another constable seriously wounded, while a third escaped with his life, it was observed that Constable Haugh (deceased) and his companion, Constable Power, were about the streets rather excited, having their rifles unslung and on the level. This was about ten o'clock a.m. Later they must have been joined by Constables Hannafin and Murphy, and carrying on to two o'clock, p.m., the four of them with their rifles went along the street or top of Mill Hill or Chapel Street, and turned to and ascendend the steps leading to Union Hall, or the new workhouse military barracks and where they—the police—are now also quartered since Saturday last, when they removed from the barracks on the Square to Mr. Biggs' commandeered private residence. They had only ascended the first flight of steps about four, and were on the first flat at foot of another flight of steps, and just behind the gable wall of Mr. Sheehan's house, when they were fired at by the attacking party, said to consist of four or five persons, was a soldier sentry on the bridge at the top of the hill says he saw immediately after the shots that number of men running from the place of attack across the shrubbery in front of the chapel and on eastward out of the grounds. The party in wait for the constables were hidden inside a stone wall about eight feet high, facing the spot where the constable was shot. They must have been perched on the wall or on some elevation behind it, so as to get themselves breast high on the wall, and on the top of which some scattered withered grass is to be seen. The spot where the constable was shot and fell is indicated by the mass of congealed and clotted blood and signs of where it flowed and trickled down the steps towards the road or street was only about four or five feet from the wall where the attacking party were ambushed. When the shot rang out and he was hit and fell, the other three constables—viz. Murphy, Hannafin and Power—fired their rifles in over the wall in the direction from which the fatal shot came. They then went for safety, and in a few paces got from the spot down over the four steps into the street, and turning to the left, they would be completely cut off from view by Mr. Sheehan's house, for the attacking party, who were enclosed in by this high surrounding wall, within which is enclosed a thick, luxurious shrubbery, affording admirable shelter and screen. The other constables who escaped ran away from the scene with all speed seeking shelter, and firing as they ran. Constables Hannafin and Murphy must have taken shelter in some house, as they were not noticed after that getting away but Constable Power, whose cap either fell or was shot off at the scene of the tragedy, ran down along the street bareheaded, with his rifle, and some say still firing on through the Square, and into licensed premises there near the old vacated barrack. Military and police were on the scene in a twinkling, and all parties were held up. A number of shots were fired either by the police or military and several people had narrow escapes. Very Revd. Canon Murphy and other priests came on the scene, and did all possible to allay the excited state of feeling. Cordons of military, with police, were drawn across all the outlets from the town and across streets, whilst a vigorous and stringent search was made of all the houses and grounds in the vicinity, including the church grounds and those of the chaplain opposite. All persons on business or otherwise, were held up and had to stop at the Post Office, moving from either side, until the order was relaxed, in the course of about three hours. It was only then that traffic or business could be resumed. It is stated that a military search party found a military rifle—others say a shotgun—in the shrubbery near where the attack was made. Numbers of soldiers were placed in various spots around the scene of the occurrence and in the adjoining grounds, keeping a close watch. Several persons were arrested, but were afterwards released, after being closely searched and questioned. The deceased constable died almost immediately. It is said he made some remarks in the nature of goodbye or farewell to his companion, Constable Power, as he was dying. The deceased constable had been stationed here about three or four years. He was unmarried, and is said to have about 15 or 17 years' service. He was a native of County Clare, from which county Constable McNamara, shot in Glengarriff the previous night, also hailed.

Chapter 41

Bantry Troubles

Cork County Eagle (28 August 1920)

The Bantry police barracks were voluntarily evacuated this morning, and the police and all their fittings etc. were removed to the military quarters at the workhouse, and recently commandeered premises in the vicinity. The process of evacuation was most imposing and elaborate. A cordon of military, with rifles and fixed bayonets, formed a large semi-circle for some distance around and in front of the barracks on the Square, outside which civilians had to pass, except those who had business with the bank, law offices and licensed and other houses within the guarded zone. At the western side of the circle, facing the Abbey road, a Lewis gun was placed in position. A number of horse-drawn military vehicles were used for transference of the constabulary goods to their new quarters. There was a large display of military, fully armed, and in charge of a number of officers, while the work was in progress. The operation was witnessed by large crowds of people. Nothing untoward occurred.

The town was quiet last night. Afer the dreadful ordeal it went through the night before [night of reprisals]. the people's nerves are unstrung, and numbers of them are saying they won't or can't stay in the town at night.

An aeroplane flew over this district last evening from the Cork direction. It circled rather low over the town, and particularly over the military headquarters, and then returned whence it came. It is thought the mail, etc., for the military will soon be brought by this means.

Claims for compensation for criminal injuries in respect of the recent burnings in the town and at Glengarriff have been lodged with the clerk of the District Council, amounting to about £45,000. They are for hearing at the Skibbereen October Sessions. The Council, so far, has taken no action as regards defending them and it is possible they will be ignored.

Increase of Lawlessness

A decree of social ostracism against all members of the RIC and their families was passed by Dáil Éireann. It had the desired effect, and as the unpopularity of the force grew, many resigned. After a series of further attacks on RIC barracks, the authorities decided to close down those in remote areas. However, as the RIC ceased to function properly, lawlessness increased in the countryside, so a body called the Republican Police was formed to uphold the law. This body existed until the Truce.

Social unrest increased as Volunteers and political prisoners refused to recognise the British courts and demanded to be treated as prisoners of war. All the law courts were boycotted and 'Republican Courts' were set up. People refused to serve on juries and court sessions ceased. Then Dáil Éireann declared the collection of income tax by the British officials in Ireland to be illegal, and ordered everyone to refuse payment. In April 1920, income tax offices all over the country were raided, and all papers and records were burnt. On the same night, 315 vacated RIC barracks were torched. A few nights later, more income tax offices and RIC barracks were burnt to the ground.

The effects were also felt in Bantry. The RIC barracks, which occupied the left corner site of the Bantry Bay Hotel, was burnt to the ground. So too were the premises occupied by the RIC officers on the north side of the Square. Other buildings either occupied by the RIC or known to be places they frequented, like Vickery's Hotel, were also put to the torch. With the unofficial execution of those captured by the British, the GOC in Cork was advised that a 'tit for tat' policy of killing and reprisal existed in the West Cork area. As the burning of houses belonging to known supporters of the Irish Brigade became widespread, the same measure of reprisal was carried out against known supporters of the English.

Martial Law was introduced and a curfew was instituted in all cities and towns. Following British courts martial, executions became common. As an act of reprisal against the townspeople, the Deal Yard was burned to the ground. The main purpose of this act was to deprive over one hundred men of a livelihood and the means of supporting their families. In time the strength of the RIC decreased from over 12,000 men to less than 10,000 and, with no recruits from Ireland, the British government was forced to advertise for recruits in Britain.

— 42 —

Berehaven: A Treaty Port

At the outbreak of the Second World War, the Treaty Ports of Cobh (then known as Queenstown), Berehaven and Bantry Bay, and Lough Swilly in County Donegal, became a serious bone of contention between the Irish Free State and the English government. All these ports had been used both during and after the First World War, with the main part of the anti-submarine war being conducted from Cobh. Although they were not fully equipped naval bases, they were extremely useful for their deep water and safe anchorages. Such shore defences as existed at that time were considered to be obsolete, despite being in reasonable working order.

It was only after the attempted invasion by Wolfe Tone and the French in 1796 that the English realised the importance of Bantry Bay to their defence of the seas around the British Isles and western Europe. Around 1800, a half-hearted attempt was made to install shore fortifications on Bere, Garnish and Whiddy Islands, but it was not until the late 1890s that any concentrated effort was made and large gun batteries were built on Bere Island, making Berehaven Sound an impregnable harbour for British warships.

Gun batteries and a submarine boom were placed across the Piper Sound, which was the western entrance to Berehaven harbour. During the fight against German submarines in the First World War, a second seaplane base was built on the south-west coast of Whiddy Island. From here, the seas from the Mizen to Loop Head could be watched for enemy shipping and submarines.

A fracas between locals and British sailors in The Square c. 1912

Sailors from the Royal Navy drilling in Bantry Square, c. 1912

In Article 6 of the Anglo-Irish Treaty of December 1921, it was laid down that, until the Irish Free State was able to undertake her own coastal defence, 'the defence by sea of Great Britain and Ireland shall be undertaken by His Majesty's Imperial Forces'. It also states, in Article 7, that 'the government of the Irish Free State shall afford to His Majesty's Imperial Forces:

(a) in time of peace such harbour and other facilities as are indicated in the Annex hereto, or such facilities as may from time to time be agreed between the British Government and the Government of the Irish Free State; and

(b) in time of war or strained relations with a Foreign Power such harbours and other facilities as the British Government may require for the purposes of such defence aforesaid.'

The British government continued its military power at these various locations with 'maintenance crews' up to 1938, when a new Anglo-Irish Agreement was drawn up, which stated that the British government unconditionally handed over the forts and harbours to the Irish government, thus abrogating the relevant articles in the prior Treaty. The new Agreement also contained articles covering financial settlement due to the 'Economic War' which had existed since 1932, as a result of de Valera's government's refusal to pay land annuities to Britain. This Agreement came into force in April 1938, but no steps were taken for the handing over of the ports until September 1938.

Both prior to and during the First World War, Berehaven and the whole of Bantry Bay was one of the main bases of the British fleet. Old black and white photographs give some idea of the number of these great warships and their escorts. The vessels had to be victualled, and with more than 10,000 crewmen in the Bay at any one time, the value of trade must have been immense. Crews came ashore at Berehaven, Bere Island, Zetland Pier, Glengarriff, Snave and Bantry. The officers were entertained at a number of well-known hotels, including the Eccles, Roche's and Vickery's. Cricket, tennis, rugby and cricket were the order of the day for those ashore.

When Admiral Jellicoe arrived in Berehaven, he immediately inspected the fleet, and having called a meeting of all senior captains and officers, he gave orders to prepare for sailing to Jutland. Some time later the major sea battle of the war was fought, resulting in a partial victory for the English fleet and the destruction of some of Germany's sea power.

The Second World War was already looming when de Valera gained unconditional possession of the sea ports. Prime Minister Chamberlain made a blunder by allowing Ireland, for the first time in its history, to take a neutral position. Churchill regarded this move as sheer madness and a serious threat to the 'defence of the realm'.

Despite the fact that Chamberlain was away in Munich attempting to dissuade Hitler from invading Czechoslovakia, and that war was likely to break out at any time, the British went ahead and handed Fort Berehaven over to the Irish army on 26 September 1938. The event itself, which guaranteed Irish neutrality and deprived the Allied Forces of a strategic port which dominated the western approaches, was somewhat farcical. The Irish force of some sixty men, under the command of 2nd Lieutenant William Rea, arrived from Bantry on the *Princess Beara*, and by road between 22 and 26 September. They arrived on Bere Island without provisions or cooking facilities, as the British gun crews were still manning the gun turrets.

At twelve noon on 26 September, the formal handover commenced with the lowering of the Union Jack and the hoisting of the Tricolour whilst Lieutenant Rea took the salute. However, as the British forces were about to leave the island, a morse code message came through from the Admiralty that the fort was not to be handed over under any circumstances. The Irish forces were ordered out of the fort and the Union Jack was apparently again hoisted. A stalemate existed, with the British and Irish governments arguing over the phone for several hours and the whole affair appearing likely to develop into a major international incident. However, the English finally capitulated and, having again lowered the Union Jack, began to evacuate their forces. By 30 September all the English forces had left the island.

It is not known who was to blame for this complete miscalculation on the part of the British government, but the following January the Joint Chiefs of Staff advised that 'the retention or the capture of ports in the face of a hostile attitude on the part of Ireland would at best involve a most formidable military commitment and might, even so, be impossible'. When Churchill became First Lord of the Admiralty he immediately requested a special report 'upon the questions arising from the so-called neutrality of the so-called Éire'. In one of his instructions for discussion on the matter of 'Southern Ireland' he said, all this talk about partition and the bitterness that would be healed by a union of Northern and Southern Ireland will amount to nothing. They will not unite at the present time and we cannot in any circumstances sell the loyalists of Northern Ireland.

A dreadnought and destroyer in Bantry Bay

A view of the British Fleet from Bere island

Following the sinking of the battleship *Royal Oak* by a German submarine, Churchill declared,

> the time has come to make it clear to the Éire Government that we must have the use of these harbours (including Berehaven) and intend in any case to use them.

All of this points to the fact that Churchill was obsessed with the retention or capture of these ports, regardless of the fact that this would have pulled Ireland into the war with Germany. Indeed, some years previously, in October 1939, when Sir John Maffey visited de Valera in Dublin with a request for the use of Cobh and Berehaven, he was politely told that if this was granted it would be the equivalent of a declaration of war with Germany.

When this matter was discussed at the war cabinet on 24 October, Churchill was incensed, and declared his view that 'Ireland's neutrality [was] illegal as the King was still the Irish head of state and Germany was the King's enemy'. In fact the Irish envoy appointed to Berlin did have his letters of credence signed by the English King. Churchill began taking steps to end Éire's Commonwealth membership, although the rest of his cabinet were not disposed to such a move. However, when he became Prime Minister a year later, he embarked on an economic policy of depriving Ireland of the goods and equipment necessary to preserve her neutrality.

Despite her neutral position, Ireland was overrun with German agents and MI5 secret service operatives from Britain. The average Irish citizen was totally unaware of the question hanging over the ports and the espionage activities of the two warring nations. Frank Aiken, at that time Minister for the Co–ordination of Defensive Measures, made sure of this by his ruthless censorship of the newspapers of the day. Only those who possessed radios were able to keep up with the worldwide news and what was in fact happening in their own country.

During the early years of the war, Churchill blamed the loss of ships in the Atlantic on enemy action and on de Valera's stand on the neutrality of Irish ports, especially Berehaven. This was in fact a fallacy as the Germans had broken the Royal Navy's secret code as early as 1936 and had accurate knowledge of all Allied shipping movements up to the summer of 1943. The British press took up Churchill's attitude and public opinion was quick to condemn the Irish for Britain's losses at sea. The cabinet secretly introduced a policy of economic sanctions, including the non-provision of shipping to meet the country's import needs.

By 1941, the 'Emergency', as it was known here, had commenced. Petrol was rationed, coal imports were non-existent, tea was severely curtailed, white bread disappeared off the shelves and coffee was no longer available.

Through Irish Shipping Limited, Ireland bought eight vessels and managed to charter another five in its first year of operation. Despite losing two ships in the following years, Ireland was able to break the economic blockade. Meanwhile, as the war progressed, the possibility of an invasion of Éire by the German forces was of grave concern to the Allies, and they were considering whether to take the ports over, by force if necessary. At this stage, de Valera and his government were walking a tightrope in the cause of neutrality and fear abounded that the British and Americans would invade from the north in order to prevent a German takeover of the country. Plans were drawn up in the War Office in London for an invasion to take over the ports, but this was eventually abandoned as it would involve too much manpower and back-up, and also because it would cause irreparable damage to the goodwill of other nations who would see it as a further imperial conquest of a neutral country, thereby playing into the hands of German propagandists. Ireland in fact could not have prevented a British invasion, due to ill-equipped armed forces and its almost non-existent naval presence, which consisted of six old timber torpedo boats.

Despite all the pressures, including the mistaken bombing of Dublin by Germany, the de Valera government stood firm until the end of the war, and Britain and the Allies were denied access to the ports, although many ships were sunk by German U-boats off the south-west coast, resulting in bodies and flotsam being washed ashore on the coastline.

Despite rumours to the contrary, there are no records available to show that either English warships or trawler spy ships came into Bantry Bay for supplies during the war years, nor that German U-boats used to surface in Dunmanus Bay (west of Kilcrohane) to charge batteries and to come ashore for food supplies. I have, however, often heard it mentioned that German officers were said to have been seen drinking in certain pubs on the Muintir mBaire peninsula.

Bantry Bay

Come help me, boys, to sing a song,
And lilt a lively roundelay;
As fast and free we boom along
And top the waves of Bantry Bay.

A fair wind fills our flowing sail—
But let it blow from where it may,
We'll woo the breeze or brave the gale
With joyful hearts on Bantry Bay!

Oh, there are harbours made with hands
With sticks and stones, with mud and clay,
With piles and beams and iron bands—
We've no such things in Bantry Bay!

We've fair Glengarriff's silvery tide,
We've grand Berehaven, where today
The fleets of half the world might ride,
With room to swing, in Bantry Bay.

Historic scenes come into view
As on we plough our water way;
For chieftains bold and clansmen true
Were long the lords of Bantry Bay.

And well we hope the world may see,
Ere many years have passed away.
The sons of patriot ancestry
Again hold sway by Bantry Bay.

So trim your sails, and ease your sheets,
And hoist your bunting bright and gay;
Our trip has been a bunch of sweets—
Hip Hip Hurrah! for Bantry Bay!

— 43 —

Gulf Oil and the Supertankers

When the representatives of Gulf Oil Corporation first visited Bantry Bay early in 1966, they assessed the eastern end of Bere Island as a suitable location for a crude oil terminal. However, they found this location was unsuitable due to the narrow entrance to the east and the large swell running on the south side. They then viewed the western end of Whiddy Island and, seeing that the heavy swell had almost subsided, came to the conclusion that this was a more suitable location. They were also impressed by the depth of water at the north side.

Soon afterwards, news filtered through that a decision had been made and that Whiddy Island had been chosen as the location for the future giant oil terminal base for Europe. Surveys were carried out both on land and at sea, planning permission was applied for and granted, and about a year later representatives of the major contractors descended on the town to prepare their tenders for the work. Three months later the equipment and heavy machinery began to roll in.

Few in the area realised that what was about to happen would change Bantry from a dead and dreary location into a 'boom town'. Bantry Bay, because of its strategic location and deep water, was once again about to be put on the historical and commercial maps of the world.

With the influx of Irish, English, Belgian, Swedish and workers from other countries, local accommodation was at a premium, from Bantry to Glengarriff. Hotels were taken over, houses and garages were quickly converted, and restaurants sprang up overnight. A fleet of boats arrived from Cork and other ports to convey both personnel and equipment to the island. South Beach took on the appearance of a major construction site and a road was built along the shoreline from North Beach (island) right around past the lakes to the main site, while a pier was built at Tranahilla on the south-western side.

The main contractors were as follows: Shellabear Price (UK) Ltd.as main civil engineering contractor; Irish Engineering and Harbour Construction Company Ltd. as main tanker jetty constructors; Ascon Ltd. as service pier constructors; and Graver/Hedlund as tank constructors.

In addition, there were many Irish and local sub-contractors, and the total number of employees varied between 650 and 700 workmen.

Most of the contractors were under tremendous pressure to complete the work on time, to coincide with the arrival of the first supertanker.

From 1971 onwards, there were an average of seventeen to twenty tankers using the facilities each month. This brought a considerable amount of revenue to the town, as crews coming ashore bought foodstuffs and other goods. Unfortunately, as Bantry lacked a harbour authority, no dues were levied on the tanker traffic. It would appear that in the early negotiations between Gulf Oil and the government of that time, an agreement was reached that no charges would be levied on the Gulf operation by way of harbour dues. This arrangement denied the marine development of the town's harbour and facilities to the tune of approximately £12 million over the period of operation (based on a charge of a halfpenny per ton in old money).

It was a known fact in world business circles that Gulf Oil had written off the total original cost of the terminal during the first year of operation due to the upward fluctuation of crude oil. Also, in the time it took a mammoth tanker to sail from the Arabian Gulf to Bantry Bay, her cargo would appreciate by over one million dollars.

During 1975 there was a general slump in the crude oil market, combined with increased usage of the Suez Canal by tankers of up to

125,000 tons. This raised the question of the viability of the Gulf operation, and the company entered into cost-cutting negotiations with its various sub-contractors. These negotiations were very protracted, due to the severity of Gulf's proposals. After about sixteen months, the negotiations concluded with minimum job losses, but with substantial cuts in weekly wages and working hours. Now, only one tug was crewed permanently, while the others lay unmanned at anchor with crew on standby at home. The same system applied to the line-boats, except that the duty boat remained at the service pier on the island.

As the tanker traffic decreased over that period (1977–79) there was a general foreboding in the town that the terminal might close. However, in the latter half of 1979, due to serious damage to the new tanker jetty at Leixeos in northern Portugal, a number of large tankers were diverted to Bantry Bay. Amongst these were the *Casiope* and the *Betelgeuse*—both tankers in the 220,000 class. After a delay of several days, due to the number of tankers awaiting discharge, the *Betelgeuse* was berthed at the offshore jetty at 23.30 hours on Saturday night, 7 January 1979, and began pumping oil ashore to the Tank Farm some hours later.

Sunday 8 January was a normal working day with the usual service boats running to and from the jetty/tanker and the island installations. Many of the tanker crew came ashore during their time off and spent some time visiting shops and making purchases. Little did they realise what that night would bring, as the joking and cheerful crew returned to their ship during the evening. The events that followed will remain in the minds of every Bantry person forever.

— 44 —

The Betelgeuse *Disaster*

As midnight approached, the tanker's discharge was progressing normally. The service boats had left Bantry and were on their way both to the island service pier and the offshore jetty with the remainder of the tanker's crew. The line-boat on duty was moored at the service jetty on call. Even though the service boats left Bantry at approximately the same time, they did not encounter each other either on the outward trip or the return journey to Bantry pier. It later transpired, at the government enquiry, neither crew observed the other boat during that hour's journey. The passenger launch, *Sea Lance*, moored at Bantry pier at about 00.35 hours and the crew went home.

The *Donemark* had meanwhile berthed for the night at the service jetty and remained on call, together with the line-boat.

At approximately 00.45 hours, a rumbling sound was heard by a number of people on the mainland, which seemed to come from the location of the terminal. To those who could see the terminal from the north mainland, the sky was lit up by what appeared to be a fire at the jetty/tanker location. This was followed by an immense explosion, with flames and smoke rising hundreds of feet into the sky. Other minor explosions followed. For some reason which has never been satisfactorily explained and was much debated during the enquiry, there appeared to be ten to fifteen minutes' delay in raising the alarm ashore.

As people ashore were awoken from their sleep and emerged into the darkness, they immediately observed that Whiddy Island was lit up by flames rising high from the north side. A black column of smoke had begun to trail towards the north of the town. As the town fire siren sounded, people began to congregate at the lower end of the Square, while others ran to the pier.

An aerial photograph of the Betelgeuse *on fire*

Very few people knew exactly what had happened and whether the fire was at the terminal itself (as it appeared) or at the jetty. Only those in direct radio contact with the terminal control knew the facts. However, word soon spread that the tanker was on fire. Within minutes Bantry pier was in a state of mayhem, with cars arriving from every direction and people running towards the moored service boats. Doors were smashed in and windows broken on those vessels which happened to be locked. Soon the roar of many engines being started broke the anxious silence as people gathered in groups. Mooring lines were cast off and all serviceable boats left the pier with crews, part crews, terminal personnel, fire officers, volunteers and managerial staff.

When those travelling out by boat learned that the fire was located at the jetty/tanker, the immediate concern was for the tanker crew and the local personnel manning the jetty. As soon as those people destined for the terminal installation had been dropped off at the service pier, some of the boats headed out through the Gearhies to the north side. What greeted them was a sight not easily forgotten.

Both the tanker *Betelgeuse* and the jetty were engulfed by a raging inferno of burning crude oil. The sea was on fire to the north and east of the tanker for a distance of about a mile, with flames leaping upwards about twenty feet. A dense black pall of smoke moved slowly north-east with the slight breeze, while the fumes and lack of oxygen made it difficult to breathe. As the service boats skirted the flaming sea for any survivors who might have escaped the inferno, they were met by the tugs coming from the north. The area was systematically searched and the western end of the jetty and the undamaged bow of the tanker were closely observed, but no sign of life could be seen (there were no survivors or bodies from these locations) as everyone seemed to have headed for the main embarking/disembarking place at Dolphin 22—the east end of the jetty.

An aerial photograph of Whiddy Island and the burning tanker

It soon became obvious to those searching that there were no survivors from the burning inferno of crude oil, so they turned their attention to standing by at the service jetty to evacuate those who were trying to prevent the large tanks exploding by spraying them with water. Some boats returned to Bantry pier to organise the search for bodies as soon as dawn arrived.

The first boats to get back to the pier were anxiously awaited by families and relatives pleading for news of their loved ones. As the news filtered through of the magnitude of the disaster, fears grew that they would not see their menfolk alive again. And so the long wait began, until the exhausted personnel from the installation finally arrived back at Bantry pier hours later as dawn broke. The waiting doctors, nurses and ambulance crews treated those suffering from exhaustion and breathing problems after the inhalation of burning gases.

As soon as crew changes were effected at about 07.30 a.m., a number of service boats went out searching for bodies. The area to be covered was the stretch of water east of the jetty and the northern shoreline of the island. By this time, the fires on the tanker had abated somewhat and the danger of the tanks at the terminal catching fire had decreased, yet the continuous watering down of the tanks continued long into the morning.

Anxious families, relations and friends of the locals who were posted as missing continued their vigil on the stone pier, huddled in groups by the wall and running across to the pier steps when the service boats called in. Press and TV crews had descended on the town from the time the earliest reports had reached the news desks. A few small planes from Cork Airport flew over the disaster area filming the final death-throes of the giant tanker which had earlier broken up into three sections—bow, mid-section, and aft wheelhouse and engine-room. The mid-section had by now sunk, while the bow and the aft part were sticking almost perpendicular out of the blackened water.

The first of the bodies were recovered late that afternoon—some with lifejackets on, others without. The bodies were impossible to identify, as the intense heat had shrunk the majority of them to the size of a three-year-old child. It was extremely traumatic for those engaged in the recovery, an experience impossible to forget. As soon as the senior representatives of both Gulf and the tanker's owners, Total of France, arrived on the scene there was a general blackout of information to the press and the public. There were no interviews given, only prepared statements issued. This was mainly due to the various rumours circulated immediately following the disaster which gave contradictory accounts concerning the time factor and where the fire had started. Later, when the government announced that there would be an enquiry, it was hoped that everything would be revealed and the full details disclosed.

Over the following days, the tankers which had been waiting in the Bay were diverted to other suitable European ports to discharge their cargoes, while the thousands of tons of oil on the sea and shoreline were contained and collected by the various boats and shore-working teams. A number of small Cessna planes were brought in and these flew from the airfield at Beach, discharging detergent on the oil-polluted sea surface.

It was approximately four to five weeks before the emergency ended and boats and men were laid off. With the scorched and blackened hull of the tanker partially sunk at the jetty, the realisation began to dawn on the workers and the people of Bantry—that this could possibly be the end of Gulf Oil in Bantry Bay and that a very high price in lives had been paid.

— 45 —

Aftermath of the Disaster

The following period saw the gradual lay–off of up to 125 part-time and permanent employees of the various sub-contractors. The employees at the terminal retained their jobs, cleaning up and repairing the installation. Negotiations had already begun between Gulf and various salvage contracting firms for the removal of the wrecked tanker from the jetty location. Smit-Tak of Rotterdam in Holland were successful in tendering and, within weeks, had their tugs and heavy lift barges on location. Work immediately began on the bow section, which was fairly intact but still joined to the submerged middle part. Having severed the joined parts by means of underwater cutting gear, the bow was eventually torn away by using three powerful tugs and was towed to the eastern moorings at Whiddy Island, where it was prepared for towage to a scrapyard on the Continent. The same procedure was followed for the aft section, which contained the engine and pump rooms. This section was eventually placed on a large pontoon barge which had been submerged beneath it and then lifted completely out of the water by powerful air pumps. It was then later towed away. The middle section proved the most difficult, but was eventually floated and towed to the eastern end of Whiddy Island, where the same procedure was used. The salvage of the tanker was not completed without cost, as one of the Dutch divers lost his life during the operation.

During the salvage operation, Smit-Tak had a number of vessels and heavy lift barges in Bantry. These included the Smit Lloyd tugs, the two Tak–Lifts and the salvage vessel *Barracuda*. At times there were over a hundred Dutchmen in Bantry. Parties were held aboard either the *Barracuda* or the Tak-Lift, where the accommodation was up to hotel standards. When Smit-Tak finally completed the work and departed from Bantry, there was many a sad farewell waved from the pier as the vessels began their journey back to Rotterdam.

The jetty was surveyed by various companies and found to be almost unsalvageable due to the damage caused by the fire and explosions which had generated over one thousand degrees of heat. In fact, the steel, aluminium and concrete had melted inside the steel piles, and the only way to rebuild the whole structure would have been to cut all the steel piles some six feet below the waterline and reconstruct them. The figure mentioned at the time, £8 million, equalled the original cost of construction of the whole complex.

During the following years, while Gulf management pondered over a decision to repair the jetty or replace it a with single buoy mooring, the terminal itself was retained on 'a care and maintenance basis'—moth-balled, with a skeleton staff on shift rotation. Sub-contractors were sometimes called in to carry out maintenance work on electrical installations, pipework and standby engine repairs.

At the time it appeared that Gulf management was in a state of general indecision globally. This was verified when the Chevron Oil Company carried out a 'midnight raid' on the stock exchanges and took over the company before anybody realised what was happening. Even the Gulf management in Bantry were unaware of the situation until they were informed the following morning by some local people.

By now the effects of the closure of the terminal were being felt in the local economy. Gone were the 170 jobs, the good wages and the general financial input into the local commerce of the region. The tugs and service vessels had departed and the busy pier became quiet again. Bantry was once more entering the doldrums of recession. The townspeople and the ex-workers waited anxiously for a decision by the new owners, Chevron. When it eventually arrived, it was not at all what had been expected. Instead of rebuilding the jetty or installing a single buoy mooring to make the terminal operational again,

Chevron negotiated a deal with the government whereby they agreed to hand over the terminal 'as is' and donated a sum of twenty-four million dollars to revitalise the terminal or the local Bantry economy.

Everyone waited in expectation of a firm government commitment to the region and detailed plans of how money was going to be spent. Would it go towards the reconstruction of the jetty or single buoy mooring and the opening of the terminal under the government department, or would it be spent in revitalising the local economy and infrastructure by promoting an expansion of industry and tourism?

No announcement was made. Some information filtered through that other West Cork towns were to benefit from the 'Bantry Package', but no government Minister was willing to explain, Instead the money just disappeared into the government coffers to meet expenses elsewhere.

However, payment was made for removing the oil terminal and jetty, to comply with one of the main conditions of the original planning permission whereby, if Gulf decided to pull out, they were obliged to remove everything from the installation site and leave the area as they had originally found it.

Mussel Farming

As no government initiative to rebuild the Bantry economy was forthcoming, the possibility of shell and fish farming was examined by a number of private individuals. Mussel farming is now a major industry, mainly funded from local sources, with assistance from government and EU funds. Two processing factories give substantial employment, mostly on a seasonal basis. Working from Bantry pier, six to seven boats, some of which are specialised, generate further employment. Even though structural repairs and certain improvements have been carried out on the pier, it is still proving totally inadequate for present usage, mainly due to the fact that the area surrounding the pier has not been dredged to allow boats to use all the berthage area on the east side—it is pointless having a reasonable facility if only a section of it can be used.

After the removal of the various sections of the wreck of the *Betelgeuse* from the north harbour, the first attempts at mussel farming were initiated. Rafts made out of timber poles and barrels were constructed on the beaches of Bantry and then anchored off Chapel Island in the inner harbour. The people involved in this early trial were Tim O'Driscoll (deceased), Vincent Roundtree and Louis Minihane amongst others. The first harvest worthy of note was some eight tons. Seeing this, many other people got involved and made additional rafts during those early years.

As the mussel rafts were vulnerable to the elements during the winter months, a new type of cultivation was introduced. This was a system whereby the mussel cultivation lines (nets and ropes) could be suspended from an anchored line of large plastic drums. With a limited number of rafts and drum lines, the results proved satisfactory and the yield was about twenty-five tons each year.

Seeing the possibilities of a viable mussel industry, a number of groups were formed, including local fishermen. In all there were about twenty-five people involved in this venture.

Within a few months, a substantial number of long mussel lines were prepared and anchored in the vicinity of Chapel Island. The following harvest amounted to about 500 tons. After this success, many more mussel lines were anchored in the harbour and its approaches, and the harvest yields increased dramatically from 500 tons to about 2,500 tons per annum. Since the early '90s, this volume of cultivated mussels has increased gradually to approximately 3,000 tons per annum. As a result, two factories have been engaged in the process of preparing the shellfish for export and for the home market.

Now, in the early months of 1996, as the town prepares for the bicentennial of Wolfe Tone's invasion, there is a new awakening. Unoccupied factories are now in production, new shops and premises are being built, redesigned or expanded. The building of private houses has gained momentum, while The Square and approaches are being redeveloped to once again make Bantry a vibrant community.

Appendix
The Bantry Charters

This indenture made on the 27th day of August One Thousand Nine Hundred and Seventy Eight BETWEEN BANTRY ESTATES COMPANY having its registered office at Gardner House, Ballsbridge, Dublin 4 (hereinafter referred to as "the Grantor") of the One Part and SEAN P. O'LUASA of Wolfe Tone Square, Bantry, County Cork and BRENDAN MINEHANE of Dromleigh South, Bantry, County Cork (hereinafter collectively referred to as "the Trustees") the present trustees of the Bantry Chamber of Commerce of the Other Part.

WHEREAS:

a) By letters Patent dated 10th of March in the Thirteenth year of the reign of His Majesty King William III of England Scotland France and Ireland the said William III did grant (*inter alia*) unto John Davis his heirs and assigns that he the said John Davis his heirs and assigns should have and hold for ever in and at the Town of Bantry a Fair or Market to be held yearly on each 20th of November together with all issues tolls customs profits revenue of selling chattels and goods, emoluments and amercements whatsoever arising from or pertaining or belonging to such kind of Fair or Market rendering yearly unto the Exchequer of the Realm of Ireland the sum of 6s 8d [33½ pence decimal currency].

b) The Grantor is now seised in fee simple of the said issues tolls customs profits revenue of selling chattels and goods emoluments and amercements (hereinafter referred to as "the Tolls') and has agreed with the said Bantry Chamber of Commerce to make a gift of the same unto the said Bantry Chamber of Commerce subject to the payment of the said reserved sum of 6s 8d.

c) The Trustees are the duly appointed trustees of the said Bantry Chamber of Commerce.

d) The said Bantry Chamber of Commerce has requested that the Tolls should be vested in the Trustees in manner hereinafter appearing.

NOW THIS INDENTURE WITNESSETH as follows:

1. In consideration of the premises and of the Grantor's desire to promote the affairs of the said Bantry Chamber of Commerce the Grantor as Settlor hereby grants and conveys unto the Trustees all that the Tolls TO HOLD the same unto the Trustees in fee simple subject only to the payment of the yearly sum of 6s 8d.

2. The Trustees shall hold the Tolls upon trust for the said Bantry Chamber of Commerce and according to the Rules thereof to deal therewith whether by sale lease mortgage charge or otherwise as the said Bantry Chamber of Commerce shall from time to time direct.

3. The Trustees and each of them hereby covenant with the Grantor that they the Trustees their successors and assigns will henceforth pay the said sum of 6s 8d reserved by the said Letters Patent and will at all times keep the Grantor and its assigns effectually indemnified against all actions and proceedings costs damages expenses claims and demands whatsoever by reason or on account of the non payment of the said sum of 6s 8d or any part thereof.

IN WITNESS whereof the Grantor has caused its Common Seal to be affixed and the Trustees have set their hands and Seals the day and year first above written.

William III by the Grace of God King of England, Scotland, France and Ireland, defender of the faith, etc., to all to whom our present letters come, greeting. Whereas our beloved subject John Davys by his petition directed to our justices general of our said realm of Ireland has humbly begged that we will deign to grant him our letters patent for a fair or market to be held yearly in and within the town of Bantry in Co. Cork in our realm of Ireland (viz) a fair or market to be held there yearly for ever on the twentieth day of November and the day next following, and whereas our writ of ad quod dampnum issued to enquire whether it were to our damage or prejudice or that of any of our subjects near adjacent that the said fair or market should be held yearly at the said town of Bantry, and whereas it appears by the return to that writ that it is not to our harm or prejudice or that of any of our subjects near adjacent that the said fair or market should be held there, we know therefore that we of our special grace and of certain knowledge and pure motive and by the advice and consent of our beloved and faithful cousins and councillors Charles Duke of Bolton, Charles Earl of Berkeley and Henry Earl of Galway, our justices and general governors of the said realm of Ireland have given and granted and by these presents give and grant for us, our heirs and successors, to our beloved and faithful subject aforesaid John Davis, his heirs and assigns, full and absolute power and authority that he the aforesaid John Davis, his heirs and assigns, and each of them for ever shall have and hold and may and can have and hold a fair or market to be held in or at the town of Bantry aforesaid yearly for ever on each twentieth day of November and the day next following yearly for ever unless either of the said days happen to be a Sunday, and as often as it so happen we will that such fair shall be held on Monday next after such Sunday and the next day then next following, together with a court of pie powder to be held there during the aforesaid fair or market, and further we will and by the presents grant for us, our heirs and successors, that the aforesaid John Davis, his heirs and assigns for ever, shall have and hold, enjoy and receive (Gaudeant, recipient et percipient) all and singular issues, tolls, customs, profits, revenue of selling chattels and goods, emoluments and amercements whatsoever arising from the aforesaid fair or market and court, or pertaining or belonging to this kind of fair or market and court without rendering account thereof to us, our heirs or successors. Having and holding the aforesaid fair or market and court with all and singular issues, tolls, customs, privileges and immunities belonging or pertaining to them to the same John Davis, his heirs and assigns for ever, Holding of us, our heirs and successors, as of our castle of Dublin in free and common socage, Rendering thence yearly to us, our heirs or successors at the receipt of our Exchequer and that of our heirs and successors of our said realm of Ireland for the time being, the sum of six shillings and eight pence current money of England, payable in equal parts at the feasts of St. Michael the Archangel and the Annunciation of the Blessed Virgin Mary for ever. We will and by the presents grant for us, our heirs and successors, to the aforesaid John Davis, his heirs and assigns, that these our letters patent of their enrolment shall be in all things good, firm, valid sufficient and efficacious in law towards and against us, our heirs and successors, as well in all courts of us, our heirs and successors, as elsewhere within our said realm of Ireland or wheresoever elsewhere, any statute, act, ordinance, provision or any other thing, cause or matter whatsoever made to the contrary of the premises in anything notwithstanding. Provided always that these our letters patent be enrolled in the rolls of our court of chancery in our said realm of Ireland within the space of six months next after the date of the presents. In testimony whereof we have made these our letters patent.

Witness our aforesaid justice of our said realm of Ireland at Dublin on the tenth day of March in the thirteenth year of our reign.

EXTRACTS FROM PATENT 32 CHARLES II TO THE EARL OF ANGLESEY.
CHARLES the 2nd by the Grace of God of England Scotland France and Ireland King Defender of the faith &c.

TO ALL TO WHOM THESE PRESENTS SHALL COME—GREETING:-

WHEREAS: our right Trusty and Right well loved Cousin and Counsellor Arthur Earl of Anglesey Lord Kaper of our Privy Seal hath humbly represented unto us that he is seized to him and to his heirs of the towns and lands of Gurteen, Killername, Garryduff, Derniarelagh, Rusky, Windy Island, Dromclagh, Seskin, Drumdoneen, Shandrum, Inchclogh, Brinny, Rindisart, Carvan & Madderagh, Crylliconagh, Glengarriff and Island Icullin, Ardnageshall and Ardnaturrish, Cooneholy and Comeholy, Crillyconagh alias Cressiconagh, Carnefadda, Killcasken, Drumlaffe, Drumgarvan, Comgiery, Cappanaparkie, Rossinacowen, Thingrehill & Agreome, Knockmore, Ballinkally, Ballyaghboy, Garoragh, Loghanmore, Glanrogh alias Glaronagh, Cloghfone, Killoghagh, Ballydonagan, Glenlisk and Glenriske, Irhin, Cahirvillboe, Kellunncky, Legganbeg, Lackerighane,

Cahircrogh, Bearehaven, Coulagh, Kilkabrin, Caherquin, Eyris, Killmacowen, Derrenehinie, Ballynekelly, Grenan, Ardagh, Connoghter &Rurin &Molesky situate lying and being in the Barony of Bere and Bantry in the County of Cork in our said Kingdom of Ireland which said towns and lands not being united in or to any manner many inconveniences and disorders do frequently happen amongst the inhabitants thereof and being remote from Market Towns and Fairs have not yet convened for venting the Commodities of the Groth thereof as other parts of the Kingdom have AND being therefore humbly besought us to create the Towns lands and premises into two Manors according to the appointment and Division of them herein after mentioned and grant divers courts priviledges benefits advantages and franchises to be held and enjoyed with the same we referred the Consideration thereof unto our Right Trusty and Right entirely beloved Cousin and Counsellor James Duke of Ormond our Lieutenant of Our said Kingdom of Ireland who made his report thereupon unto us bearing date the * * * day of January 1679—That he had considered of the Draft of a Letter in lieu of the said Earl of Anglesey presented to us for creating several of the said Earls Lands into Two Mannors and granting him and his heirs several franchises and liberties to be enjoyed therewith and that in regard the same are only such priviledges as have been heretofore granted by us to several other persons in that our Kingdom and by the granting thereof our Revenue will not be lessened but rather encreased by an addition of Twenty shillings per annum thereunto which is to be reserved out of the Markets and Fairs thereby intended to be granted be therefore humbly conceived the same to be proper for our Signature if we should think so fit KNOW YE, that we of our Special Grace certain knowledge and mere motion by and with the advice and consent of our said Right Trusty and right entirely beloved Cousin and Counsellor James Duke of Ormond Our Liet, General &General Governor of our said Kingdom of Ireland and according to the Tenor of our Letters under our Privy Signet and Sign Manual bearing date at our Court at Whitehall the 6th day of February in the Two &Thirtieth year of our Reign and in the year of Our Lord 1679—now Inrolled in the Rolls of Our High Court of Chancery in our said Kingdom of Ireland have given and granted by those presents for us our heirs and successors we do give and grant unto the said Arthur Earl of Anglesey his heirs and assigns and we do hereby ordain constitte and appoint that all and singular the towns and lands of Gurteene, Killername, Garryduffe, Demienelagh, Rusky, Whiddy Island, Dromclogh, Seskin, Drumdoneen, Shandrum, Inchyclogh, Brinny, Rynedisart, Carvan & Maddecagh, Crillyconagh, Glanarriffe and Island Icullin, Ardnagashell and Ardeturrish, Cooneholy alias Cooneholly, Crillyconagh alias Chrishyconagh, Carruffadde, Kellkashane, Drumlaffe, Dromgarvan, Connigerg and Cappanaparkie, Rossenacowen, Thingeryhell and Agroome shall from thenceforth be reputed and be in Deed and in name one Entire Manor to all intents constructions and purposes whatsoever and all and singular the said last recited lands into one entire Manor WE do for us our heirs and successors erect and create by these presents and we do by these presents for us our heirs and successors strictly charge and command the said several last recited Towns lands tenements and hereditaments be and shall be from thenceforth reputed and taken for one entire Manor to be called and known by the name of the Manor of Bantry AND FURTHER we have given and granted and by these presents for us our heirs and successors we do give and grant unto the said Arthur Earl of Anglesey his heirs and assigns and we do likewise hereby ordain constitute & appoint that all and Singular the towns and lands of Knockmore, Ballinkelly, Ballyaghboy, Gawragh, Laghanmore, Glanrogh alias Glawrogh, Cloghfone, Killoghagh, Ballydonagan, Glenlisk alias Glenisk, Irhin, Cahirvillaboe, Killkennehy, Laghanbegg, Lackerryane, Cahircrogh, Bearehaven, Clonlagh, Killcabrin, Cahirquin, Eyris, Killnacowen, Derrehehine alias Denehine, Ballynekelly, Grenane, Ardagh, Connoghlin, Rurrin & Molasky afd. shall from henceforth be reputed and be in Deed and in name one entire Manner to all Intents constructions and purposes whatsoever and all and singular the said last mentioned lands into one entire manner WE do for us our heirs and successors strictly charge and command that the said several last mentioned towns lands tenements and hereditaments be and shall be from henceforth reputed and taken for one entire Manner to be called and known by the name of the Manor of Althem AND FUR. of our Special Grace certain knowl and meere motion by and within the advise and consent aforesaid and in psuance of our said letters we do by these presents for us and our heirs and successors give and grant and confirm unto the said Earl of Anglesey his heirs and assigns full and absolute power and authority to have and to hold from henceforth for ever to hold and keep a markett upon every Wednesday and Saturday weekley at Ballygobbane als. Oldtown within the said Manor of Bantry and also to hold and keep three fairs yearly at Ballygobbane als, Oldtown aforesaid one of the said Fairs to be held or kept on the twenty-ninth day of May & the day after another on the tenth day of August & the day after and the other on the fourth day of October and the day after yearly for ever unless the said twenty-ninth day of May tenth day of August and fourth day of October or either of them shall happen to be on the Lords Day commonly called Sunday then and in such case the said fair so happening to fall on Sunday shall be kept on the Monday following and the day after AND FUR. of our more ample grace certain knowled. and meere motion by and with the advice and consent afd. and according to the tenor of Our afd. Letters we do by these presents for us our heirs and successors grant unto the said Arthur Earl of Anglesey his heirs and assigns full and absolute power & authority that he the said Arthur Earl of Angl. his heirs and assigns for ever shall from time to time at his and their will and pleasure make constitute nominate and appoint one or more person or persons from time to time to be Paymaster & Clerk of the Market in & within the said Manors & that such person or persons so to be constituted nominated and appointed by the said Earl of Anglesey his heirs and assigns to be Clerk or Clerks of the Market as afd. shall from time to time have enjoy use and execute all and all manner of power jurisdiction & preheminance fees perquisites emoluments and advantages in and within the said Manors which do in anywise belong to the Office of Clerk of the Market or which any other Clke of the Market of us our heirs or successors within our said realm of Ireland hath enjoyed useth or executeth or may or ought to have enjoy use or execute by virtue of the said office that no other Clke of the Market of us our heirs and successors shall hereafter enter into the said manors or any part thereof to exercise or execute the said Office or in default of the Clke of the Market so to be nominated by the said Earl his heirs or assigns any Statute Act ordinance provision or any other cause matter or thing whatsoever to the contrary in anywise notwithstanding AND we do by these presents for us our heirs & successors give and grant unto the said Arthur Earl of Anglesey his heirs and assigns full free and absolute power and authority that he the said Arthur Earl of Anglesey his heirs and assigns shall and may have and one or more Court or Courts of Bipowder and all things to a Court of Bipowder belonging and within the said Manor of Bantry during the continuance of the said Markets and Fairs respectly and likewise that he the said Arthur Earl of Anglesey his heirs and assigns and may from time to time have hold and enjoy all and singr. Tolls perquisites profit that no writ or writs of quod dampnum hath not before the making of these our Letters patents issued to enquire what damage or hindrance the said Markets and Fairs or any of them would be to any other neighbouring markets and fairs TO HAVE AND TO HOLD the said several Fairs and Markets with all the profits thereout arising unto the said Arthur Earl of Anglesey his heirs and assigns for ever to be holden of us our heirs and successors as of our Castle of Dublin in free and common Soccage and not in capite nor in Soccage in Capite nor by Knights Service YIELDING AND PAYING unto us our heirs and successors at the rect. of our Excheqr. in our said realm of Ireland yearly for the said Markets and Fairs the yearly rent of twenty shillings to be paid at the feast of St. Michael the Archangle & the Annunciation of the blessed Virgin St. Mary half yearly by even & equal portions AND FURTHER of our Special Grace certain knowledge and meere motion by and with the advice and consent aforesaid we do by these presents for us our heirs and successors grant unto the said Arthur Earl of Anglesey his heirs and assigns that these our Letters Patents or the Inrollmt. thereof shall be in all things firm good valid and sufft. and effectual in the Law agst. us our heirs and successors as well as in all our Courts within our said Realm of Ireland as elsewhere wheresoever according to the purport and tenor of our afd. Letters without any other or further Grant Licence or Confirmation from us our heirs or successors by the said Arthur Earl of Anglesey his heirs or assigns to be had procured or obtained AND ALSO that these our Letters Patents and ALL AND SINGULAR the articles and clauses therein contained and specified as well in Sence Intention & meaning as in words shall be construed and interpreted to the best advantage benefit and behoof of the said Arthur Earl of Anglesey his heirs and assigns as well as in all the Courts of us our heirs and successors within our said Kingdom of Ireland as elsewhere wheresoever witht. any objection or exception whatsoever notwithstanding the not naming or ill naming ill reciting or not reciting in these presents the prems. and parts or parcels thereof or the Tenor thereof to Coy. Barony Parish or place wherein the premes. or any part thereof do lye and notwithstanding the not recital or misrecital not naming or misnaming of any of the said offices Franchises Libertys and priviledges or the not recital or misrecital of our right title or int. in or to the premes. or any part thereof and notwithstanding no writ of ad quod dampnum hath issued to enquire of the Markets and Fairs AND notwithstanding any Statute act ordinance provision or restriction or any other Cause matter or thing whatsoever to the Enervation Evacuation or annihilation of these our Letters patents PROVIDED ALWAYS that these our Letters patent be Inrolled in the rolls of our high court of Chancry in our said Kingdom of Ireland within the space of 6 months next ensuing the date of these presents although no express mention &c.

IN WITNESS whereof we have caused these our Letters Patents witness of Lieut. Genl. & Genl. Govr. of our said Kingdom of Ireland at Dublin the 15th day of March in the two and thirtieth year of our Reign.

Irrot decimodie aprilis anno RK Caroli Sedi
Tricesimo Secundo Mr. Paterson & Fras. Perry D Clk & Keepr. of the Rolls

Bibliography

Analecta Hibernica, *No. 4*
Anderson, R. C., *Oared Fighting Ships*
Anwyl, E., *Celtic Religion*
Archives de la Marine, *Journal de Morard de Galles*
Archives de la Guerre, *Carton de L'Expedition de L'Irlande*

Bagwell, *Ireland Under the Tudors*
Bennett, G., *History of Bandon and the Principal Towns in the West Riding of Cork*
Berleth, R., *The Twilight Lords*
Bonnechose, E., *Lazare Hoche*
Bowra, C. M., *Language and Background of Homer*
Bradley, P. Brendan, *Bantry Bay, Ireland in the Days of Napoleon and Wolfe Tone*
Burke, Rev. U. J., *The Aryan Original of the Gaelic Race and Language*
Butler, W., *Confiscation in Irish History*

Caesar, *De Bello Gallico*
Casson, *The Ancient Mariners*
Chadwick, N. K., *The Druids*
Chausee, Le Comte de la, *Memoire Sur Bantry*
Chevalier, E. Capitaine de Vaisseau, *Histoire de la Marine Franciase Pendant la Guerre de L'Independance Amercaine*

Childe, V. G., *Pre-Historic Communities of the British Isles*
Clarke & Piggot, *Pre-Historic Societies*
Clarke, G., *World Pre-History*
Connellan, *Annals of the Four Masters*
Corkery, D., *The Hidden Ireland*
Croker, T. Crofton, *Popular Songs Illustrative of the Invasions of Ireland*
Croker, T. C., *Fairy Legends of Ireland*
Curry, E., *The Battle of Magh Leane*

D'Alton, Rev. E., *History of Ireland*
D'Arbois de Joubainville, *Les Druides*
De la Graviere, *La Marines des Anciens*
De Grouchy, Marquis, *Le General de Grouchy et L'Irlande en 1796*
Duro, F., *La Armada Invencible*

Eliade, M., *Shamanism*
Eliade, M., *The Myth of the Eternal Return*
Ellis, P. B., *Hell or Connaught*
Everett Hale, E., *Letter on Irish Emigration*

Fallon, N., *The Armada in Ireland*
Ferguson, Lady, *Story of the Irish before the Conquest*
Fernandez-Armesto, F., *The Spanish Armada*
Froude, J. A., *The Spanish Story of the Armada*

Gibson, Revd. C. B., *History of the County and City of Cork*
Gordon, C. H., *Riddles in History*
Gore-Booth, B., *Report of the Select Committee on Colonisation from Ireland*
Guillon, E., *La France et L'Irlande Pendant la Revolution*
Gwynne, Revd. Aubrey, *Cromwell's Policy of Transportation*
Gwynne, Revd. Aubrey, *Studies December 1920*
Gwynne, Revd. Aubrey, *Studies June 1931*
Gwynne, Revd. Aubrey, *Early Irish Emigration to the West Indies 1612–43*
Gwynne, Revd. Aubrey, *Studies September 1929*
Gwynne, Revd. Aubrey, *Studies December 1929*

Hardiman, *Irish Minstrelsy*
Hawkes, Dr. Richard, *The Last Invasion of Ireland*
Holland, Revd. E., *History of West Cork and the Diocese of Ross*
Homet, M. F., *On the Trail of the Sun Gods*

Joyce, Dr., *Irish Names and Places*
Jubainville, *Cours de la Literature Celtique*

Keating, G., *History of Ireland*
Kelleher, D. L., *Ireland of the Welcomes*

Lanigan, Revd., *Ecclesiastical History of Ireland*
Le Roy, *La Marine des Ancients Peuples*
Le Roy, *Les Navires des Anciens*
London Records Office, *C. O. I. to 1688*

MacDermot, Frank, *Theobald Wolfe Tone*
Markham, R., *The History of Persia*
Marshman, J., *The History of India*
Martin, C. P., *Pre-Historic Man in Ireland*
McAllister, R. A. S., *Ireland in Pre-Celtic Times*
McAllister, R. A. S., *Tara–A Pagan Sanctuary of Ancient Ireland*
McAllister, R. A. S., *Ancient Ireland*
Morgan, Edward, *Journal of the Movements of the French Fleet*
Murphy, Revd. D., *Deportation of the Irish to the West Indies in the Seventeenth Century*

Nilsson, N. P., *Primitive Time Reckoning*

O'Brennan, *Ancient Ireland*
O'Brien, H., *The Round Towers of Ireland*
O'Brien, H., *Phoenician Ireland*
O'Connor, *Dissertation on Ancient Ireland*
O'Curry, *Manuscript Materials of Irish History*
O'Donoghue, B., *Parish Histories and Place Names of West Cork*
O'Donovan, J., *The Four Masters*
O'Donovan, J., *Miscellany of the Celtic Society*

O'Flaherty, *Ogygia*
O'Flaherty, *Leabhar Na gCeart (Book of Rights)*
O'Flaherty, *Chronicles of Fire*
O'Hanlon, Revd. J., *The Irish American History of the United States*
O'Mahony, J. *West Cork and its Story*
O'Riordain, S. P., *Antiquities of the Irish Countryside*
O'Rourke, Cannon, *The Battle for the Faith in Ireland*
O'Sullivan, Don P., *Ireland under Elizabeth*

Parati, Luigi, *The Ancient World*
Petrie, *Tara*
Phene, Dr., *Serpent Worship*
Piggott, S., *The Druids*
Pitt & Fox (Notes), *History of the Abolition of the Slave Trade*
Prichard, J. C., *The Eastern Origins of the Celtic Nations*

Rawley, J. A., *The Trans-Atlantic Slave Trade*
Rawlingson, G., *Religions of the Ancient World*
Richey, Dr., *Lectures on the History of Ireland*
Rushe, Revd. J., *A Second Thebaid*
Rutledge, *Anglo-Irish Trade in the Sixteenth Century*

Savory, H. N., *The Pre-History of the Iberian Peninsula*
Scott Eliot, G. F., *Pre-History Man and his Story*
Shearman, J., *Loca Patriciana*
Stuart Jones, E. H., *An Invasion that Failed*

Taylor & Skinner, *Maps of the Roads of Ireland*
Toor, *Ancient Ships*
Troude, O., *Batailles Navales de la France*
Tuckey, F., *Cork Remembrancer*

Vallencey, Lt. Col., *Vindication of the Ancient History of Ireland*

Wakeman, W. E., *Archaeologia Hibernica*
Weech, W. N., *The History of the World*
Wilde, J. P., *Papyrus in Pre-Roman Britain*

Wilde, Lady, *Ancient Legends of Ireland*
Wilde, Lady, *An Tain Bo Cuailnge*
Wilde, Lady, *Antiquities*
Wilkes, Mrs. E., *Ireland—Ur of the Chaldees*
Williams, J. B., *Regicides in Ireland Part 3*
Williams, R. A., *The Berehaven Copper Mines*
Wood, J. E., *Sun, Moon, and Standing Stones*

Correspondence de l'Armee des Cotes de l'Ocean
Irish Ecclesiastical Records *1893*
Irish Ecclesiastical Records *1914*
Registrie de l'Armee des Cotes de l'Ocean
Act of the Privy Council (Colonial Series)
Calendar of State Papers (Colonial Series)
Council Books on 'Cromwellian Period'
British Museum
Egerton MSS 2395–Island of St. Christophers (*1626–27*)
Sloan MSS 17913–West Indies Colonies
Sloan MSS 11411–West Indies Colonies
Sloan MSS 3662–West Indies Colonies
West Indian Archives–West Indies Colonies
Darnell Davis Collection of papers on Barbados
Lansdowne MSS
Lansdowne MSS 2395–Folio 54–59 re debts owing O'Sullivan, O'Driscoll, O'Callaghan etc.
Darnell Transcripts–See Irish Indentures
Public Records Office–London
The Virginia Archives
Cork County Library and other Irish sources
Life of Theobald Wolfe Tone, edited by his son, two volumes, Washington 1826.

Chronology

1250 BC	Famous battle on Beara peninsula.
c. 500 BC	The arrival of Heremon, son of Milesius, King of Spain, precursor of the Celts.
AD 125–145	Modha—Conn Cead Catha—returned from Iberia with royal wife Beara, daughter of 'Heber' Mor, with an army of two thousand men including Beara's brother Fraech. Many battles followed and the Beara peninsula was divided into Leath Chahonn and Leath Mhodha with the Eiscin Riada as the boundary.
	Fearing a possible Roman invasion from Britain, the clans and septs of Ireland came together and agreed to raise a special army to defend the country. These were called 'Na Fianna'—from *fian*, meaning fierce ones.
AD 350	Irish raids on Britain.
AD 352	St. Ciaran born on Cape Clear—*The Annals of Inisfallen (AI).*
c. AD 400	Oilioll Olum is King of Munster.
AD 402	Ciaran and Deaglan, both bishops, came from Rome to preach the Gospel *(AI).*
AD 432	St Patrick brings Christianity.
AD 448	Earthquakes destroyed most of the round towers of Ireland.
AD 548	Great plague all over Ireland.
AD 600	St. Fachna, Bishop of Ross, died *(AI).*
AD 685	Another plague.
AD 795	Arrival of first Scandinavians—Norsemen, Vikings and Danes.
AD 822	Rending of the islands in Roaring Water Bay—division due to abnormal seas.
AD 823	Norsemen plundered Valentia, County Kerry.

Chronology

AD 837 Danes plundered Cape Clear.

AD 916 Danes defeated by tribes.

AD 923 Norsemen plundered Sceilig Michil and made Dursey their southern base.

AD 960 War with the Irish in Munster.

AD 978 Battle of Bealach-Leachta. This was a disaster for the southern tribes who were decimated at the time of the Viking/Danish incursions. The exact location of Bealach-Leachta is unknown—it was possibly a 'cairn roadway' (*AI*).

1012 Danes laid waste the countryside.

1057 Mughron Ua-Mutain, successor of Bairre, Bishop of Cork, was killed by robbers (*AFM*).

1063 Cathal O'Dunchadha, King of Ui nEathach and the south of Ireland, died (*AI*).

1072 Mudan O'Driscoll, prince of Corca Laidhe, killed in battle (*AI*).

1089 Danes defeated at Oneachach in South Carbery.

1104 The son of O'Driscoll, with twenty-five others, set out fishing and never returned (*AI*).

1136 Pestilence broke out in Ireland.

1169 Normans landed at Bannow in County Wexford. Among them FitzStephens, Henry, Miler, David, Harvey, Gerald. Irish warring amongst themselves.

Diarmuid MacMurrough, King of Leinster, had brought these foreigners. They were called 'Flemings' by the Four Masters.

Maccon O'Driscoll was slain in Waterford by Strongbow's forces while fighting for the McCarthys.

1170 Synod of the Church at Armagh abolished slavery. Henry ordered Strongbow and his followers home. Strongbow disobeyed.

1171 Henry arrived in Waterford on 18 October. Amongst those who swore loyalty was Dermod McCarthy, King of Desmond.

1172 Charter of Cork and Kerry by Henry II to his noblemen Robert FitzStephens and Milo de Cogan.

1175 Council of Windsor began English domination of Ireland. Henry, with the permission of Pope Alexander III, declared his son, John, King of Ireland.

1182 Richard de Carew was in the Bantry region.

1183 Insurrection in Munster against the English.

1196 Conflict over succession to the Diocese of Ross. Daniel—a secular priest—consecrated in 1197 by order of Celestine III.

1198 Richard de Carew in Donemark Castle. Florence consecrated by Archbishop of Cashel (Innocent III).

1215	English forces conquered most of Munster (*AI*). Lord Barnwell took over Caislean Mhic Mhiarmuda (Castletown Castle).
1232	Cormac McCarthy Mór invaded and conquered the area of Cairbre.
1235	Many of the forces of Corca Laidhe were slain at the Battle of Tralee against the English forces (*AI*).
1260	Inter-tribal warfare between the McCarthys, O'Driscolls, O'Donovans, MacDonaghs, MacMahons and MacSwineys.
1260–1305	Many of the castles held by the English in Corca Laidhe were destroyed by the Irish (*AI*).
1261	Battle of Callan. Finghin McCarthaig repossessed Caislean Mhic Mhiarmuda (Castletown Castle).
1332	McCarthys were defeated by English.
1348	Appearance of Black Death.
1349	John de Carew became Lord Chief Justice of Ireland.
1359	On the death of Maurice, son of the Earl of Desmond, the King granted lands to the Earl's brother in order to quell Munster uprising.
1361	Pestilence in County Cork.
1367	Statute forbidding intermarriage between Normans and native Irish women.
1370	Plague.
1377	James Warner was Sheriff of the County.
1383	Another great plague.
1406	Yearly income of Marquis Carew—excluding Dorzey-haven and other creeks—£2,200. Lord Barnewale of Bearhaven and other creeks, £1,600.
1412	John Galwey of Kinsale—Newtown Fish Palace.
1460	Dermot Sullivan built a house for minorities at Bantry near the seashore. Franciscan monastery founded at Inis Arcainn (possibly 'hog island') (*AI*).
1531	O'Sullivan related how Dermot brought an English and a Spanish ship into Berehaven. He hung the English captain and set free the Spaniards.
1549	Dermot O'Sullivan of Berehaven was blown up in his castle and his successor Amlavus was killed soon afterwards.
1552	O'Sullivan Beare received a large ransom from the English for the release of John Tomson and other pirates.
1558	Finin O'Driscoll attended parliament in Dublin and accepted British laws as to land rights and inheritance, thus ending Brehon Law.
1562	Ireland divided into counties.

1565 McCarthy More and O'Sullivan Beare went to London and were created an Earl and a Knight respectively.

1567 Daniel McCarthy More assumed title of King of Munster and with O'Sullivan More, MacSwiney and others invaded Roche country.

Atrocities committed by the Earl of Desmond.

1568 Arrival of Sir Peter Carew in Cork claiming the properties of his ancestors the de Carews.

1569–83 Revolt and suppression of Earls of Desmond.

1569 McCarthy More repudiated his earlship and led rising in the south-west; this area was much frequented by Spaniards—fishing and shipping beef, hides and tallow to Spain.

1580 Landing of Spanish and Italians at Smerwick Harbour. 700 slaughtered.

1583 List of forces of south-west Irish lords submitted to Queen, together with expenses.

1585 Parliament convened in Dublin on 26 April. West Cork chieftains went, but many did not take their seats. All the properties of the late Earl of Desmond were confiscated. The vast estate—from Dingle to the Blackwater—were apportioned among English settlers such as Beacher, St. Leger, Grynfield, Fleetwood and the Lord Chancellor.

1586 Bishopric of Ross was annexed to that of Cork.

1588 Inquisition at Shandon Castle as to who assisted the Earl of Desmond in his uprising. Richard Boyle arrived in Cork, later became Earl of Cork. Roger, Lord Broghill, his youngest son, married Margaret Howard, second daughter of the Royalist Earl of Suffolk. He joined Cromwell under threat of imprisonment in the Tower of London.

1589 Sir Francis Drake, chased by the Spaniards, sought refuge in Carrigaline inlet.

1599 Sir George Carew made Lord President of Munster. He augmented powers of courts, etc. All lands without male heirs were forfeited to the Crown.

1601 Dunboy Castle delivered to Spaniards.

1602 Dunboy Castle taken by Carew. Spanish vessels with gold landed at Kenmare. Money entrusted to the 'non-elected' Bishop of Ross, Owen McEgan. Jesuit Fr. Archer received £150. Captain Taaffe raided cattle to feed his army. Earl of Thomond with 2,500 men and 50 horses laid waste to West Cork.

1603 Captain Morgan sent to Cork by Lord Deputy to proclaim King James I.

1604 Sir Richard Boyle paid £1,000 to the King and received patent to all Sir Walter Raleigh's lands.

1609	Cork, Youghal, Kinsale and other towns obtained new charters from the King which augmented their privileges.
1611	Systematic destruction of the Irish woods commenced. Most English ships were built of Irish wood after this date.
1620	Richard Boyle, Bishop of Cork, Cloyne and Ross, repaired many ruined churches.
1631	Pirate named 'Nut' had three privateers working on the south-west coast. He accepted a king's pardon and worked out of Crookhaven.
1636	All the septs paid tribute to the McCarthy Reagh.
1641	According to Petty, the population of Ireland was 1,448,000.
1642	Carriganass taken from the rebels.
1645	Nuncio from Pope Urban VIII arrived in Kenmare with arms and ammunition.
1647	Emergence of the guerrilla bands known as 'tories' (*toiridhe*).
1649	Oliver Cromwell appointed General for Ireland and landed in Dublin on 14 August with 9,000 troops and 1,000 horses.
1650	Mass was forbidden. £20 offered for a live priest and £5 for a head.
1651	Destruction of crops and livestock. Cattle had to be imported from Wales. Act prohibiting the importation of Irish goods into Britain except on British-owned ships (9 October).
1652	Population decreased by about half a million. 40,000 men departed to foreign armies and over 100,000 were transported to the West Indies. A notable increase in wolf packs recorded in Munster. Lord Fleetwood, son-in-law of Cromwell, arrived accompanied by William Petty as General Physician to the Army on a salary of £365 per annum.
1660	Edward III granted Cork, Kerry and Waterford to his brother John, succeeded by brother Gerard.
1662	Act of Settlement passed by Lords Orrery and Mountrath, and Sir Maurice Eustace and Sir John Percival. Formation of great estates.
1667	English Act excluding export of Irish livestock to English markets.
1686	Uprising and general unrest in the west of the country.
1689	French fleet in Bantry Bay (1 May).
1690	A Dutch merchant ship taken by the Irish in Bantry Bay recaptured by Colonel Becher.
1691	Seventy rebels killed and fifteen taken prisoner in skirmish with Colonel Becher. He later landed on Whiddy Island. Colonel Townsend defeated Raparees, killing one hundred near Bantry and seventeen in Muintir mBaire.
1692	A twenty-two gun privateer from St. Malo sank in a great storm.
1697	Transport ships arrived from Flanders and landed troops in the service of William III at Bantry.

1748 Methodists arrived in Cork.

1749 Sir Richard Meade of Bantry obtained a premium after catching and curing 380,800 fish.

1750 Whiddy Island had many good orchards and a hop yard.

1752 Change from Gregorain to Julian Calendar.

1761 Emergence of Whiteboys in West Cork.

1762 Building of coastguard stations.

1767 Complaint to Cork that fifty French vessels were fishing for mackerel off Bantry Bay.

1778 Sixty-four West Indian transporters sailed out of Cork in January. On 24 September, 40 sailed from Cobh.

1779 False alarm that a French fleet had entered Bantry Bay.

1780 Bantry parish record commenced.

1785 200,000 herrings taken in one haul in Bantry Bay.

1790s Whiddy Island population given as 714.

1797 Lord Lieutenant in Bantry inspecting defence forces. Introduction of martial law in Ireland.

1798 News of Nelson's victory over the French fleet at the Nile celebrated in Cork (5 October).

1799 General Lake ordered a curfew in the County (16 March).

1800 General Barber inspected forts at Bantry (November).

1801 Union between Great Britain and Ireland on 1 January. Lord Lieutenant ordered all cattle in sea ports to be driven inland (8 September). Martello tower of 240 feet interior diameter built on north-west of Whiddy Island (October). Military work commenced on the Bantry batteries (16 December). Stables of O'Mahony, constructor of the batteries, destroyed by fire with loss of 25 horses.

1814 Fortieth regiment left Bantry by sea for Cork, having lost all their baggage (21 October) in a hurricane. Grain trade to England collapsed.

1815 Dr. Moylan, Bishop of Cork, died on 13 February. On 10 November, a number of prisoners from Bantry escaped while being transported to Cork.

1817 On 12 September Sir Francis Burdett arrived in Bantry to great acclaim. He stayed at Ardnagashel, seat of Arthur Hutchins, Esq.

1818 Establishment of Southern Fisheries Association at Kinsale.

1820 Commencement of 'cabin suburbs' of Bantry town. Mass migration from countryside to town.

1845–7 The Great Famine. Population drops from eight million to six and a half million through starvation and emigration.

1848	Abortive rising by William Smith O Brien and the Young Irelanders, many of whom are deported to Australia.
1849	Visit of Queen Victoria and Prince Albert. Queen's Colleges at Belfast, Cork and Galway opened.
1855	Year of the Great Snow.
1880–90	Period of greatest destruction of national monuments.
1891	Downfall and death of Parnell.
1893	Gladstone's second Home Rule Bill defeated. Gaelic League founded by Douglas Hyde who becomes its first president.
1896	Irish Race Convention held in Dublin.
1903	Wyndham Land Act, headed by Lord Dunraven (*see* Quinn), abolishes landlordism.
1912	Irish Home Rule Bill passed by British House of Commons due to come into effect in 1914; its provisions are defied by Ulster Volunteers. Bill suspended for duration of First World War in which 200,000 Irish enlisted.
1916	Irish Republic declared during Easter Week Rising. The insurrection is crushed and its leaders executed.
1921	Treaty with Britain establishes a 26-county Irish Free State, the six counties of Ulster having voted themselves out.
1922–23	Civil War between Free Staters and Republicans.
1922	Treaty approved by Dáil Éireann. General election majority pro-Treaty. Republicans led by de Valera disagree and Civil War begins.
1923	End of Civil War. Ireland (Free State) joins League of Nations.
1926	Inauguration of radio service, 2 RN, later Radio Éireann.
1939–45	Second World War, in which Ireland remains neutral. However, thousands of Irish men and women enlist in British services and over 50,000 are killed in action.
1948	The Taoiseach John Costello confirms that the External Relations Act will be repealed. Ireland leaves the Commonwealth.
1955	Ireland joins the United Nations.
1960	Ireland sends troops to serve with the United Nations in the Congo.
1961	Lowest recorded population for Bantry—2,234. Ireland joins UNESCO. Television service inaugurated.
1973	Ireland joins the European Economic Community.
1985	Anglo-Irish Agreement signed.
1996	Bantry celebrates bicentenary of the Wolfe Tone invasion.

Glengarriff Harbour c. *1912, the Martello Towers on Garinish are in the background*

View of the west side of the present Glengarriff Pier c. *1900*

Roche's Hotel Glengarriff early this century

Eccles Hotel Glengarriff c. 1922

Flooding in Bantry Square c. 1947

The tunnel and a cottage on the Kenmare Road

Two views of Bantry House and Bantry Bay c. 1900

Sioux representatives at the Cork Exhibition of 1902

Lord Bantry's cottage

A view of Bantry c. 1896

Artist's impression of Donemark Falls

Tennis at Newtown, Bantry c. *1922*

A view of Bantry c. *1896*

Bantry House, dreadnoughts in background

English sailors in Bantry Square

Royal yacht in Glengarriff

Steam yacht in Glengarriff harbour

Dreadnought in Bantry Bay

Dreadnoughts in Berehaven harbour

Puxley's Mansion, Berehaven

Guinness yacht in Bantry harbour